JESUS CHRIST
in the FLESH

Precept Three

JESUS CHRIST in the FLESH

David Jenkins

Jesus Christ in the Flesh

Copyright © 2023 by David Jenkins. All rights reserved.

No part of this publication may be reproduced, stored in a retrieval system or transmitted in any way by any means, electronic, mechanical, photocopy, recording or otherwise without the prior permission of the author except as provided by USA copyright law.

The opinions expressed by the author are not necessarily those of URLink Print and Media.

1603 Capitol Ave., Suite 310 Cheyenne, Wyoming USA 82001
1-888-980-6523 | admin@urlinkpublishing.com

URLink Print and Media is committed to excellence in the publishing industry.

Book design copyright © 2023 by URLink Print and Media. All rights reserved.

Published in the United States of America
Library of Congress Control Number: 2023919338
ISBN 978-1-68486-550-5 (Paperback)
ISBN 978-1-68486-551-2 (Hardback)
ISBN 978-1-68486-552-9 (Digital)

12.09.23

CONTENTS

Precept Three 7
Introduction 9
Believing 13
The Thousand-Year Reign 95
Reincarnation 173
Where is Satan locked up? 187
The Rock 227
Conclusion 255

PRECEPT THREE

This is the republication of the third book our Father had me write. Nothing of the contents of the third book has been changed. The only thing changed is the cover with the precept three, and my new website on the back cover. davidofpsalm89.com, is the name of the website where you can download any or all the manuscripts for free if you cannot or do not want to pay for the books.

As I was finishing the sixth book, I felt the Father was telling me to republish the books. And have something referring to the six books that we have written as a series or something like that. And because our Father has been teaching me precept upon precept, line upon line, little bit here and a little bit there, I thought it would be a good idea to call each book a precept.

And Because each book is a continuation of the previous book. And at the same time, each book takes me and the reader deeper into the scriptures. With a better understanding of who our Father is and what He is doing, and why He is doing what He is doing. And hopefully you will come to agree with Him as I do.

> Whom shall he teach knowledge? and whom shall he make to understand doctrine? them that are weaned from the milk, and drawn from the breasts. For precept must be upon precept, precept upon precept; line upon line, line upon line; here a little, and there a little: (Isaiah 28:9-10)

If you have read the first two books, or precepts, then this book will be a lot easier to understand. And if you have read the first two precepts, then you should be starting to understand that milk, honey, water, and meat are all levels of knowledge and understanding. You will also be learning that the bread that we are to eat, is knowledge. All this knowledge comes from the entire King James Version of the Bible. This knowledge and understanding starts in the first verse of Genesis through the 22nd book of Revelation.

And again, if you have read the fist two precepts, then your conscience is already starting to enjoy being in the land of milk and honey. And if you continue to read precept upon precept, you will be drinking of the water that I will provide to you.

> But whosoever drinketh of the water that I shall give him shall never thirst; but the water that I shall give him shall be in him a well of water springing up into everlasting life. (John 4:14)

If you are starting with this book, then you are jumping precepts. You will be taking on to much knowledge or milk and honey so that you will not except our marvelous Father or His loving kindness that He has shown since the foundation of the world. You will then vomit, (reject) everything about Him.

> Hast thou found honey? eat so much as is sufficient for thee, lest thou be filled therewith, and vomit it. (Proverbs 25:16)

> It is not good to eat much honey: so for men to search their own glory is not glory. (Proverbs 25::27)

In this precept, you are going to learn that our Father commanded me to make my name known. This happened in June of 2019. After this commandment came, I wrote the book and it was published in September of 2019.

INTRODUCTION

The first thing I am going to mention is that I do not take credit for writing this book again. For it is our Father in which teaches me and I just try to help others understand what I have been learning from our Father. He is the ultimate teacher. I am a man in the flesh so yes, I do make mistakes and my education level is not that high. I only have a ninth-grade education and have failed and colleges and such. The only thing I know about is the bible. Our Father is using my vessel of God to show that nobody needs a fancy education or degrees if you will. I know the bible and I know our Father. In fact, this is my third time of redoing this book so that the publisher could publish it. I am not too proud to say I had to many tabs and I did not know how to do a page break. I got the suggestion from the publisher's office so that I could do this correctly. I laugh because my lack of education on computers does not make me love mankind any less.

We are naming this book a little different than the other two, yet as you will notice as you read this one, they all go together. I am the servant or vessel of God in which He chooses to use to reveal secrets in which have kept since the beginning of the world. Our Father is the true author of this book as He had me show in the first two books. All glory goes to our Father and not me.

Remember as you read through this that we must worship God in spirit. John 4:23 **But the hour cometh, and now is, when the true worshippers shall worship the Father in spirit and in truth: for the Father seeketh such to worship him. 24 God is a Spirit: and they that worship him must worship him in spirit and in truth.** So humble yourself and let your guard down. This message is all about love, but it also shows how this world hates love.

As I stated in the last book, I am in school with our Father and my knowledge of Him and what He is doing will never stop growing as long as I am in the flesh. Once again, He is using this foolish old man to show how far this world is from knowing who He is and what He is doing. I will say now that there will most likely be type errors in here and we will be jumping around and maybe even repeating certain things. Just as the last book, this book will not be formatted to be fancy or even practical for that matter. I do not use big fancy words for I, well I just don't really know any. I am not going to spend my time trying to figure out how to make things in a way that might please some people. What I mean is I am not trying to please any man; the message is within the words and not in how the words are formatted. With that being said, ask our Father to help you understand for I am in the flesh and do not teach as well as He does. I will say right now though this book is a little different than the other two. This one is going to show my thought process through all this teaching so that you as a reader can know without a doubt that I do come in my Father's name and not my own. We are going to be learning that our Father has offered His love for each person and that His love is for all people. It does not matter what color, race, nationality, size, or shape someone is. It does not matter what a person has done, doing, or will do. His love is unconventional to all of mankind. It is just man that truly does not want to know Him and what He is doing. I will say you really need to let go of your pride. Humble yourself and realize that this is a time in which is going to be very devastating for the world.

We will be learning that the old testament and the new testament is all knitted together as one long letter for instructions as to how we are to live our lives today and not the people of the past. We will be learning that reincarnation is talked about in our bibles. This is a topic in which was covered in the last book, yet I felt that we needed to see more biblical truth behind it. We will be learning that Job of the bible is alive today. Just as our Father has had me put in all three books, the bible is one long letter of instructions on how we are to live our lives and not just about the people of the past.

We will be learning of our Father's magnificent power, and you will be learning how the scriptures are truly being fulfilled. Down to the letter of the bible. Just by looking at the cover of this book, how do think this world had a good idea of what I would look like? I will be honest; I didn't even know that I would wind up looking as I do. We will be learning how to build our house. As shown in the last book, each one of us is our own personal house of God.

We will be taking you through my thought process. What I mean by that is how my thoughts towards the bible and our Father formed. How I got to the stage of believing what I believe now. There will be times in which I will show how I didn't think I was supposed to say anything about who I am. We will also be realizing that our Father has kept all of this secret, without keeping it secret for everything that He has and is teaching me is in our bibles. I will say that I only use the King James version of the bible and I strongly feel our Father will not allow me to use any other. I did use a different bible in the first book for one sample, but our Father brought me right back to the King James. I truly believe this is because man has altered the bible to make it say what they want it to say so they do not have to hear the truth. Then let us listen to Ezra 6:11 Also I have made a decree, **that whosoever shall alter this word, let timber be pulled down from his house,** and being set up, let him be hanged thereon; and let his house be made a dunghill for this.

I will say at this time this book is not going to tickle your ears and will probably offend many. However, we are at a time of history in which the truth must be revealed. For the rest of the introduction, I think the name of the book says it all. So, sit back, get a cup of coffee or preferred drink and enjoy learning more and more about our Father and how brilliantly He is doing everything that He is doing. And as always, ask our Father to help you understand as you read through this for it is not the doctrine you will hear in any church, and He is a much better teacher than I am.

I do want to add this before you get into this book any further. There are things in which have been added after the initial manuscript was sent in. So, there might be times in which might seem out of place or even repeat something that you might have already read. There will also be times that I might mention something that has not been explained yet so please bear with us and we will hopefully have it explained better by the time you finish the book.

BELIEVING

In this chapter we are going to be showing within the scriptures what believing in God our savior is. We must do this chapter because recently I asked our Father why He continues teaching me all that He teaches me and why He still shows mercy towards me for I am a sinful and rebellious man. For He has been teaching me obedience now for just over three years now and there are still days that I do resist of what I am being commanded to do. The answer I received almost immediately is because you believe. So, this took my mind on a journey through the scriptures and I quickly realized that there are very many that believe but we need to look into what believing is all about.

Let us look at John 3:16 For God so loved the world, that he gave his only begotten Son, that whosoever believeth in him should not perish, but have everlasting life.17 For God sent not his Son into the world to condemn the world; but that the world through him might be saved. 18 **He that believeth on him is not condemned: but he that believeth not is condemned already, because he hath not believed in the name of the only begotten Son of God.**

At first glance at these two verses one might believe that this is a man that came to earth several years ago and died on the cross for our sins and if you believe that you will have ever lasting life with our Father. If this is the case, then this would be the entire bible. We need to listen to the words of Jesus in Matthew 11:25 At that time Jesus answered and said, I thank thee, O Father, Lord of heaven and earth, **because thou hast hid these things from the wise and prudent, and hast revealed them unto babes.** Now with just these few verses we can know without a doubt that there must be more than just believing that that son of God came into this world and died on the cross and your sins are forgiven.

Through this entire book we are going to be learning that because Jesus laid down his life is why we are here today. This is not just for us or for people born just a couple thousand years ago. As showed in the last book our Father had me write, if it wasn't for Jesus doing this, Adam and Eve in the very beginning of the bible wouldn't have existed either. Just a quick look back at a couple of verses without going into all the details again, let us look at John 14:6 Jesus saith unto him, I am the way, the truth, **and the life:** no man cometh unto the Father, but by me. And now we need to look back into the beginning of the bible. Genesis 2:7 And the Lord God formed man of the dust of the ground, **and breathed into his nostrils the breath of life; and man became a living soul.** The life that Jesus states that he is, is the very life that our Father breathed into man in the very beginning.

As our Father had me show in the first and second book, our bible is one long letter of instructions for us to learn. It is not just parts of the bible, it is not just the new testament nor just parts of the old testament. It is the entire bible from the first verse in Genesis all the way to the last verse in the book of Revelation. This is probably the first and foremost thing to believe. What I mean by that is if you believe that the old testament was only for the people of the past, then you will never understand the new testament. And of course, if you believe that you are in the new testament now and only need the new testament then you do not even believe the words of Jesus Christ as he stated in John 5:39 Search the scriptures; for in them ye think ye have eternal life: and they are they which testify of me. 40 And ye will not come to me, that ye might have life. 41 I receive not honour from men. 42 But I know you, that ye have not the love of God in you. 43 I am come in my Father's name, and ye receive me not: if another shall come in his own name, him ye will receive. 44 How can ye believe, which receive honour one of another, and seek not the honour that cometh from God only? 45 Do not think that I will accuse you to the Father: there is one that accuseth you, even Moses, in whom ye trust. 46 **For had ye believed Moses, ye would have believed me; for he wrote of me. 47 But if ye believe not his writings, how shall ye believe my words?** This is Jesus telling us right here, we must believe the writings of Moses if there is any chance that we will believe his sayings. Even if we do believe the writings of Moses, it will not guarantee that we will believe the sayings of Jesus. This stems off us actually believing that our Father is perfect, righteous, and justified in everything that He has done, doing, and will do.

At some time in this book we will also be looking at how Adam is not one man but several people as one man as we introduced in the last book. But for now, we need to be focusing on what this believing is all about. To do this we need to be looking at a few areas of the bible that mention believing. And yes, we will be looking at quite a few for this is a matter that is greatly misunderstood. Let us start with Genesis 15 After these things the word of the Lord came unto Abram in a vision, saying, Fear not, Abram: I am thy shield, and thy exceeding great reward. 2 And Abram said, Lord God, what wilt thou give me, seeing I go childless, and the steward of my house is this Eliezer of Damascus? 3 And Abram said, Behold, to me thou hast given no seed: and, lo, one born in my house is mine heir. 4 And, behold, the word of the Lord came unto him, saying, This shall not be thine heir; but he that shall come forth out of thine own bowels shall be thine heir. 5 And he brought him forth abroad, and said, Look now toward heaven, and tell the stars, if thou be able to number them: and he said unto him, So shall thy seed be. 6 **And he believed in the Lord; and he counted it to him for righteousness.** Notice how Abram believed in the Lord and not someone that came and changed the Lord. Also note that this is in the very first book of the bible.

I am backing up in the bible for I want to show all how my mind works. I mentioned above that this is in the very first book of the bible, so this automatically brought my mind to think of Noah. Now our bible does not exactly state how long it took Noah to build the ark. We need to look at a couple different areas to kind of get a grasp of how long it took. First let us look at how old Noah was when he begat his three sons. Genesis 5:32 And Noah was five hundred years old:

and Noah begat Shem, Ham, and Japheth. Then we need to look at Genesis 6:10 And Noah begat three sons, Shem, Ham, and Japheth. 11 The earth also was corrupt before God, and the earth was filled with violence. 12 And God looked upon the earth, and, behold, it was corrupt; for all flesh had corrupted his way upon the earth. 13 And God said unto Noah, The end of all flesh is come before me; for the earth is filled with violence through them; and, behold, I will destroy them with the earth. 14 Make thee an ark of gopher wood; rooms shalt thou make in the ark, and shalt pitch it within and without with pitch. Now without being told exactly when Noah was commanded to build the ark, we can hear that it must not have been long after he begat his three sons.

Now let us look at when Noah entered into the ark. Genesis 7:6 And Noah was six hundred years old when the flood of waters was upon the earth. 7 And Noah went in, and his sons, and his wife, and his sons' wives with him, into the ark, because of the waters of the flood. Now let us look at 1 Peter 3:20 Which sometime were disobedient, when once the longsuffering of God waited in the days of Noah, while the ark was a preparing, wherein few, that is, eight souls were saved by water. Without going into all the timetables of knowing how long each child was when they entered into the ark, we can easily figure that it took some time to build but must have been less than a hundred years to build the ark. All this time in which he was building this ark, do you think he was being ridiculed for what he was doing? Do you think all the people that he saw daily thought he was doing something for nothing? Do you think that many people were telling Noah that he was doing a good thing? Can you hear how it is because Noah believed God and not man? He believed what God said. That God is our Father and not some god that was thought to change our Father.

Now we mentioned that we are not going to look into all the timetables and such of the age of each child. This is because this is how our Father has taught me. He has taught me to just listen to what is being said and not to try to make more of what it is. We could go on forever trying to figure out what is being said and how it should work, or we could just listen to the simplicity of the matter. That is one of the ways our Father has hidden this from the wise and prudent. The wise figure that they must do all the math and figure the genetics and such behind the message. But, if we just listen to what is being said, it makes our bibles easier to understand.

Just to make a quick side note here, we need to listen to what our Father told Noah about the animals that he was to take with him into the ark. Genesis 7 And the Lord said unto Noah, Come thou and all thy house into the ark; for thee have I seen righteous before me in this generation. 2 **Of every clean beast thou shalt take to thee by sevens, the male and his female: and of beasts that are not clean by two, the male and his female.** 3 Of fowls also of the air by sevens, the male and the female; to keep seed alive upon the face of all the earth. Notice how this is only the seventh chapter of the first book of the bible. Our Father didn't give us a list of the clean and unclean animals until the third book of the bible. We bring this up for this is something we should be having in the back of our minds as we read this book. Now we need to look at something else about Noah's sons. Genesis 9:19 And the sons of Noah, that went forth of the ark, were Shem, and Ham, and Japheth: and Ham is the father of Canaan. 19 **These are the three sons of Noah: and of them was the whole earth overspread.** Let us use E-sword, an online bible concordance so that we can break down what this verse shows. We are hearing that these three sons overspread the entire earth. The word overspread is H5310 nâphats naw-fats'm A primitive root; to dash to pieces, or scatter:–be beaten in sunder, break (in pieces), broken, dash (in pieces), **cause to be discharged, dispersed, be overspread, scatter.** These three souls covered the entire earth. 22 Remember man became a living soul? This all ties in with many people being as one man or one man as many people. These spirits of the bible are a lot bigger than we are. Remember, we are only in their image. By the time we get to the end, it should make a lot more since to all.

Now we will jump back into the topic of believing. Let us look at Jonah 3 And the word of the Lord came unto Jonah the second time, saying, 2 Arise, go unto Nineveh, that great city, and preach unto it the preaching that I bid thee. 3 So Jonah arose, and went unto Nineveh, according to the word of the Lord. Now Nineveh was an exceeding great city of three days' journey. 4 And Jonah began to enter into the city a day's journey, and he cried, and said, Yet forty days, and Nineveh shall be overthrown. 5 **So the people of Nineveh believed God, and proclaimed a fast, and put on sackcloth, from the greatest of them even to the least of them.** 6 For word came unto the king of Nineveh, and he arose from his throne, and he laid his robe from him, and covered him with sackcloth, and sat in ashes. 7 And he caused it to be proclaimed and published through Nineveh by the decree of the king and his nobles, saying, Let neither man nor beast, herd nor flock, taste any thing: let them not feed, nor drink water: 8 But let man and beast be covered with sackcloth, and cry mightily unto God: yea, let them turn every one from his evil way, and from the violence that is in their hands. 9 Who can tell if God will turn and repent, and turn away from his fierce anger, that we perish not? 10 **And God saw their works, that they turned from their evil way; and God repented of the evil, that he had said that he would do unto them; and he did it not.**

As we showed you all in the last book, the city of Nineveh covers the entire earth so I will not show all of the explanation of that, but I will show a bit. Remember what Jesus tells us in John 4:23 But the hour cometh, and now is, when the true worshippers shall worship the Father in spirit and in truth: for the Father seeketh such to worship him. 24 **God is a Spirit: and they that worship him must worship him in spirit and in truth.** The earth took three days for our Father to finish. The spirit of Jonas was commanded to warn the entire earth that our Father was going to overthrow it. Notice how the people of this time, believed God and proclaimed a fast and put on sackcloth. This is not because they took God's name in vein, nor did they believe that He would change. However, they did believe that, maybe our Father would have mercy on them, and they hoped that He would repent of the evil our Father had planned.

Now we need to listen to a couple of times that Jesus mentions how important it is to believe. John 5:43 I am come in my Father's name, and ye receive me not: if another shall come in his own name, him ye will receive. 44 How can ye believe, which receive honour one of another, and seek not the honour that cometh from God only? 45 Do not think that I will accuse you to the Father: there is one that accuseth you, even Moses, in whom ye trust. 46 **For had ye believed Moses, ye would have believed me; for he wrote of me. 47 But if ye believe not his writings, how shall ye believe my word.** John 17 These words spake Jesus, and lifted up his eyes to heaven, and said, Father, the hour is come; glorify thy Son, that thy Son also may glorify thee: 2 As thou hast given him power over all flesh, that he should give eternal life to as many as thou hast given him. 3 And this is life eternal, **that they might know thee the only true God, and Jesus Christ, whom thou hast sent.** 4 I have glorified thee on the earth: I have finished the work which thou gavest me to do. 5 And now, O Father, glorify thou me with thine own self with the glory which I had with thee before the world was. 6 I have manifested thy name unto the men which thou gavest me out of the world: thine they were, and thou gavest them me; and they have kept thy word. 7 Now they have known that all things whatsoever thou hast given me are of thee. 8 For I have given unto them the words which thou gavest me; and they have received them, and have known surely that I came out from thee, **and they have believed that thou didst send me**.

When you put these few verses with what Jesus tells us in the book of John. John 6:43 Jesus therefore answered and said unto them, Murmur not among yourselves. 44 No man can come to me, except the Father which hath sent me draw him: and I will raise him up at the last day. 45 It is written in the prophets, **And they shall be all taught of God. Every man therefore that hath heard, and hath learned of the Father, cometh unto me.** 46 Not that any man hath seen the Father, save he which is of God, he hath seen the Father. We can hear right away that if we do not know our Father, there is absolutely no chance we are going to be given to Jesus. Or better said we are not going to have the spirit of the son of God rise within our own bodies.

Remember that our Father is working a works that no man will believe. Habakkuk 1:5 Behold ye among the heathen, and regard, and wonder marvelously: **for I will work a work in your days which ye will not believe, though it be told you.** Acts 13:41 **Behold, ye despisers, and wonder, and perish: for I work a work in your days, a work which ye shall in no wise believe, though a man declare it unto you.** With these two verses alone should tell all that we need to try to understand what God our Father is doing.

I know there are lot of people that believe that if they believe this man came and died on the cross, then that is all they must believe. But what is that really believing? Is that believing that you are justified in all of your works? Or is that believing that this man died so that everybody, including yourself could learn what our Father wants from us? As our Father had me show in the last book, everybody is part of the son of God and not just one person as you or me. We are all in this together and not just you and the people around you. If you believe that Jesus dying on the cross is all that you need to believe, then just listen to this one verse. 1 Corinthians 1:18 **For the preaching of the cross is to them that perish foolishness; but unto us which are saved it is the power of God.** As our Father had me show in the last book, everybody on this planet carries the cross from the time they come out of the womb until they die. We all bleed the same one blood. Acts 17:26 **And hath made of one blood all nations of men for to dwell on all the face of the earth,** and hath determined the times before appointed, and the bounds of their habitation; Malachi 2:10 **Have we not all one father? hath not one God created us? why do we deal treacherously every man against his brother, by profaning the** covenant of our fathers?

Now this does not mean that you should believe that there are some that are doing better or worse of what our Father's will is. Let us listen to what Jesus said if we think we know whether or not someone is doing the will of God. Matthew 21:28 But what think ye? A certain man had two sons; and he came to the first, and said, Son, go work to day in my vineyard. 29 He answered and said, I will not: but afterward he repented, and went. 30 And he came to the second, and said likewise. And he answered and said, I go, sir: and went not. 31 Whether of them twain did the will of his father? They say unto him, **The first. Jesus saith unto them, Verily I say unto you, That the publicans and the harlots go into the kingdom of God before you.**

This does not mean that believing people that live in different areas of the world are loved by God more or less than others. This does not mean that some people make up the one body of Christ. This does not mean that because someone has a different skin color than you, that they are not part of the son of God. It does not matter what color, race, or nationality someone is. It does not matter what size or shape someone is. It does not matter what someone has done, doing, or will do, they still have the same blood as you do. They breath the same air you do, and they walk on the same type of ground as you do.

It is not believing that our Father changed just so people could go about their day ignoring Him and not trying to get to know who He is and what He is all about because you have better things to do or you just don't have time for Him. Let us listen to what our Father tells us in Malachi 3:6 For I am the Lord, **I change not;** therefore ye sons of Jacob are not consumed. This is actually telling us that if our Father made a commandment, this commandment will NEVER change. Now I know that there are a lot of people that believe that Jesus changed the laws of God and to that, I say that this is only because you don't truly want to find out what it will do to your life if you have to actually try to learn of and try to obey of what our Father has said. Who benefits when the laws of God change? Do you realize that Jesus was and example for us and not a changer of God? 1 Peter 2:21 For even hereunto were ye called: because Christ also suffered for us, **leaving us an example, that ye should follow his steps:** 22 Who did no sin, neither was guile found in his mouth: 23 Who, when he was reviled, reviled not again; when he suffered, he threatened not; but committed himself to him that judgeth righteously: 24 Who his own self bare our sins in his own body on the tree, that we, being dead to sins, should live unto righteousness: by whose stripes ye were healed. 25 For ye were as sheep going astray; but are now returned unto the Shepherd and Bishop of your souls. Are not Jesus and our Father one? John 10:29 My Father, which gave them me, is greater than all; and no man is able to pluck them out of my Father's hand. 30 **I and my**

Father are one. Now if the Father and Jesus are one, then why in the world would Jesus try to change Him. Jesus is all about the Father and everything that He is for. He knew and knows without a doubt that our Father is perfect, righteous, and justified in all His works in which our Father has ever done, is doing, and will ever do.

This is where you need to ask yourself, what spirit is telling you that our Father changed His ways just so you do not have to change yours? It is not our Father. If you remember from the last book our Father had me write showed that the laws, ruling, judgments, testimonies, commandments, and such are a mixture of laws, ruling, and commandments for man, the soul inside man, Jesus, the kings of the old testament, and Satan. If you remember we showed, you that you are the house of God in which houses all these spirits. Which spirit is it that you believe?

At this time, we feel that we need to show an entire chapter in Hebrews and as you read through this, ask yourself if these people thought to change the ways of God. Hebrews 11 Now faith is the substance of things hoped for, the evidence of things not seen. 2 For by it the elders obtained a good report. 3 Through faith we understand that the worlds were framed by the word of God, so that things which are seen were not made of things which do appear. 4 By faith Abel offered unto God a more excellent sacrifice than Cain, by which he obtained witness that he was righteous, God testifying of his gifts: and by it he being dead yet speaketh. 5 By faith Enoch was translated that he should not see death; and was not found, because God had translated him: for before his translation he had this testimony, that he pleased God. 6 **But without faith it is impossible to please him: for he that cometh to God must believe that he is, and that he is a rewarder of them that diligently seek him.** 7 By faith Noah, being warned of God of things not seen as yet, moved with fear, prepared an ark to the saving of his house; by the which he condemned the world, and became heir of the righteousness which is by faith. 8 By faith Abraham, when he was called to go out into a place which he should after receive for an inheritance, obeyed; and he went out, not knowing whither he went. 9 By faith he sojourned in the land of promise, as in a strange country, dwelling in tabernacles with Isaac and Jacob, the heirs with him of the same promise: 10 For he looked for a city which hath foundations, whose builder and maker is God. 11 Through faith also Sara herself received strength to conceive seed, and was delivered of a child when she was past age, because she judged him faithful who had promised. 12 Therefore sprang there even of one, and him as good as dead, so many as the stars of the sky in multitude, and as the sand which is by the sea shore innumerable. 13 These all died in faith, not having received the promises, but having seen them afar off, and were persuaded of them, and embraced them, and confessed that they were strangers and pilgrims on the earth. 14 For they that say such things declare plainly that they seek a country. 15 And truly, if they had been mindful of that country from whence they came out, they might have had opportunity to have returned. 16 But now they desire a better country, that is, an heavenly: wherefore God is not ashamed to be called their God: for he hath prepared for them a city. 17 By faith Abraham, when he was tried, offered up Isaac: and he that had received the promises offered up his only begotten son, 18 Of whom it was said, That in Isaac shall thy seed be called: 19 Accounting that God was able to raise him up, even from the dead; from whence also he received him in a figure. 20 By faith Isaac blessed Jacob and Esau concerning things to come. 21 By faith Jacob, when he was a dying, blessed both the sons of Joseph; and worshipped, leaning upon the top of his staff. 22 By faith Joseph, when he died, made mention of the departing of the children of Israel; and gave commandment concerning his bones. 23 By faith Moses, when he was born, was hid three months of his parents, because they saw he was a proper child; and they were not afraid of the king's commandment. 24 By faith Moses, when he was come to years, refused to be called the son of Pharaoh's daughter; 25 Choosing rather to suffer affliction with the people of God, than to enjoy the pleasures of sin for a season; 26 Esteeming the reproach of Christ greater riches than the treasures in Egypt: for he had respect unto the recompence of the reward. 27 By faith he forsook Egypt, not fearing the wrath of the king: for he endured, as seeing him who is invisible. 28 Through faith he kept the passover, and the sprinkling of blood, lest he that destroyed the firstborn should touch them. 29 By faith they passed through the Red sea as by dry land: which the Egyptians assaying to do were drowned. 30 By faith the walls of Jericho fell down, after they were compassed about seven days. 31 By faith the harlot Rahab perished not with them that believed not, when she had received the spies with peace. 32 And what shall I more say? for the time would fail me to tell of Gedeon, and of Barak, and of Samson, and of Jephthae; of David also, and Samuel, and of the prophets: 33 Who through faith subdued kingdoms, wrought righteousness, obtained promises, stopped the mouths of lions. 34 Quenched the violence of fire, escaped the edge of the sword, out of weakness were made strong, waxed valiant in fight, turned to flight the armies of the aliens. 35 Women received their dead raised to life again: and others were tortured, not accepting deliverance; that they might obtain a better resurrection: 36 And others had trial of cruel mockings and scourgings, yea, moreover of bonds and imprisonment: 37 They were stoned, they were sawn asunder, were tempted, were slain with the sword: they wandered about in sheepskins and goatskins; being destitute, afflicted, tormented; 38 (Of whom the world was not worthy:) they wandered in deserts, and in mountains, and in dens and caves of the earth. 39 And these all, having obtained a good report through faith, received not the promise: 40 God having provided some better thing for us, that they without us should not be made perfect.

Notice in verse 6 that without faith it impossible to please Him; 6 But without faith it is impossible to please him: for he that cometh to God must believe that he is, **and that he is a rewarder of them that diligently seek him.** This is not telling us that we should seek someone else other than God. Note that all these people mentioned after this, are the people of the old testament and not of the new testament. This isn't telling us to investigate the old testament and then go find other books that man has written to explain what it was about. It is simply telling us to seek God and as Jesus said in John 6:**45 It is written in the prophets, And they shall be all taught of God. Every man therefore that hath heard, and hath learned of the Father, cometh**

unto me. These are the words of Jesus himself; he is saying that if you do not learn of the Father in the old testament, you're not coming to Jesus. If you will recall in the last book, we showed you all that it is the spirit of Jesus that our Father raises up inside of us.

That comes from a fear of our Father. Malachi 4 For, behold, the day cometh, that shall burn as an oven; and all the proud, yea, and all that do wickedly, shall be stubble: and the day that cometh shall burn them up, saith the Lord of hosts, that it shall leave them neither root nor branch. 2 **But unto you that fear my name shall the Sun of righteousness arise with healing in his wings; and ye shall go forth, and grow up as calves of the stall.** 3 And ye shall tread down the wicked; for they shall be ashes under the soles of your feet in the day that I shall do this, saith the Lord of hosts. 4 Remember ye the law of Moses my servant, which I commanded unto him in Horeb for all Israel, with the statutes and judgments. 5 Behold, I will send you Elijah the prophet before the coming of the great and dreadful day of the Lord:6 And he shall turn the heart of the fathers to the children, and the heart of the children to their fathers, lest I come and smite the earth with a curse. Proverbs 16:6 By mercy and truth iniquity is purged: **and by the fear of the Lord men depart from evil.** Remember faith comes by hearing the word of God so I ask that read verse two out loud and listen to what you read and hear the son of righteousness. Romans 10:17 **So then faith cometh by hearing, and hearing by the word of God.**

Now I have been asked by people why we should fear our Father? And the simple answer is believing that He is the one that can make life easy or hard. Believing that our Father has control over everything, every minute of every day. Now my faith has grown to be the size of the entire earth and yes it did grow from something less than the size of a mustard seed. I want to explain this a bit for it does have a lot to do with me believing. As I told you all in the last book, I wouldn't even talk about the bible before I was 41 years old because I did not understand it. I was called by our Father in an odd way. I tuned into a radio talk show in which was talking a rapture that they thought would happen in a few months. I decided to investigate this concept a little further for I had never heard of such a thing. I first got on YouTube to see all these areas of the bible that people were talking about and went and bought a King James bible for myself. I looked for all the verses or passages that people were referring to. I could not see how anyone could see a rapture or anything like that.

So, I made a few videos on what I could see and understand by the same verses that a lot of people were using. It was a couple of months of that and then I felt that I needed to read the bible from the very beginning. Now this is the very first time that I read the bible from the front to back and there were three things that caught my attention in the old testament. Now remember this is shortly after I came out of a nine-year relationship with a woman that had a child when we met, and we had one child together. This was my fifth child in which at that time, I didn't have much contact with any of my other children. I can remember as if it was just yesterday, as I am reading the bible, I come across Leviticus 26:18 And if ye will not yet for all this hearken unto me, then I will punish you seven times more for your sins. 19 And I will break the pride of your power; and I will make your heaven as iron, and your earth as brass: 20 And your strength shall be spent in vain: for your land shall not yield her increase, neither shall the trees of the land yield their fruits. 21 And if ye walk contrary unto me, and will not hearken unto me; I will bring seven times more plagues upon you according to your sins. 22 **I will also send wild beasts among you, which shall rob you of your children,** and destroy your cattle, and make you few in number; and your high ways shall be desolate. 23 And if ye will not be reformed by me by these things, but will walk contrary unto me; 24 Then will I also walk contrary unto you, and will punish you yet seven times for your sins. 25 And I will bring a sword upon you, that shall avenge the quarrel of my covenant: and when ye are gathered together within your cities, I will send the pestilence among you; and ye shall be delivered into the hand of the enemy. 26 And when I have broken the staff of your bread, ten women shall bake your bread in one oven, and they shall deliver you your bread again by weight: and ye shall eat, and not be satisfied.27 And if ye will not for all this hearken unto me, but walk contrary unto me; 28 Then I will walk contrary unto you also in fury; and I, even I, will chastise you seven times for your sins. Oh my gosh, I have been through several things in my life and have had all five children taken from me. These were the thoughts that were going through my head at the very time I was reading this and yes it still connects today. I knew right then and there that this wasn't just about the people of the past. It was about me. I believed, and still believe with all of my heart, soul, and mind that the old testament is about us living today and not just about the people of the past. As I continue reading, I notice a couple other spots that just didn't seem right if this old testament was only for those of the past. Deuteronomy 28:64 And the Lord shall scatter thee among all people, from the one end of the earth even unto the other; and there thou shalt serve other gods, which neither thou nor thy fathers have known, even wood and stone. 65 **And among these nations shalt thou find no ease, neither shall the sole of thy foot have rest: but the Lord shall give thee there a trembling heart, and failing of eyes, and sorrow of mind:** 66 And thy life shall hang in doubt before thee; and thou shalt fear day and night, and shalt have none assurance of thy life:

Now picture this in your minds, I am sitting there reading this and have already read and felt that the bible was about the people of today and not just the past and then I come upon this. This was in 2011 and had just about a year and half since I had tried to take my own life for, I was tired of failing at, at that time, seemed to be everything I tried. I wore glasses and still wear glasses as of today. I can see fairly well, and my eyes are not all that bad, but I am required to wear them when I drive. I have failing eyesight; it is not 20/20. Can you see how this was connecting with me and not just the people of the past?

Now I come across another spot in the bible that seemed to connect but not as much as the first two. Amos 4: **And I also have given you cleanness of teeth in all your cities,** and want of bread in all your places: yet have ye not returned unto me, saith the Lord. At the time of reading this, my thought was the people from thousands of years ago, did not have a way to clean their teeth. Today we have all ways imaginable to whiten our teeth. This just seemed to really stick out in my mind as another way of showing that this is about us and not just the people of the past.

That is how I got to the point of believing what I believe today, it wasn't because I felt I needed to go and get a bunch of books explaining what the bible meant. It wasn't me believing that once I got to the new testament that I no longer needed the old testament. It wasn't me believing that I have read the bible once and now I can just go about my life and everything will be okay. It was about me believing that my life was in this humongous book and I wanted to know more. There was only one place that this book could tell me more and it is the book itself. That is how I have gotten to know my Father and will continue to get to know my Father even more each day of my life.

Yes, there was a time I did watch and listen to other bible scholars and theologians but what they taught was not connecting of what I could hear and see in the same bible. This was before I was baptized with the Holy Ghost. It didn't make since on how they could not see or hear what I could. Same bible, same verses, same words, but I could see and hear something completely different from what they could. Well of course this just made me desire to seek the truth in the bible further.

Then after believing that I could only find the truth from the bible and bible only, I got to the point of believing the words of Moses and yes, I did everything in my power to try to obey everything that Moses commanded. At this time I did not know that the unclean things listed in Leviticus 11 was the forbidden fruit from the tree in the midst of the garden, but I knew that if our perfect Father had said not to eat of it, I trusted Him and that it was not good for me, so I did quit eating of the unclean things. Skipping a lot of details, I did and do to this day, hear loud and clear of what Jesus tells us in John 5:45 Do not think that I will accuse you to the Father: there is one that accuseth you, even Moses, in whom ye trust. 46 For had ye believed Moses, ye would have believed me; for he wrote of me. 47 **But if ye believe not his writings, how shall ye believe my words?**

Now it wasn't just Moses that I listened to however, I listened to the prophets of the old testament. Because I believed that all the bible was or is about our lives today and not just a book of the people of the past. I got to the point of believing what I heard in Isaiah 58 Cry aloud, spare not, lift up thy voice like a trumpet, and shew my people their transgression, and the house of Jacob their sins. 2 Yet they seek me daily, and delight to know my ways, as a nation that did righteousness, and forsook not the ordinance of their God: they ask of me the ordinances of justice; they take delight in approaching to God. 3 Wherefore have we fasted, say they, and thou seest not? wherefore have we afflicted our soul, and thou takest no knowledge? Behold, in the day of your fast ye find pleasure, and exact all your labours. 4 Behold, ye fast for strife and debate, and to smite with the fist of wickedness: ye shall not fast as ye do this day, to make your voice to be heard on high. 5 Is it such a fast that I have chosen? a day for a man to afflict his soul? is it to bow down his head as a bulrush, and to spread sackcloth and ashes under him? wilt thou call this a fast, and an acceptable day to the Lord? 6 Is not this the fast that I have chosen? to loose the bands of wickedness, to undo the heavy burdens, and to let the oppressed go free, and that ye break every yoke? 7 Is it not to deal thy bread to the hungry, and that thou bring the poor that are cast out to thy house? when thou seest the naked, that thou cover him; and that thou hide not thyself from thine own flesh? 8 Then shall thy light break forth as the morning, and thine health shall spring forth speedily: and thy righteousness shall go before thee; the glory of the Lord shall be thy reward. 9 Then shalt thou call, and the Lord shall answer; thou shalt cry, and he shall say, Here I am. If thou take away from the midst of thee the yoke, the putting forth of the finger, and speaking vanity; 10 And if thou draw out thy soul to the hungry, and satisfy the afflicted soul; then shall thy light rise in obscurity, and thy darkness be as the noon day: 11 And the Lord shall guide thee continually, and satisfy thy soul in drought, and make fat thy bones: and thou shalt be like a watered garden, and like a spring of water, whose waters fail not. 12 And they that shall be of thee shall build the old waste places: thou shalt raise up the foundations of many generations; and thou shalt be called, The repairer of the breach, The restorer of paths to dwell in. 13 **If thou turn away thy foot from the sabbath, from doing thy pleasure on my holy day; and call the sabbath a delight, the holy of the Lord, honourable; and shalt honour him, not doing thine own ways, nor finding thine own pleasure, nor speaking thine own words: 14 Then shalt thou delight thyself in the Lord; and I will cause thee to ride upon the high places of the earth, and feed thee with the heritage of Jacob thy father: for the mouth of the Lord hath spoken it.**

We placed the entire chapter for there is a very important message in here that we will cover in just a minute but to keep on track let us just pay attention to the area in bold. Yes, I got to the point that as soon as the sun set on Friday evening, for that is when the day begins according to the bible. I will not show all the details in our bibles for that is something that each person must do so that they can spiritually tell our Father they believe Him. As shown in Exodus 31:13 Speak thou also unto the children of Israel, saying, **Verily my sabbaths ye shall keep: for it is a sign between me and you throughout your generations;** that ye may know that I am the Lord that doth sanctify you. 14 Ye shall keep the sabbath therefore; for it is holy unto you: every one that defileth it shall surely be put to death: for whosoever doeth any work therein, that soul shall be cut off from among his people. 15 Six days may work be done; but in the seventh is the sabbath of rest, holy to the Lord: whosoever doeth any work in the sabbath day, he shall surely be put to death. 16 Wherefore the children of Israel shall keep the sabbath, to observe the sabbath throughout their generations, for a perpetual covenant. 17 **It is a sign between me and the children of Israel for ever:** for in six days the Lord made heaven and earth, and on the seventh day he rested, and was refreshed.

Quick side note here, notice how in verses 14 and 15 that a person shall be cut off and or put to death. Remember how we showed in the last book that the putting to death in the old testament is a spiritual death. They are the same thing, if you are cut off from working with our Father, then that is the same thing as being put to death. Your heart still pumps the same blood and you will still be breathing.

I got to the point that I would come home from work on Fridays and as soon as the sun would set, I would start listening to the bible online and would not stop listening till I went to bed. I got up Saturday morning and immediately started listening to the bible again. I would listen until the sun would set on Saturday evening. I had that same desire as Jesus did and does to be obedient to every word that proceedeth out of the mouth of God.

This was me allowing the spirit of Moses, lead me out of Egypt just as it is described in the old testament. Yes, this world still lives in Egypt and yes, Egypt covers the entire earth. Now just listen to what our Father is saying in **Isaiah 19:3 And the spirit of Egypt shall fail in the midst thereof; and I will destroy the counsel thereof: and they shall seek to the idols, and to the charmers, and to them that have familiar spirits, and to the wizards.** Now we need to listen to **Jeremiah 46:8 Egypt riseth up like a flood, and his waters are moved like the rivers; and he saith, I will go up, and will cover the earth; I will destroy the city and the inhabitants thereof.** When we truly listen here, we can hear that Egypt is a spirit and is a he. And he covers the entire earth and is water as a flood. Remember this is all spiritual workings. Therefore, Jesus tells us that we need to **believe** the writings of Moses. So yes, if Egypt is a he and covers the entire earth, we can know that this is one of the kings of the old testament that has dominion over our bodies as we showed in the last book. And if we do come out of Egypt, we need to stay on that path, or our Father will lead us right back into Egypt.

We feel a need to place the second half of Deuteronomy 1 so we can truly hear what happens if, and when we do not trust our Father to lead us all the way to the end. Deuteronomy 1:18 And I commanded you at that time all the things which ye should do. 19 And when we departed from Horeb, we went through all that great and terrible wilderness, which ye saw by the way of the mountain of the Amorites, as the Lord our God commanded us; and we came to Kadeshbarnea. 20 And I said unto you, Ye are come unto the mountain of the Amorites, which the Lord our God doth give unto us. 21 Behold, the Lord thy God hath set the land before thee: go up and possess it, as the Lord God of thy fathers hath said unto thee; fear not, neither be discouraged. 22 And ye came near unto me every one of you, and said, We will send men before us, and they shall search us out the land, and bring us word again by what way we must go up, and into what cities we shall come. 23 And the saying pleased me well: and I took twelve men of you, one of a tribe: 24 And they turned and went up into the mountain, and came unto the valley of Eshcol, and searched it out. 25 And they took of the fruit of the land in their hands, and brought it down unto us, and brought us word again, and said, It is a good land which the Lord our God doth give us. 26 Notwithstanding ye would not go up, but rebelled against the commandment of the Lord your God: 27 And ye murmured in your tents, and said, Because the Lord hated us, he hath brought us forth out of the land of Egypt, to deliver us into the hand of the Amorites, to destroy us. 28 Whither shall we go up? our brethren have discouraged our heart, saying, The people is greater and taller than we; the cities are great and walled up to heaven; and moreover we have seen the sons of the Anakims there. 29 Then I said unto you, Dread not, neither be afraid of them. 30 The Lord your God which goeth before you, he shall fight for you, according to all that he did for you in Egypt before your eyes; 31 And in the wilderness, where thou hast seen how that the Lord thy God bare thee, as a man doth bear his son, in all the way that ye went, until ye came into this place. 32 Yet in this thing ye did not believe the Lord your God, 33 Who went in the way before you, to search you out a place to pitch your tents in, in fire by night, to shew you by what way ye should go, and in a cloud by day. 34 And the Lord heard the voice of your words, and was wroth, and sware, saying, 35 Surely there shall not one of these men of this evil generation see that good land, which I sware to give unto your fathers. 36 Save Caleb the son of Jephunneh; he shall see it, and to him will I give the land that he hath trodden upon, and to his children, because he hath wholly followed the Lord. 37 Also the Lord was angry with me for your sakes, saying, Thou also shalt not go in thither. 38 But Joshua the son of Nun, which standeth before thee, he shall go in thither: encourage him: for he shall cause Israel to inherit it. 39 Moreover your little ones, which ye said should be a prey, and your children, which in that day had no knowledge between good and evil, they shall go in thither, and unto them will I give it, and they shall possess it. 40 But as for you, turn you, and take your journey into the wilderness by the way of the Red sea. 41 Then ye answered and said unto me, We have sinned against the Lord, we will go up and fight, according to all that the Lord our God commanded us. And when ye had girded on every man his weapons of war, ye were ready to go up into the hill. 42 And the Lord said unto me, Say unto them. Go not up, neither fight; for I am not among you; lest ye be smitten before your enemies. 43 So I spake unto you; and ye would not hear, but rebelled against the commandment of the Lord, and went presumptuously up into the hill. 44 And the Amorites, which dwelt in that mountain, came out against you, and chased you, as bees do, and destroyed you in Seir, even unto Hormah. 45 And ye returned and wept before the Lord; **but the Lord would not hearken to your voice, nor give ear unto you.** 46 So ye abode in Kadesh many days, according unto the days that ye abode there.

Now this is an area of this book we will be covering some of what our Father had me show in the last book. However, it will go more into detail. We showed how our Father had me give everything away. The reason we are covering this in detail is so our Father can show all how believing truly works. As showed in the first book, our Father woke me up on my 45th birthday with the knowledge He had me write in the first book. I had stopped celebrating b-days and all holidays, some years before this. I do not remember how many years, but I do know that I stopped because I believed that our Father was and is perfect in everything He has ever done or said, is doing and will do. He never gives a commandment of celebrating holidays and such, so I trusted Him and believed that I didn't need or want any kind of celebration of these days. After I realized that our Father had given me a very great gift on my b-day, and that gift came from above and not from man, I became a bible junky if you will.

About two months after He had me write the first book, my wife, by man's definition, left me. Well about two months after it was published in April of 2015. My heart was breaking again and after weeping for about a week, I received a commandment to just follow her and love her with everything I had to offer. I immediately called into work and told them I had to quit in a week even though I had just started working there a couple weeks before this. I made decent money, about $1,200 a week. I quit that job and moved to where she was. I did not move in with her for I knew this was going to take time. It took a couple of days, but I did find a reasonable apartment and started a job search. I found a job in a factory, making just over $9 an hour. I was bringing home about $280 a week. Quite the pay difference but, I believed that our Father had given me a commandment to just go love your wife. He did not say get a good paying job, nor did He say just think about doing this. He commanded me to just go and love your wife. Nothing else mattered for I was doing what I was being commanded to do. Acts 5:29 Then Peter and the other apostles answered and said, **We ought to obey God rather than men.** Yes, I was being ridiculed for what I was doing by everybody I knew and even my wife when I contacted her and told her what I had been commanded.

I want to show something that happened while I was working at this factory. At this time in my life I am all about God and what He is doing. And yes, He was all I could think about. I was at work one evening and a couple of women seemed to be really interested in how our Father had me write the first book. I kept telling them about it and then all the sudden, the supervisor came to me and said one of the women were complaining about how I was talking about God. He asked me not to talk to her anymore. I said okay and went on doing my job. A few minutes later I chuckled and said within myself that I will be hated by all. I didn't give it much thought but knew that I would look it up once I got home. Matthew 10:22 **And ye shall be hated of all men for my name's sake: but he that endureth to the end shall be saved.** I laugh now, but that night when I got home and seen this, I told our Father that I was not going to do this. Needless to say, that was only a feeling I had for a short while. I was truly fascinated with everything the bible said, was coming to pass.

After a few weeks of talking with my wife, she started to understand, and things started to go well for a while. Everything that she couldn't stand at the time she left, I changed and started doing the complete opposite. We were building a good relationship for about six months. She stayed with her family and I stayed in my apartment. Then things turned sour. What I mean is now she complained about all the things I changed for her. It was like no matter what I did, I was wrong. This is when our Father put on my conscience about hearing the word of God. Romans 10:17 **So then faith cometh by hearing, and hearing by the word of God.** So, I started with Genesis and listened to the bible online for the first time. Oh yes, it seemed so much more exciting than reading and I seemed to comprehend it a little better. I started hearing things like tell them you are their sign in the book of Ezekiel 12:11 **Say, I am your sign: like as I have done, so shall it be done unto them: they shall remove and go into captivity.** This really caught my attention. I felt strongly that our Father was telling me to do this right now. So, I did and sent out messages on Facebook to all on my friends list. I did not know what it meant at the time; however, I just knew our Father was giving me a commandment. I continued to listen to the bible and then I started to hear certain things like take no food or drink, nor script for your journey. After a month or so of this is when our Father led me out into the wilderness to be baptized with the Holy Ghost.

Now we must get sidetracked here for a few minutes. In the last book our Father had me show that and say that I am your sign. And I just showed above of what I heard, so now our Father is making me feel that I need to show in the scriptures as to why I feel I am your sign of the end of the world. First and foremost, the first time I listened to the bible, this almost made the hair on the back of my neck stand. I paused the bible and immediately said within myself, you have got to be kidding. I hit rewind and listened to it over and over and just started knowing how deeply I felt that this was personally talking to me. Just another small taste of the power of God. Then Now we are going to skip a couple of years of me intensely listening to the complete bible over and over. In the last book we mentioned that looking for sign like asteroids and such keeps us from doing the two greatest commandments. Matthew 22:36 Master, which is the great commandment in the law? 37 Jesus said unto him, **Thou shalt love the Lord thy God with all thy heart, and with all thy soul, and with all thy mind. 38 This is the first and great commandment. 39 And the second is like unto it, Thou shalt love thy neighbour as thyself. 40 On these two commandments hang all the law and the prophets**.

So here is where we realize how looking for these things distracts us from following these commandments. Who are you looking out for when you look for these things? Are you watching these things so much, that you disregard the entire bible and only look for prophecies to be fulfilled? Are you hearing that engrafted word that can save your soul? Or are you more worried about surviving when all hell breaks loose? The entire bible is about loving and helping others more than yourself. Listen to a little of Psalm 74 O God, why hast thou cast us off for ever? why doth thine anger smoke against the sheep of thy pasture? 2 Remember thy congregation, which thou hast purchased of old; the rod of thine inheritance, which thou hast redeemed; this mount Zion, wherein thou hast dwelt. 3 Lift up thy feet unto the perpetual desolations; even all that the enemy hath done wickedly in the sanctuary. 4 **Thine enemies roar in the midst of thy congregations; they set up their ensigns for signs.** Looking for these signs in which Jesus tells us are just signs of the end but the end is not yet. Matthew 24:6 **And ye shall hear of wars and rumours of wars: see that ye be not troubled: for all these things must come to pass, but the end is not yet.**

Now we need to listen to what we are being told about what our Father will do. Isaiah 11 And there shall come forth a rod out of the stem of Jesse, and a Branch shall grow out of his roots: 2 And the spirit of the Lord shall rest upon him, **the spirit of wisdom and understanding, the spirit of counsel and might, the spirit of knowledge and of the fear of the Lord; 3 And shall make him of quick understanding in the fear of the Lord: and he shall not judge after the sight of his eyes, neither reprove after the hearing of his ears:** 4 But with righteousness shall he judge the poor, and reprove with equity for the meek of the earth: and he shall smite the earth: with the rod of his mouth, and with the breath of his lips shall he slay the wicked. 5 And righteousness shall be the girdle of his loins, and faithfulness the girdle of his reins. 6 The wolf also shall dwell with the lamb, and the leopard shall lie down with the kid; and the calf and the young lion and the fatling together; and a little child shall lead them. 7 And the cow and the bear shall feed; their young ones shall lie down together: and the lion shall eat straw like the ox. 8 And the sucking child shall play on the hole of the asp, and the weaned child shall put his hand on the cockatrice' den. 9 They shall not hurt nor destroy in all my holy mountain: for the earth shall be full of the knowledge of the Lord, as the waters cover the sea. 10 **And in that day there shall be a root of Jesse, which shall stand for an ensign of the people; to it shall the Gentiles seek: and his rest shall be glorious.** 11 And it shall come to pass in that day, that the Lord shall set his hand again the second time to recover the remnant of his people, which shall be left, from Assyria, and from Egypt, and from Pathros, and from Cush, and from Elam, and from Shinar, and from Hamath, and from the islands of the sea. 12 **And he shall set up an ensign for the nations, and shall assemble the outcasts of Israel, and gather together the dispersed of Judah from the four corners of the earth.**

Now when our Father was first telling me to put this in this book, I almost refused for it made me feels as if I am saying that I am Jesus. But then our Father remined me of Ecclesiastes 1:9 **The thing that hath been, it is that which shall be; and that which is done is that which shall be done: and there is no new thing under the sun. 10 Is there any thing whereof it may be said, See, this is new? it hath been already of old time, which was before us. 11 There is no remembrance of former things; neither shall there be any remembrance of things that are to come with those that shall come after.** 12 I the Preacher was king over Israel in Jerusalem. 13 **And I gave my heart to seek and search out by wisdom concerning all things that are done under heaven: this sore travail hath God given to the sons of man to be exercised therewith.** This is telling us right here, if it happened in the past it will happen again, and if is happening now, it happened in the past. I can say without a doubt that I am your sign for my understanding and knowledge of our Father. Even though I am a high school drop out and didn't even look at the bible until I was 41, I have the utmost confidence that I could show anyone things that they have never heard of before. That is because our Father is backing me up in everything that I do. This is why you always hear me say we feel or something of that sort. The Father and I are one. Try to remember we are going through my thought process.

Now to back on the topic of believing. Now picture this in your mind if you will, I just came out of another relationship and was totally sick of living this life. I started hearing things like take no food or drink for your journey. Matthew 10:8 Heal the sick, cleanse the lepers, raise the dead, cast out devils: freely ye have received, freely give. 9 **Provide neither gold, nor silver, nor brass in your purses, 10 Nor scrip for your journey, neither two coats, neither shoes, nor yet staves: for the workman is worthy of his meat.** Luke 9:3 And he said unto them, **Take nothing for your journey, neither staves, nor scrip, neither bread, neither money; neither have two coats apiece.** This is something I am adding for I feel our Father is saying show it all. Remember, this is something that we must believe and hear in our hearts and not something we can just do so that we can do things right by our Father.

Skipping a lot of details, with me hearing these particular sections of the bible I was thinking I am going out by myself so that I can die and go to work for our Father in the spiritual world. I was being commanded to go out into the wilderness so that I could die alone. I was excited for I didn't know what I know now so I truly believed I was going to go be with our Father and not be here on earth anymore. So, I gave everything I owned to the poor and needy. Matthew 19:21 Jesus said unto him, **If thou wilt be perfect, go and sell that thou hast, and give to the poor, and thou shalt have treasure in heaven: and come and follow me.** I was truly believing that this is what I must do so that I could become perfect, just like our Father and Jesus. I will not give details of what I gave away for as Jesus states in John 6, we are to give our alms in secret. I truly believed that I was going out in the wilderness to die so I gave everything away except one pair of shoes, one pair of socks, one pair of jeans, one pair of undershorts, and two shirts for I always where and undershirt. I believed I was not going to be here anymore, so I listened to what the scriptures told me to do. By the way script is money. I knew that I couldn't take anything with when I died so why not give it to someone that needed the help. 1 Timothy 6:6 **But godliness with contentment is great gain. 7 For we brought nothing into this world, and it is certain we can carry nothing out.** Job 1:20 Then Job arose, and rent his mantle, and shaved his head, and fell down upon the ground, and worshipped, 21 **And said, Naked came I out of my mother's womb, and naked shall I return thither:** the Lord gave, and the Lord hath taken away; blessed be the name of the Lord. 22 In all this Job sinned not, nor charged God foolishly.

At this time, I thought I could do this on the day I choose, so I tried this on March 5th, 2016. It was a Saturday evening, and I walked out about five miles from my apartment and found a somewhat secluded area and laid there till I fell asleep. I awoke around three am, freezing. I got up, telling our Father I failed Him, and walked back to the apartment. Carl was looking over some of the stuff I had given him, so I was able to get back into the apartment. In our conversation I figured that maybe I needed to move out of the apartment and pay off utilities and return the cable box. So, I asked Carl for a little money back so I could do this, however I knew I was not giving up. Come Monday I moved everything out of my apartment in the daylight as the scriptures said to do. Ezekiel 12 The word of the Lord also came unto me, saying, 2 Son of man, thou dwellest in the midst of a rebellious house, which have eyes to see, and see not; they have ears to hear, and hear not: for they are a rebellious house. 3 **Therefore, thou son of man, prepare thee stuff for removing, and remove by day in their sight; and thou shalt remove from thy place to another place in their sight: it may be they will consider, though they be a rebellious house. 4 Then shalt thou bring forth thy stuff by day in their sight, as stuff for removing: and thou shalt go forth at even in their sight, as they that go forth into captivity.** 5 Dig thou through the wall in their sight, and carry out thereby. 6 In their sight shalt thou bear it upon thy shoulders, and carry it forth in the twilight: thou shalt cover thy face, that thou see not the ground: **for I have set thee for a sign unto the house of Israel.** 7 And I did so as I was commanded: I brought forth my stuff by day, as stuff for captivity, and in the even I digged through the wall with mine hand; I brought it forth in the twilight, and I bare it upon my shoulder in their sight.

That wall that we are to dig through is a spiritual wall. It is the same wall that Jesus breaks down inside of us. Ephesians 2:13 **But now in Christ Jesus ye who sometimes were far off are made nigh by the blood of Christ. 14 For he is our peace, who hath made both one, and hath broken down the middle wall of partition between us;**

Are you starting to see how I believed what I was hearing in the scriptures? Then I asked Carl if I could sleep in his car for one night until I figured out what I was going to do. I awoke from a dream Tuesday morning at 4:13 am. This was actually the first day of the year of the Hebraic calendar. Not showing the details and research I did for this for this is a way of showing our Father yourself, that you have a desire to be obedient. And when this happened, I had was not paying attention to any calendar. This is something I realized a couple of weeks after it happened. But this was not the day I chose; however, it was on March 8-9, of 2016. In this dream, I was watching the news and the broadcaster announced all those to report to duty is David Jenkins and Randy for jerry rigging. The place that I was working at when all this started had a guy there that was very good a jerry rigging. So, I figured our Father does make jokes. Funny, but the owner's name was Jerry also. I knew this is now the time I am going out to die. I was now staying where Carl was staying; however, I was sleeping in the car I gave him. This place was already out in the country, so I just walked out on the gravel road. As I am walking, I asked the Father to lead me to the place this is going to happen. After a couple hours of walking and daylight being broke, I found a creek that looked to lead to nowhere. I walked back about ¾ of a mile back into the woods along this creek and set up camp there if you will.

Okay, I mentioned in the last book that I tried to take my life in 09, right? I was doing it again, but it was different this time. Remember how we showed you all in the last book that the sacrifices that our Father likes are of a broken spirit and so forth. That was the kings and spirits making a sacrifice to get me to the bible the last time. This time I was giving up my life on what I felt on my terms, but as the scriptures instructed. I did this with my free will. 1 Chronicles 29:9 Then the people rejoiced, **for that they offered willingly, because with perfect heart they offered willingly to the Lord:** and David the king also rejoiced with great joy. 10 Wherefore David blessed the Lord before all the congregation: and David said, Blessed be thou, Lord God of Israel our father, for ever and ever. 11 Thine, O Lord is the greatness, and the power, and the glory, and the victory, and the majesty: for all that is in the heaven and in the earth is thine; thine is the kingdom, O Lord, and thou art exalted as head above all. 12 Both riches and honour come of thee, and thou reignest over all; and in thine hand is power and might; and in thine hand it is to make great, and to give strength unto all. 13 Now therefore, our God, we thank thee, and praise thy glorious name. 14 But who am I, and what is my people, that we should be able to offer so willingly after this sort? for all things come of thee, and of thine own have we given thee. 15 For we are strangers before thee, and sojourners, as were all our fathers: our days on the earth are as a shadow, and there is none abiding. 16 O Lord our God, all this store that we have prepared to build thee an house for thine holy name cometh of thine hand, and is all thine own. 17 I know also, my God, that thou triest the heart, and hast pleasure in uprightness. **As for me, in the uprightness of mine heart I have willingly offered all these things: and now have I seen with joy thy people, which are present here, to offer willingly unto thee.** I tried to take my life the first time for I just couldn't stand this life anymore. Pretty much the same reason the second time but now I was allowing our Father to take my life. But now I remembered what Jesus said. Luke 14:26 **If any man come to me, and hate not his father, and mother, and wife, and children, and brethren, and sisters, yea,**

and his own life also, he cannot be my disciple. I just knew I must be doing something right.

That was me believing the writings of Moses and me believing what the prophets wrote. And yes, believing the true sayings of Jesus. After about 40 hours of being out there with no food nor drink, I got to the point that I started walking back to where Carl was staying, thinking and telling the Father that I have failed Him again. After this our Father sent me to my mom's for three weeks so that I could get my head straightened out and realize that I did die but not the death as man thinks of. I was telling everybody I talked to that we needed to repent for the kingdom of God was at hand. I thought the world was going to end right away. I did not know what was going on.

We feel that we need to place just one chapter of many in which helped me understand what I just went through. Colossians 2 For I would that ye knew what great conflict I have for you, and for them at Laodicea, and for as many as have not seen my face in the flesh; 2 That their hearts might be comforted, being knit together in love, and unto all riches of the full assurance of understanding, to the acknowledgement of the mystery of God, and of the Father, and of Christ; 3 In whom are hid all the treasures of wisdom and knowledge. 4 And this I say, lest any man should beguile you with enticing words. 5 For though I be absent in the flesh, yet am I with you in the spirit, joying and beholding your order, and the stedfastness of your faith in Christ. 6 As ye have therefore received Christ Jesus the Lord, so walk ye in him: 7 Rooted and built up in him, and stablished in the faith, as ye have been taught, abounding therein with thanksgiving. 8 Beware lest any man spoil you through philosophy and vain deceit, after the tradition of men, after the rudiments of the world, and not after Christ. 9 For in him dwelleth all the fulness of the Godhead bodily. 10 And ye are complete in him, which is the head of all principality and power: 11 In whom also ye are circumcised with the circumcision made without hands, in putting off the body of the sins of the flesh by the circumcision of Christ: 12 **Buried with him in baptism, wherein also ye are risen with him through the faith of the operation of God, who hath raised him from the dead.** 13 And you,

being dead in your sins and the uncircumcision of your flesh, hath he quickened together with him, having forgiven you all trespasses; 14 Blotting out the handwriting of ordinances that was against us, which was contrary to us, and took it out of the way, nailing it to his cross; 15 And having spoiled principalities and powers, he made a shew of them openly, triumphing over them in it. 16 Let no man therefore judge you in meat, or in drink, or in respect of an holyday, or of the new moon, or of the sabbath days: 17 Which are a shadow of things to come; but the body is of Christ. 18 Let no man beguile you of your reward in a voluntary humility and worshipping of angels, intruding into those things which he hath not seen, vainly puffed up by his fleshly mind, 19 And not holding the Head, from which all the body by joints and bands having nourishment ministered, and knit together, increaseth with the increase of God. 20 **Wherefore if ye be dead with Christ from the rudiments of the world, why, as though living in the world, are ye subject to ordinances, 21 (Touch not; taste not; handle not; 22 Which all are to perish with the using;) after the commandments and doctrines of men? 23 Which things have indeed a shew of wisdom in will worship, and humility, and neglecting of the body: not in any honour to the satisfying of the flesh.**

Jeremiah 46:8 **Egypt riseth up like a flood, and his waters are moved like the rivers; and he saith, I will go up, and will cover the earth; I will destroy the city and the inhabitants thereof.** This is the water in which I came out of when I was baptized by the Holy Ghost. This is when the upper grades of my schooling took place. Remember this is a spiritual works that our Father is working. I was now dead but still alive. I was buried and risen with Christ. I was and am truly working with our Father one on one, hands on training. Want to bring something up right here. Think about this for a minute. We just read that this world is covered with a spiritual water. What happens if man is under water. They drown and become dead, right? Now listen to Jesus in Matthew 8:20 And Jesus saith unto him, The foxes have holes, and the birds of the air have nests; but the Son of man hath not where to lay his head. 21 And another of his disciples said unto him, Lord, suffer me first to go and bury my father. 22 **But Jesus said unto him, Follow me; and let the dead bury their dead.** Can you now see how the dead can bury the dead?

I gave up my life of the flesh and the things of this world so that I could be with our Father for our Father and Jesus are not of this world. During this time, one of my brothers, tried to convince me to go to a hospital to seek drugs so I could stop thinking of our Father and the bible so much. I obviously replied with no way. Now with my brother saying this, we need to look at a couple of things so that we can hear the damage I would have done if I would have agreed to such a thing. First and foremost, I remember thinking and telling him that he shouldn't temp God. Matthew 4:7 Jesus said unto him, **It is written again, Thou shalt not tempt the Lord thy God.** Let us look at where it is written. Deuteronomy 6:16 **Ye shall not tempt the Lord your God,** as ye tempted him in Massah. It wasn't him that would have been tempting God, but rather it would have been me. I would have been telling our Father, by my spiritual works, that I needed more proof than everything that had already happened so that I would believe Him. NO, I DID NOT need more proof. Now because this was a statement made by my brother and not God, who would have I been trying to please? John 12:42 Nevertheless among the chief rulers also many believed on him; but because of the Pharisees they did not confess him, lest they should be put out of the synagogue: 43 **For they loved the praise of men more than the praise of God.** John 5:41 I receive not honour from men. 42 But I know you, that ye have not the love of God in you. 43 I am come in my Father's name, and ye receive me not: if another shall come in his own name, him ye will receive. 44 **How can ye believe, which receive honour one of another, and seek not the honour that cometh from God only?** I don't do what I do so that I can please anyone for our Father is the one I am trying to please. If I would have went and got some drugs, I would have been blocking out the voice of our Father. I would have been putting that vail over my heart just as most of the world has when it comes to the reading of the old testament. 2 Corinthians 3:13And not as Moses, which put a veil over his face, that the children of Israel could not stedfastly look to the end of that which is abolished: 14 **But their minds were blinded: for until this day remaineth the same vail untaken away** in the reading of the old testament; which vail is done away in Christ.

I want to make a side note here. One of the things my brother said to me is that I couldn't be right with God for I smoke cigarettes. Nowhere in the bible does it say that we cannot smoke cigarettes. Before you reading this, cast a stone, just as my brother did, and think that I am wrong for smoking, let me ask you if you are without sin? It is not what goes into the mouth that defiles a man. Matthew 15 Then came to Jesus scribes and Pharisees, which were of Jerusalem, saying, 2 Why do thy disciples transgress the tradition of the elders? for they wash not their hands when they eat bread. 3 But he answered and said unto them, Why do ye also transgress the commandment of God by your tradition? 4 For God commanded, saying, Honour thy father and mother: and, He that curseth father or mother, let him die the death. 5 But ye say, Whosoever shall say to his father or his mother, It is a gift, by whatsoever thou mightest be profited by me; 6 And honour not his father or his mother, he shall be free. Thus have ye made the commandment of God of none effect by your tradition. 7 Ye hypocrites, well did Esaias prophesy of you, saying, 8 This people draweth nigh unto me with their mouth, and honoureth me with their lips; but their heart is far from me. 9 But in vain they do worship me, teaching for doctrines the commandments of men. 10 And he called the multitude, and said unto them, Hear, and understand: 11 **Not that which goeth into the mouth defileth a man; but that which cometh out of the mouth, this defileth a man**. My smoking cigarettes does not make me love man less, nor does it make me think that anyone else's life is not just as important to our Father as mine is. These are the thoughts that man has, in which comes from the heart that defile a man. Now I want to mention something that had happened in this conversation that happened for one of the first times of many now.

When my brother was telling me this, I was smoking a cigarette, and all the sudden it came to mind. I looked him straight in the eye and told him that if I quit smoking so that I can live longer than I will lose my life with the Father. This is when we need to listen to what the scriptures tell us. Matthew 10:19 **But when they deliver you up, take no thought how or what ye shall speak: for it shall be given you in that same hour what ye shall speak. 20 For it is not ye that speak, but the Spirit of your Father which speaketh in you.** And when this happens, I can tell, for there are times that I will say something and then have to look it up to see if I spoke correctly. This is just a small example of what it means when we hear "those that save their life will lose it" is about. This will be explained in detail later in the book. For me, I could feel, see, and hear how every word of the scripture was being fulfilled to the letter as Jesus stated on Matthew 5:17 Think not that I am come to destroy the law, or the prophets: I am not come to destroy, but to fulfil. 18 For verily I say unto you, **Till heaven and earth pass, one jot or one tittle shall in no wise pass from the law, till all be fulfilled.**

Then I was sent to my oldest brother's place in South Dakota so that I could help a different brother with his business. I told my brother, before going, that he will not pay me. I was there for about seven weeks. I was afraid to get paid for my labor for I wasn't sure what was going on here, however I remembered the scriptures telling me not to take my life back. Luke 9:62 And Jesus said unto him, **No man, having put his hand to the plough, and looking back, is fit for the kingdom of God.** I was not taking my life back for I just knew something was happening. About six weeks in my stay with my brother, we had a big falling out. You guessed it; it was about the scriptures. There was no way I would say anything of the law had changed.

Now we need to bring up the forbidden fruit as man calls it. If you all can recall, we showed in the last book that this fruit is a tree of life and that tree is detailed in Leviticus 11. There was about eight months of me being down where I was trying to patch things up with my wife. There was a time, about six weeks before the baptism of the Holy Ghost, that I started to eat pork or swine. Not because I didn't believe, but rather because I was commanded to just go and love your wife. She did not have the same beliefs as I did, however I was just trying to show her that I would do anything at that time. In my mind,

I was only doing what our Father commanded of me. Obviously, our Father put it on my conscience to stop doing that and shortly after that is when I got baptized by the Holy Ghost. Side note here, I did not know what was happening when this baptism happened. Our Father showed me several months after He did this. The reason we bring this up is because to work for our Father in the manner I am, we need to be by ourselves. 1 Corinthians 7:32 But I would have you without carefulness. **He that is unmarried careth for the things that belong to the Lord, how he may please the Lord: 33 But he that is married careth for the things that are of the world, how he may please his wife.** I am by myself but yet I am never alone.

Then when I was sent to my brothers in South Dakota, about two weeks before our Father took me from there, there was one night that my brother fixed porkchops. He also did and does not believe in the manner that I do. I chose to eat this not because of me not believing, but rather because I remembered the scriptures. Luke 10:8 And into whatsoever city ye enter, and they receive you, **eat such things as are set before you.** So, some might ask, why? It is so that you do not make others feel as if they are doing wrong. Remember the bible is about loving and not condemning.

Now we are going to show something that our Father has just very recently brought to my attention. There are many people that believe that Jesus was the ultimate sacrifice, and now the law is changed. Yes, Jesus did sacrifice himself, but not to change our Father's law. To understand this better, let us listen to 1 Corinthians 10 Moreover, brethren, I would not that ye should be ignorant, how that all our fathers were under the cloud, and all passed through the sea; 2 And were all baptized unto Moses in the cloud and in the sea; 3 **And did all eat the same spiritual meat; 4 And did all drink the same spiritual drink: for they drank of that spiritual Rock that followed them: and that Rock was Christ.** 5 But with many of them God was not well pleased: for they were overthrown in the wilderness. 6 Now these things were our examples, to the intent we should not lust after evil things, as they also lusted. 7 Neither be ye idolaters, as were some of them; as it is written, The people sat down to eat and drink, and rose up to play. 8 Neither let us commit fornication, as some of them committed, and fell in one day three and twenty thousand. 9 Neither let us tempt Christ, as some of them also tempted, and were destroyed of serpents. 10 Neither murmur ye, as some of them also murmured, and were destroyed of the destroyer. 11 Now all these things happened unto them for examples: and they are written for our admonition, upon whom the ends of the world are come. 12 Wherefore let him that thinketh he standeth take heed lest he fall. 13 There hath no temptation taken you but such as is common to man: but God is faithful, who will not suffer you to be tempted above that ye are able; but will with the temptation also make a way to escape, that ye may be able to bear it. 14 Wherefore, my dearly beloved, flee from idolatry. 15 I speak as to wise men; judge ye what I say. 16 The cup of blessing which we bless, is it not the communion of the blood of Christ? The bread which we break, is it not the communion of the body of Christ? 17 For we being many are one bread, and one body: for we are all partakers of that one bread. 18 Behold Israel after the flesh: are not they which eat of the sacrifices partakers of the altar? 19 What say I then? that the idol is any thing, or that which is offered in sacrifice to idols is any thing? 20 But I say, that the things which the Gentiles sacrifice, they sacrifice to devils, and not to God: and I would not that ye should have fellowship with devils. 21 Ye cannot drink the cup of the Lord, and the cup of devils: ye cannot be partakers of the Lord's table, and of the table of devils. 22 Do we provoke the Lord to jealousy? are we stronger than he? 23 All things are lawful for me, but all things are not expedient: all things are lawful for me, but all things edify not. 24 Let no man seek his own, but every man another's wealth. 25 Whatsoever is sold in the shambles, that eat, asking no question for conscience sake: 26 For the earth is the Lord's, and the fulness thereof. 27 If any of them that believe not bid you to a feast, and ye be disposed to go; whatsoever is set before you, eat, asking no question for conscience sake. 28 **But if any man say unto you, this is offered in sacrifice unto idols, eat not for his sake that shewed it, and for conscience sake: for the earth is the Lord's, and the fulness thereof:** 29 Conscience, I say, not thine own, but of the other: for why is my liberty judged of another man's conscience? 30 For if I by grace be a partaker, why am I evil spoken of for that for which I give thanks? 31 Whether therefore ye eat, or drink, or whatsoever ye do, do all to the glory of God. 32 Give none offence, neither to the Jews, nor to the Gentiles, nor to the church of God: 33 Even as I please all men in all things, not seeking mine own profit, but the profit of many, that they may be saved. When some think that we can eat all things because Jesus was sacrificed, we can hear that is wrong. Jesus gave his life so that we might be saved by doing the same as him.

Now back on topic. This is when our Father severed me from all other people. Leviticus 20:24 But I have said unto you, Ye shall inherit their land, and I will give it unto you to possess it, a land that floweth with milk and honey: I am the Lord your God, **which have separated you from other people. 25 Ye shall therefore put difference between clean beasts and unclean, and between unclean fowls and clean: and ye shall not make your souls abominable by beast, or by fowl, or by any manner of living thing that creepeth on the ground, which I have separated from you as unclean. 26 And ye shall be holy unto me: for I the Lord am holy, and have severed you from other people, that ye should be mine.** 27 A man also or woman that hath a familiar spirit, or that is a wizard, shall surely be put to death: they shall stone them with stones: their blood shall be upon them.

Very shortly after our Father severed me from others and placed me in the truck to be myself, He showed me when I was listening to the bible for about the 5th or 6th time, that this tree is a tree of life and that tree is listed in Leviticus 11. Then He showed me what He tells us in 2 Corinthians 6:16 And what agreement hath the temple of God with idols? for ye are the temple of the living God; as God hath said, I will dwell in them, and walk in them; and I will be their God, and they shall be my people. 17 Wherefore come out from among them, and be ye separate, saith the Lord, and touch not the unclean thing; and I will receive you. 18 And will be a Father unto you, and ye shall be my sons and daughters, saith the Lord Almighty.

Now I am to the point that I would rather die before I eat the unclean things. I always eat by myself and I have absolutely no desire to eat the unclean things. It was the very first thing that are Father commanded us not to do, so I won't. Now if I am wrong for this, no one else suffers because of my inability to understand of what our Father is commanding of me. I am only trying to work out my own salvation as we are commanded to do, Philippians 2:12 Wherefore, my beloved, as ye have always obeyed, not as in my presence only, but now much more in my absence, **work out your own salvation with fear and trembling.** At the same time, I try to share what our Father has taught me for I do know that He does not respect or favor any person.

Now we are going to show something that we showed in the last book; however, it just seems to fit in with believing. And we are going to be going through some of my life and my thought process pretty much the same I did back then for all I do is think about our Father. I was now driving a truck and listening to the bible and I heard something as I was listening. I won't post the entire chapter for it is just a few verses that really stuck out. 1Chronicles 17:16 And David the king came and sat before the Lord, and said, **Who am I, O Lord God, and what is mine house, that thou hast brought me hitherto?** 17 And yet this was a small thing in thine eyes, O God; for thou hast also spoken of thy servant's house for a great while to come, and hast regarded me according to the estate of a man of high degree, O Lord God. 18 What can David speak more to thee for the honour of thy servant? for thou knowest thy servant. 19 O Lord, for thy servant's sake, and according to thine own heart, hast thou done all this greatness, in making known all these great things. I paused the bible immediately and asked the Father same thing. I awoke the next morning with a car accident that I had when I was 16 on my conscience, heavy. This accident happened on March 28th Good Friday of 1986. I was in a coma from Friday afternoon, till Monday morning, or for three days and three nights. Then He started reminding of the date that I went out in the woods and thought I was going to die. This was me being baptized with the Holy Ghost. This baptism took place almost 30 years later to the day. On March 8-9 of 2016. I immediately remembered the scriptures and how old Jesus was when he was baptized. Luke 30:21 Now when all the people were baptized, it came to pass, that Jesus also being baptized, and praying, the heaven was opened, 22 And the Holy Ghost descended in a bodily shape like a dove upon him, and a voice came from heaven, which said, Thou art my beloved Son; in thee I am well pleased. 23 **And Jesus himself began to be about thirty years of age, being (as was supposed) the son of Joseph, which was the son of Heli,** I still didn't connect anything but now am starting to remember of what I heard in the book of Ezekiel and am almost feeling as if my very own life is in the bible. Of course, this just made me want to learn more and learn fast. And now at the same time I am also remembering the scripture in which Jesus spoke. Matthew 12:38 Then certain of the scribes and of the Pharisees answered, saying, Master, we would see a sign from thee. 39 But he answered and said unto them, An evil and adulterous generation seeketh after a sign; and there shall no sign be given to it, but the sign of the prophet Jonas:40 **For as Jonas was three days and three nights in the whale's belly; so shall the Son of man be three days and , three nights in the heart of the earth.** As we showed you all in the last book, our Father gives us instructions while we sleep. Job 33:14 For God speaketh once, yea twice, yet man perceiveth it not. 15 **In a dream, in a vision of the night, when deep sleep falleth upon men, in slumberings upon the bed; 16 Then he openeth the ears of men, and sealeth their instruction, 17 That he may withdraw man from his purpose, and hide pride from man.** 18 He keepeth back his soul from the pit, and his life from perishing by the sword.

Then a few weeks had went along with me listening to the bible every day, all day long as long as I was driving. Now at the same time, I had personal stuff going on with my son. He had gotten to a point in his life that all he wanted to do is play video games and not work. He has a family with two children but would not work and always wanted money. Our Father kept reminding me of the scriptures about a person that would not work. 2 Thessalonians 3:10 For even when we were with you, this we commanded you, **that if any would not work, neither should he eat. 11 For we hear that there are some which walk among you disorderly, working not at all, but are busybodies. 12 Now them that are such we command and exhort**

by our Lord Jesus Christ, that with quietness they work, and eat their own bread. This is the only son of mine out of four that I had and have any contact with at all. But because of my fear of God and trying everything in my power to be obedient, I stopped helping my son financially. I wouldn't even give him money for a pack of gum. I kept talking with him on the phone and such, but the funds were cut off completely for I strongly felt our Father was commanding me to do just that until he got a job. This went on for a couple of months and then one day I got a call from him. He told me he just got a job and that he was going to be starting in a couple of days. He explained where he was going to be working and everything. This was great and now I figured I could start to help him financially again for he now has a job.

Now check this out, about an hour after my son called me and told me of the good news, I got a call from my second to oldest brother. He called and told me he was stuck at a Walmart in Colorado. He told me they had food and everything, but he wanted a $100 so that he could by his family hot food instead of eating what they had. I immediately thought that the money our Father allows me to have goes to the poor and needy and not for the people that just want better. Then I told my brother that I would have to ask the Father for HE is the true owner of the money I have, and I try to do with it of what He tells me to do with it. I got off the phone and was immediately reminded of some scriptures. Genesis 22 And it came to pass after these things, that God did tempt Abraham, and said unto him, Abraham: and he said, Behold, here I am. 2 And he said, Take now thy son, thine only son Isaac, whom thou lovest, and get thee into the land of Moriah; and offer him there for a burnt offering upon one of the mountains which I will tell thee of. 3 And Abraham rose up early in the morning, and saddled his ass, and took two of his young men with him, and Isaac his son, and clave the wood for the burnt offering, and rose up, and went unto the place of which God had told him. 4 Then on the third day Abraham lifted up his eyes, and saw the place afar off. 5 And Abraham said unto his young men, Abide ye here with the ass; and I and the lad will go yonder and worship, and come again to you. 6

And Abraham took the wood of the burnt offering, and laid it upon Isaac his son; and he took the fire in his hand, and a knife; and they went both of them together. 7 And Isaac spake unto Abraham his father, and said, My father: and he said, Here am I, my son. And he said, Behold the fire and the wood: but where is the lamb for a burnt offering? 8 And Abraham said, My son, God will provide himself a lamb for a burnt offering: so they went both of them together. 9 And they came to the place which God had told him of; and Abraham built an altar there, and laid the wood in order, and bound Isaac his son, and laid him on the altar upon the wood. 10 And Abraham stretched forth his hand, and took the knife to slay his son. 11 And the angel of the Lord called unto him out of heaven, and said, Abraham, Abraham: and he said, Here am I. 12 And he said, Lay not thine hand upon the lad, neither do thou any thing unto him: for now I know that thou fearest God, seeing thou hast not withheld thy son, thine only son from me. 13 **And Abraham lifted up his eyes, and looked, and behold behind him a ram caught in a thicket by his horns: and Abraham went and took the ram, and offered him up for a burnt offering in the stead of his son.** 14 And Abraham called the name of that place Jehovahjireh: as it is said to this day, In the mount of the Lord it shall be seen. 15 And the angel of the Lord called unto Abraham out of heaven the second time, 16 And said, By myself have I sworn, saith the Lord, for because thou hast done this thing, and hast not withheld thy son, thine only son: My brother was the ram caught in a thicket by his horns. I did not send my brother money.

I am not trying to tell you all my alms for I do try to do these in secret as commanded in Matthew 6, but I am explaining how I believe. But, my very next load went through where my son lives, so I helped them purchase a car for now he had a job and he needed reliable transportation that his entire family could be safe in. I now knew what we showed in the last book. God never commanded us to sacrifice animals and that He is not as vindictive as this world portrays Him to be. I couldn't connect it in the bible at that time, but I now knew that had my only son on that same alter as Abraham. We are the beast that the kings, Lords, and spirits are commanded to sacrifice as we showed in the last book. Now I am remembering the scriptures in which tell us that we will sit in the kingdom with Abraham. Matthew 8:11 And I say unto you, **That many shall come from the east and west, and shall sit down with Abraham, and Isaac, and Jacob, in the kingdom of heaven.** 12 But the children of the kingdom shall be cast out into outer darkness: there shall be weeping and gnashing of teeth.

Now that we have brought up on how I have sat with Abraham, we need to see how I have sat with Isaac, and Jacob also. Without showing all the scriptures, we think most are familiar with how Isaac blessed Jacob first even though he was younger than Esau. I am the youngest boy in the family. My sister is younger than me, but I have three older brothers. And I am despised by all three of my brothers for my knowledge and blessing I have received from our Father.

Now I know one of the first things our Father allowed me to hear after I got in the truck was Psalm 89:19 Then thou spakest in vision to thy holy one, and saidst, I have laid help upon one that is mighty; I have exalted one chosen out of the people. 20 I have found David my servant; with my holy oil have I anointed him: 21 With whom my hand shall be established: mine arm also shall strengthen him. 22 The enemy shall not exact upon him; nor the son of wickedness afflict him. 23 And I will beat down his foes before his face, and plague them that hate him. 24 But my faithfulness and my mercy shall be with him: and in my name shall his horn be exalted. 25 I will set his hand also in the sea, and his right hand in the rivers. 26 **He shall cry unto me, Thou art my father, my God, and the rock of my salvation. 27 Also I will make him my firstborn, higher than the kings of the earth. 28 My mercy will I keep for him for evermore, and my covenant shall stand fast with him.** 29 His seed also will I make to endure for ever, and his throne as the days of heaven. 30 If his children forsake my law, and walk not in my judgments; 31 If they break my statutes, and keep not my commandments; 32 Then will I visit their transgression with the rod, and their iniquity with stripes. 33 Nevertheless my lovingkindness will I not utterly take from him, nor suffer my faithfulness to fail. 34 My covenant will I not break, nor alter the thing that is gone out of my lips. 35 Once have I sworn by my holiness that I will not lie unto David. 36 His seed shall endure for ever, and his throne as the sun before me. I had to show this to my son for our Father allowed me to hear it and I wanted my son to hear what it said about my children. I just knew this was me because this is exactly what I do. I had been doing this for quite some time now. At this point of my life, there was absolutely no way anybody was going to convince that the bible isn't about our very own lives today. Our Father had me write that in the first book. The bible is one long letter on how we are to live our lives today and not about the people of the past.

It had been some time now that I have been doing this, but now I could hear that our Father would raise one man that would call on Him when he arrises. Isaiah 41:25 I have raised up one from the north, and he shall come: from the rising of the sun shall he call upon my name: and he shall come upon princes as upon morter, and as the potter treadeth clay. This connected strongly for I had been doing this for some time. I don't just mean that I awake and pray. If I am awake at 11 pm the night before, I will go to bible gateway to see what the verse of the day is for tomorrow. This gives me an idea of what I am going to be listening to when I awake. Wherever the verse is in the bible, I know there is something that our Father is wanting to hear for that day, within three chapters of the bible surrounding that verse. When I wake up, I will listen to these three chapters at least two times. And when the next day rolls around and the next verse of the day stays in the same area, I know that I didn't hear what I needed to hear, so I will listen to these chapter three times or maybe four. To show how real this is, I need to explain how this worked just today. Yesterday I was writing and knew that I need to show this, but I couldn't remember where it was in the bible. I could remember what it said, but I could not remember how it was worded. So, let us listen to the verse of the day. Isaiah 40:31 But they that wait upon the Lord shall renew their strength; they shall mount up with wings as eagles; they shall run, and not be weary; and they shall walk, and not faint. Now this is what the verse of the day is but notice how the area that shows how I call on our Father when I awake is in Isaiah 41.

David Jenkins

Now I am not remembering exactly when this happened, but I do know for certain that I hadn't been in the truck very long. Before we dive into this, we need to do a little bit of background on myself. This goes back to 2003 or 2004. I was with Cathy, the mother of my daughter that has my granddaughter in which is my mom and dad as one flesh. This was explained in the last book as well. I was driving for a local concrete company at the time. I had finished my shift one day with my odometer ending with 777. I got home from work that day and told Cathy that I really felt that I needed to go to the casino. Now we will pause for I know there are many that think that going to a casino is wrong. As we showed in the last book everybody one the planet makes up the one son of God. So let us remind you of this. John 1 In the beginning was the Word, and the Word was with God, and the Word was God. 2 The same was in the beginning with God. 3 **All things were made by him; and without him was not any thing made that was made.** The casinos belong to our Father and are also for the son of God. So, to go on, it was the spring season and the hours were pretty short at work. Cathy was running a at home daycare but did not have that many children at the time. We were almost two months behind on rent of $650 a month and over a month behind on utilities. I told Cathy that I would only take a hundred dollars and just see what happens for I strongly felt I needed to go. That hundred dollars was not going to pay the bills as needed but if something good happened at the casino, then we could pay our bills. These were the thoughts going through my head as I was heading to the casino. I went to one slot machine, played for a bit and lost $65 of the $100 and figured well maybe nothing was going to happen. So, I cashed out and started walking to the exit, when all the sudden, I figured hey I came with $100 and I mays as well try the $1 Wheel of Fortune slot with the remaining $35. I stuck my $35 dollars in and played max credits. I spun once and nothing hit. I spun the second time and hit $1,000. I stepped back and said you have got to be kidding. I stepped up and spun it a few more times getting it up to around $1,670. I spun a few more times and it got down to $1,600. I stopped and said to myself, the bills are paid. I cashed out and went home. We had no way of paying the bills before this. Now we are caught up with a couple hundred extra in our pockets. And that got us through till the hours picked up at work.

Now I know that we are really getting off track here, but I truly feel our Father is telling me to tell of a couple things that have happened to show some things that He did so that I could also know something miraculous was happening. This was shortly after I had read the bible for the first time. I had taken my daughter to Macon, Mo. For a weekend visit with my mom. We were leaving to go back to Iowa. My daughter was in the car, my mom was watching at the door. The screen door was closed. I had my door open and was just about to sit in the car and all the sudden, the globe off the porch light fell. I instantly thought that this was very weird for there was no movement around that door for at least 3-4 minutes. Erin and I got the glass, and everything cleaned up for my mom so that shew wouldn't have to worry about stepping on broken glass. This took about 15 minutes or so. Now as we are driving back to Iowa, we are going up US 27 when a cop car blew by us with his lights and sirens blasting. My daughter's reply is wow, he is going fast. Then about 2 or 3 minutes later. another goes by with just his lights going but he seemed to be going fast than the first. Obviously, my daughter commented on how he was going faster than the last. I told her that there must be an accident or something somewhere. We get to US 92 and head east for this is the way we are taking to Davenport. We go about 4 or 5 miles and are now seeing where these police were heading. When we got to the scene, the ambulance was just getting there. There was a pick up that had side swiped something like a blazer or something like that. My daughter tells me there were three vehicles involved, but I only remember two. Now I can't say for certain, but if we would have not taken the time to clean up that glass from the globe at my mom's. We would have been a lot closer to that accident, if not involved. Coincidence? I think not.

Then it was just a couple of weeks later I was driving to Kankakee, Illinois to get certified for advance open water scuba diving. I am certified scuba diver, but this would allow me to dive deeper to stay within regulations. I had just gotten off work on a Friday evening. This was taking place just shortly after our Father had called me to the bible, so I wasn't observing the sabbath at that time. I was still in darkness. Ephesians 5:8 **For ye were sometimes darkness, but now are ye light in the Lord: walk as children of light:** It was dark out and I had seen a deer about 10 feet off the highway. Me being a truck driver, see them all the time, so I didn't give it much thought. About 10 minutes later or so, I see two or three more, but these were pretty close to the road. I immediately thought within myself that maybe I should kick the cruise down a few mph, jut incase. So, I did and about an hour later, I am looking forward and notice headlights coming around a curve in front of me. In my direction, the curve goes to the right and to the oncoming vehicle, it goes to the left. Then I notice that after this vehicle completed the curve, it kept going as if it was still on a curve. The vehicle crossed my lane and went into the ditch and flipped. Immediate reaction, I stopped to see if the person was okay. The gravel was still rolling from where the vehicle flipped over. That is how close this was in front of me. I called 911 and told them of my location. I asked the driver of the vehicle if he was okay and he replied that he was good. When the police arrived, I gave them my statement and they advised me that this driver was drunk. The officer then asked me where I was heading, so I told him. Then he said something that took my breath away. He said, you almost didn't get to where you were going. I knew instantly that if I would have not slowed down for those deer, I would have been a few seconds further than I was. That would have put me right there in the spot that driver came into my lane.

    With everything that our Father has been teaching me now I can say with all certainty that was being fed manna without me knowing about it. Deuteronomy 8 All the commandments which I command thee this day shall ye observe to do, that ye may live, and multiply, and go in and possess the land which the Lord sware unto your fathers.2 **And thou shalt remember all the way which the Lord thy God led thee these forty years in the wilderness, to humble thee, and to prove thee, to know what was in thine heart, whether thou**

wouldest keep his commandments, or no. 3 And he humbled thee, and suffered thee to hunger, and fed thee with manna, which thou knewest not, neither did thy fathers know; that he might make thee know that man doth not live by bread only, but by every word that proceedeth out of the mouth of the Lord doth man live. Can you see how I can see how this is relating to my very own life. He didn't call me to the bible until shortly after I turned 41.

Let us get back on topic now. Now very shortly after being in the truck, I felt this urge to go to the casino. I stopped in Council Bluffs, Ia. And went in to play some poker for I had went to a poker school back in 2010. I no longer was playing the slot machines because I discovered poker. Now I am thinking, I know God uses the casinos to help people, speaking from experience. When I started playing cash poker, I noticed they had a tournament going on, but it had started about and hour and a half ago. The blinds were very high. I wanted to join but with the blinds being so high I weighed against it. I played for six or seven hours and lost around $400. I had no problems with losing for I knew God helped me, so who was I to say it was wrong if He used the money, He allowed me to have to help someone else out. The very next day I was heading south east and had to go through St louis, MO. I kept having this strong over whelming sensation that I needed to go to another casino. I am asking our Father why, I just lost $400 last night? Anyway, the closer I got to St. Louis, the stronger the urge got. So, I stopped, and they had a tournament starting in just over an hour. I am thinking okay; I can do this for it only cost $110 and that will be a controlled loss if I lose. The tournament is now starting and there is about 120 people registered. I am thinking this is going to be fun. This is the biggest tourney that I had ever joined. About 10 minutes into the game, I am sitting in seat 3, not remembering the table number, and it just came out of my mouth, loud enough that the entire table could hear. I am just here to watch. I did now know what it meant, but I laughed my butt off. About six hours into the tourney, the blinds were getting very high. I got down to one half blind in my stack and now was convinced that I was going to bust out soon. There are about 30 people left, I get big cards and decide to go all in. I won that pot and the next four or five more after that. I now am the chip leader. I am excited beyond belief. They decide to break my table and as I am stacking my chips so that I could move, I tell the dealer that I am just here to watch. I now knew what it meant. Our Father was the one actually playing the game. David was just there to watch. Well as I am stacking my chips, I dropped one of my chips into my cup of coffee. I couldn't get it out with my finger. I remembered the scriptures saying nothing that I drink will hurt me. Mark 16:18 They shall take up serpents; **and if they drink any deadly thing, it shall not hurt them;** they shall lay hands on the sick, and they shall recover. I gulped the coffee down so that I could get my chip out. The dealer looked at me and said, I would drink that if I was you. I laughed and told her that I could drink anything I want, and it will not hurt me. So now we are getting down to the last 15-18 people left. We are about seven hours into the game, I am not chip leader but am third or fourth in chips. This is a different kind of tourney. The last nine people of the game win a thousand dollars. I am feeling pretty confident that I can make it to the end. And after eight hours of playing. My self and eight other players won $1,000 each.

Now with reading and hearing what we just did a bit ago in John 1, who do you think was playing that game. This is what is going through my mind. Our Father is playing, He is shuffling the cards and dealing them the way He wants them to be dealt. He dwells in all of us. He is the one that is causing people to fold when they shouldn't or call a raise when the shouldn't. He is the one in control of everything down to the very minute. This is when I started to realize that there is no such thing as a coincidence, nor good or bad luck. He uses these casinos to help people, chastise people, or even take vengeance on people. I am speaking of experience and not just a simple belief. Of course, after this happened, I got quite the big head and did start going to a few casinos. I would win some and lose some. But there were times that I thought I was going in so that I would win big and could use the money to help others or maybe take another trip to Israel. I would lose. So, as a reader, please do not think this is an open-door policy to go to the casinos. If our Father does not want you there, you will lose big. But at the same time, don't allow anyone to convince you that it is a sin to be in a casino. If you conscience allows it, then maybe you are being guided there. Remember they do have dominion over our bodies.

Now during this time that I would go to the casinos and play poker for cash, He taught me another very good lesson. I stopped in a casino in Kansas and was having a pretty good night. I was playing $1-$2 no limit hold'em poker. I picked up something like suited jack-eight. I don't remember exactly how that hand played out, but I do remember that when all cards were on the table, I had the nut full house. All three players got all their money in and I won like $700 in one hand. I do know one player had a smaller full house and the other had a straight. I walked out with over $1,000 that night. The very next time I went into a casino to play poker, not remembering what the cards were, I had a straight once all the cards were on the table. There was two other players in. One of them had a small full house and the other had the nut full house. I immediately remembered what Jesus said in Matthew 7:12 **Therefore all things whatsoever ye would that men should do to you, do ye even so to them: for this is the law and the prophets.** I was all in with about $200 and now I just lost a hand that I had won with, just the last time I played. I won a big hand with the nut full house but, now that tables were turned and now, I just lost a big hand with the exact same circumstances. So yes, He even uses the casinos to teach us lessons in life. There is not one thing in this world, nor heaven that does not belong to our Father and everything has a reason.

It is believing that everybody on the planet is the son of God. My wife that I had problems within Missouri, my brothers, and my sister. It was not them personally doing what they did, however it was our Father commanding them to do what they were doing so that I could learn who I am and what our Father had planned for my life. They are servants, and or vessels of God. All that was happening is that our Father used these servants to help get me on the path He needed me to be on.

It is not making people feel less important to God by insulting them, telling them they are doing wrong, This is why we are told what we are in Romans 3:13 **Their throat is an open sepulchre; with their tongues they have used deceit; the poison of asps is under their lips:** As we showed just a bit ago in Matthew 21, if you think anyone has done or doing wrong by our Father, you will not enter into the kingdom of God. Now the kingdom of God is not something that is going to be set up at the end of the world for the kingdom of God is within each of us. Luke 17:20 And when he was demanded of the Pharisees, when the kingdom of God should come, he answered them and said, **The kingdom of God cometh not with observation: 21 Neither shall they say, Lo here! or, lo there! for, behold, the kingdom of God is within you.**

This is what we really tried to explain in the last book. That everybody on the planet makes up the son of God and not just one person. Our Father is up there in heaven looking down on us and just watching all the pain and anguish that we are causing for His son. We are all familiar with Matthew 1:23 **Behold, a virgin shall be with child, and shall bring forth a son, and they shall call his name Emmanuel, which being interpreted is, God with us.** And as we showed you in the last book, we are hearing conversations being held in heaven when we listen to the scriptures. Now listen to what we can hear in Isaiah 8:5 The Lord spake also unto me again, saying, 6 Forasmuch as this people refuseth the waters of Shiloah that go softly, and rejoice in Rezin and Remaliah's son; 7 Now therefore, behold, the Lord bringeth up upon them the waters of the river, strong and many, even the king of Assyria, and all his glory: and he shall come up over all his channels, and go over all his banks: 8 **And he shall pass through Judah; he shall overflow and go over, he shall reach even to the neck; and the stretching out of his wings shall fill the breadth of thy land, O Immanuel.** Spelled a little different however, sound just alike when you hear them. I have listened to both in the bible and on google or You tube, and I can hear no difference when listening to both names. The son of God or Emmanuel covers the entire earth.

This is where we need to look at how we are to pray. Matthew 6 After this manner therefore pray ye: Our Father which art in heaven, Hallowed be thy name.10 Thy kingdom come, **Thy will be done in earth, as it is in heaven.**11 Give us this day our daily bread.12 And forgive us our debts, as we forgive our debtors.13 And lead us not into temptation, but deliver us from evil: For thine is the kingdom, and the power, and the glory, for ever. Amen. In the last book on how when we see the earth trough our Fathers eyes from above, we can see the entire son of God consisting of about 8 billion body parts. We are being told that it will happen in earth as it is in heaven.

I started to write the last book in May of 2018, I finished around the end of September. BEHOLD, A GREATER THAN JONAS IS HERE!!! After I sent the manuscript to the publisher, I called to ask how many pages it was. On my program on the laptop showed one thing of 295, and then another showing 315, or something like that. I couldn't tell. While I was on the phone with them, they looked it up. They told me it is 316 pages long. I instantly remembered John 3:16 **For God so loved the world, that he gave his only begotten Son, that whosoever believeth in him should not perish, but have everlasting life.** So, I want to ask a question. Do you think that when I started writing the book in May, I had any idea of how many pages the book would be?

We are going to get sidetracked for a few minutes here. Now I mentioned that we placed the entire chapter of Isaiah 58 earlier for there is a very important message in there. I am going to place the first few verses of it again so that we can actually hear this message. Isaiah 58 Cry aloud, spare not, lift up thy voice like a trumpet, and shew my people their transgression, and the house of Jacob their sins. 2 Yet they seek me daily, and delight to know my ways, as a nation that did righteousness, and forsook not the ordinance of their God: they ask of me the ordinances of justice; they take delight in approaching to God. 3 Wherefore have we fasted, say they, and thou seest not? wherefore have we afflicted our soul, and thou takest no knowledge? Behold, in the day of your fast ye find pleasure, and exact all your labours. 4 Behold, ye fast for strife and debate, and to smite with the fist of wickedness: ye shall not fast as ye do this day, to make your voice to be heard on high. 5 **Is it such a fast that I have chosen? a day for a man to afflict his soul? is it to bow down his head as a bulrush, and to spread sackcloth and ashes under him? wilt thou call this a fast, and an acceptable day to the Lord? 6 Is not this the fast that I have chosen? to loose the bands of wickedness, to undo the heavy burdens, and to let the oppressed go free, and that ye break every yoke? 7 Is it not to deal thy bread to the hungry, and that thou bring the poor that are cast out to thy house? when thou seest the naked, that thou cover him; and that thou hide not thyself from thine own flesh?** 8 Then shall thy light break forth as the morning, and thine health shall spring forth speedily: and thy righteousness shall go before thee; the glory of the Lord shall be thy reward. 9 Then shalt thou call, and the Lord shall answer; thou shalt cry, and he shall say, Here I am. If thou take away from the midst of thee the yoke, the putting forth of the finger, and speaking vanity; 10 And if thou draw out thy soul to the hungry, and satisfy the afflicted soul; then shall thy light rise in obscurity, and thy darkness be as the noon day: 11 And the Lord shall guide thee continually, and satisfy thy soul in drought, and make fat thy bones: and thou shalt be like a watered garden, and like a spring of water, whose waters fail not. 12 And they that shall be of thee shall build the old waste places: thou shalt raise up the foundations of many generations; and thou shalt be called, The repairer of the breach, The restorer of paths to dwell in.

that our Father never commanded us to starve ourselves at the time we fast. First and foremost, we should be mindful of what Jesus tells us about fasting. Matthew 6:16 Moreover when ye fast, be not, as the hypocrites, of a sad countenance: for they disfigure their faces, that they may appear unto men to fast. Verily I say unto you, They have their reward. 17 But thou, when thou fastest, anoint thine head, and wash thy face; 18 That thou appear not unto men to fast, but unto thy Father which is in secret: and thy Father, which seeth in secret, shall reward thee openly. This is not telling us to make a public scene, nor is it telling us that we should let anyone know of when we fast. With that being said, if we truly listen to what our Father is saying above, we can hear that a fast that He commands is about helping others. It is about taking the burden of someone else's shoulders. It is about undoing heavy burdens on others. It is about clothing the naked, feeding the needy, and even housing those that go without. Remember the two greatest commandments. Matthew 22:36 Then one of them, which was a lawyer, asked him a question, tempting him, and saying, 36 Master, which is the great commandment in the law? 37 **Jesus said unto him, Thou shalt love the Lord thy God with all thy heart, and with all thy soul, and with all thy mind. 38 This is the first and great commandment.** 39 **And the second is like unto it, Thou shalt love thy neighbour as thyself. 40 On these two commandments hang all the law and the prophets.**

Nowhere in our bible does are we commanded to starve ourselves or even to go without food for any particular length of time. In fact, we are told that food is necessary. Job 23:12 Neither have I gone back from the commandment of his lips; **I have esteemed the words of his mouth more than my necessary food.** We need food to help keep or maintain our health. If we do not eat regularly, we suffer from weakness of muscles, weakening of the immune system, phycological, and emotional problems. All these can affect us and all those that we interreact with on a daily basis. It can also not keep us from working. If we cannot work, how can we do all these things listed as what a true fast is?

Matthew 16:24 Then said Jesus unto his disciples, If any man will come after me, **let him deny himself, and take up his cross, and follow me.** 25 For whosoever will save his life shall lose it: and whosoever will lose his life for my sake shall find it. 26 For what is a man profited, if he shall gain the whole world, and lose his own soul? or what shall a man give in exchange for his soul? Helping others out and denying our own wants and desires is what this entire bible is about. It is not about knowing that you will benefit from helping others. It is not thinking that you can't help someone out because you will not get anything in return. As we showed in the last book, it is learning to love in the same manner as our Father loves us. When you listen to verses 8-12 of Isaiah 58, we can hear that our Father will reward us after we do this fast in which He commands. He is not going to do this before, or so that we will help others out. It is showing Him with our spiritual works that we think of and love others at least as much as we think of ourselves.

Now we showed you all just a bit ago in Malachi 4 that is those that truly fear our Father, it is to them that the sun or son of righteousness is risen up in, That fear is the beginning of all wisdom in which comes from our Father. Proverbs 9:10 **The fear of the Lord is the beginning of wisdom: and the knowledge of the holy is understanding**. That fear is not a fear that He is going to knock your teeth out or cut your throat or something like that. It is a fear of knowing and believing that He does have control of everything, and He is the one in which can make your own life a living hell or He can bring some peace within you. Yes, Jesus is the king of peace, but this king will not rise inside you unless you show our Father that you love Him with all of your heart, soul, and mind. The only way this can be done is by seeking Him and the only place we can learn about our Father is Moses and the prophets. Not my words but the very words of Jesus Christ, as we showed you all earlier in John 5 and 6.

I truly feel that this all starts with us truly believing that our Father is perfect, righteous, and justified in everything He has done, doing and will do. If you truly, and I do mean truly believe that He is perfect, then you will have the same desire as Jesus did to be obedient in all that our Father commanded or is commanding him to do. Hebrews 5:8 **Though he were a Son, yet learned he obedience by the things which he suffered; 9 And being made perfect, he became the author of eternal salvation unto all them that obey him;** I do remember that I did come to truly believe that our Father is perfect before He had me write the first book. To me, that makes since for how could He have me write a book about something I didn't agree with, with all my heart? No, this does not mean that I understood anything as I do today, but I do know that with me believing that He is perfect is why I still continue to seek His perfection. There are a lot of people that I talk with, that tell me that they know our Father is perfect yet refuse to learn about Him. They always make a comment as I don't have time, or I don't understand the old testament. There is a humongous difference in believing that He is perfect and knowing and believing that the scriptures say that He is perfect.

Once we get to the stage of truly believing is when our Father raises up Jesus inside of us and that is when we are sealed as shown in Ephesians 1:13 **In whom ye also trusted, after that ye heard the word of truth, the gospel of your salvation: in whom also after that ye believed, ye were sealed with that holy Spirit of promise, 14 Which is the earnest of our inheritance until the redemption of the purchased possession, unto the praise of his glory.**

We do not get sealed if we believe that our Father has changed His perfection. Our Father's house is perfect and is functioning perfectly. If you believe that this perfection has or is going to change, then how can it still be perfect? This is where you need to ask yourself, do you truly believe our Father is perfect? Or are you believing the son of perdition that is sitting inside the temple of God. Remember, you are the temple of God and the son of perdition sits inside the temple of God. This is a spirit in which our Father will allow to have dominion over your body for you have made the choice not to take the time to get to know our Father and who and what He is all about.

We can hear this when we listen to what we are being told in 2 Thessalonians Now we beseech you, brethren, by the coming of our Lord Jesus Christ, and by our gathering together unto him. 2 That ye be not soon shaken in mind, or be troubled, neither by spirit, nor by word, nor by letter as from us, as that the day of Christ is at hand. 3 Let no man deceive you by any means: for that day shall not come, except there come a falling away first, and that man of sin be revealed, the son of perdition; 4 **Who opposeth and exalteth himself above all that is called God, or that is worshipped; so that he as God sitteth in the temple of God, shewing himself that he is God.** 5 Remember ye not, that, when I was yet with you, I told you these things? 6 And now ye know what withholdeth that he might be revealed in his time. 7 For the mystery of iniquity doth already work: only he who now letteth will let, until he be taken out of the way. 8 And then shall that Wicked be revealed, whom the Lord shall consume with the spirit of his mouth, and shall destroy with the brightness of his coming: 9 Even him, whose coming is after the working of Satan with all power and signs and lying wonders, 10 And with all deceivableness of unrighteousness in them that perish; because they received not the love of the truth, that they might be saved. 11 **And for this cause God shall send them strong delusion, that they should believe a lie: 12 That they all might be damned who believed not the truth, but had pleasure in unrighteousness.**

Now we need to be listening to a couple more spots of our bibles in the closing of this chapter. Romans 10 Brethren, my heart's desire and prayer to God for Israel is, that they might be saved. 2 For I bear them record that they have a zeal of God, but not according to knowledge. 3 **For they being ignorant of God's righteousness, and going about to establish their own righteousness, have not submitted themselves unto the righteousness of God. 4 For Christ is the end of the law for righteousness to every one that believeth.** 5 For Moses describeth the righteousness which is of the law, That the man which doeth those things shall live by them. 6 But the righteousness which is of faith speaketh on this wise, Say not in thine heart, Who shall ascend into heaven? (that is, to bring Christ down from above:) 7 Or, Who shall descend into the deep? (that is, to bring up Christ again from the dead.) 8 But what saith it? The word is nigh thee, even in thy mouth, and in thy heart: that is, the word of faith, which we preach; 9 That if thou shalt confess with thy mouth the Lord Jesus, and shalt believe in thine heart that God hath raised him from the dead, thou shalt be saved. 10 For with the heart man believeth unto righteousness; and with the mouth confession is made unto salvation. 11 For the scripture saith, Whosoever believeth on him shall not be ashamed. 12 For there is no difference between the Jew and the Greek: for the same Lord over all is rich unto all that call upon him. 13 For whosoever shall call upon the name of the Lord shall be saved. 14 **How then shall they call on him in whom they have not believed? and how shall they believe in him of whom they have not heard?** and how shall they hear without a preacher? 15 And how shall they preach, except they be sent? as it is written, How beautiful are the feet of them that preach the gospel of peace, and bring glad tidings of good things! 16 But they have not all obeyed the gospel. For Esaias saith, Lord, who hath believed our report? 17 So then faith cometh by hearing, and hearing by the word of God. 18 But I say, Have they not heard? Yes verily, their sound went into all the earth, and their words unto the ends of the world. 19 But I say, Did not Israel know? First Moses saith, I will provoke you to jealousy by them that are no people, and by a foolish nation I will anger you. 20 But Esaias is very bold, and saith, I was found of them that sought me not; I was made manifest unto them that asked not after me. 21 But to Israel he saith, All day long I have stretched forth my hands unto a disobedient and gainsaying people.

As we can hear in here, it is about believing in our Father. If we do not believe in our Father in which is perfect, righteous, and justified in everything that He has done, doing, and will do, then we do not believe God. How can someone call on God to save them from troubles if they show God with their spiritual works, that they do not want anything to do with Him? Why would God want anything to do with you if you do not want anything to do with Him?

Now I have heard of and have spoken with people saying things like, why should we believe the bible for it was written by man. To that I say is a copout or and just another way of saying you do not believe in the power of God. Listen to what we are told in 2 Peter 1:17 For he received from God the Father honour and glory, when there came such a voice to him from the excellent glory, This is my beloved Son, in whom I am well pleased. 18 And this voice which came from heaven we heard, when we were with him in the holy mount. 19 We have also a more sure word of prophecy; whereunto ye do well that ye take heed, as unto a light that shineth in a dark place, until the day dawn, and the day star arise in your hearts: 20 Knowing this first, that no prophecy of the scripture is of any private interpretation. 21 **For the prophecy came not in old time by the will of man: but holy men of God spake as they were moved by the Holy Ghost.** Now with everything that our Father has taught me, I can say without a doubt that our bible is written by our Father. He just used these holy men as servants and or vessels to write the bible.

Okay, I thought we were done with this chapter, so I stepped away for a few minutes to think of how to start the next chapter, when our Father reminded me of something I said in the very beginning of this chapter. I mentioned that our Father has been teaching me obedience for just over three years now. We are going to explain this obedience without showing how I am commanded for that will cause more harm than good if someone tries to skip all the stages that our Father has put me through. This didn't happen until after He had severed me from all other people. He had to do this for if there are other people around me, I get distracted a lot, they disagree with what He is teaching me, and I believe the best way to teach me anything is one on one. He is constantly teaching me so yes; I prefer to be by myself. Yet, I never feel as if I am alone. What I mean by it can cause more harm than good is talked about in the bible. Exodus 19:12 And thou shalt set bounds unto the people round about, saying, Take heed to yourselves, that ye go not up into the mount, or touch the border of it: **whosoever toucheth the mount shall be surely put to death:** Hebrew 12:19 And the sound of a trumpet, and the voice of words; which voice they that heard intreated that the word should not be spoken to them any more: 20 (For they could not endure that which was commanded, **And if so much as a beast touch the mountain, it shall be stoned, or thrust through with a dart:**

This is where we need to remember that we are counted as beast in the bible. We showed that in the last book and it will be covered more, later in this book. This is a spiritual mountain and if we do not go through the process of allowing Moses and the prophets lead us unto this mountain, we have no right to be there. Our Father will not tolerate it, under no circumstances. Therefore, He teaches us a little at a time, and continually testing our hearts to make sure that we do have the true desire to continue to seek His wisdom and not man's. It is like we have to climb the mountain but only by His instructions. Again, showing why the entire bible is one long letter from our Father, giving us instructions on how we are to live our lives today.

Listen to what He tells us about the way He will teach us. Isaiah 28:9 **Whom shall he teach knowledge? and whom shall he make** to understand doctrine? them that are weaned from the milk, and drawn from the breasts. 10 For precept must be upon precept, precept upon precept; line upon line, line upon line; here a little, and there a little:** Now while He is teaching us in this manner, He is also continually testing our hearts. Job 7:18 And that thou shouldest visit him every morning, **and try him every moment?** Deuteronomy 8:2 And thou shalt remember all the way which the Lord thy God led thee these forty years in the wilderness, to humble thee, and to prove thee, **to know what was in thine heart, whether thou wouldest keep his commandments, or no.** Then if we desire the honor of men rather than God as shown just a bit ago, He will, well listen to Isaiah 28:11 For with stammering lips and another tongue will he speak to this people. 12 To whom he said, This is the rest wherewith ye may cause the weary to rest; and this is the refreshing: yet they would not hear. 13 **But the word of the Lord was unto them precept upon precept, precept upon precept; line upon line, line upon line; here a little, and there a little; that they might go, and fall backward, and be broken, and snared, and taken.**

Now that we have shown that, we want to show you all how what He has been teaching me. I am a truck driver and drive 11 to 14,000 miles a month. This does stem from **believing** that everybody on the planet is a servant and or vessel of God. Or better yet said, makes up the one son of God. I am shown what lane to be in. I am shown when to merge to a different lane. I am given about a three to five- mile advance notice if there is a traffic jam coming up. I am shown when traffic is getting ready to be heavy. I am shown where to stop the truck so that I can find a parking spot. I am usually told, without calling ahead, if I can sleep at the customers. I am shown in advance if I am going to have to wait a short or long time when I arrive to a shipper or receiver. I am usually shown if I am going to be inspected by D.O.T. I always run legal, but it is kind of nice to know if I am picking up a trailer with a light out or something. I know I need to get it fixed before crossing the scale. There are other things in which I am shown how to do but I think you get the idea. This is because I **believe**. And I believe what I hear when I am told this. John 16:13 Howbeit when he, the Spirit of truth, is come, he will guide you into all truth: for he shall not speak of himself; but whatsoever he shall hear, **that shall he speak: and he will shew you things to come.** All these things and more are me being told or shewed of things to come.

When this first started to happen, I freaked out. It was like you have got to be kidding me. Then there was also a time shortly after this started, I kept telling my mom, that it wasn't fair to other drivers. She kept telling me that it isn't for them to understand. I understand that now, but I didn't then. That was our Father using my mom as a vessel of God to tell me that. Then about two months before my mom passed away, I was shown that she was going to be passing away soon. I could not tell family members, but I was shown. I was sitting in Maine when I was shown that she was not coming home from the hospital. I am not told these things because I do not believe in our Father. I am not told or shown these things because I think our Father changed from His perfection. I am told these things for I know, way beyond believing, our Father is perfect, righteous, and justified in everything He has done, doing, and will do and I know that He is perfect righteous, and justified in everything that He has ever said, saying, and will say. For me, it is almost like I can't unbelieve if you will. These things that happen that show me of what is to come, keep happening. That is why I stated in the beginning that I am a rebellious man. There are times that I do screw up or sometimes just ignore of what I am being showed. But I always talk to Him about whatever I am doing. And am constantly asking for His mercy And I do take full responsibility for my transgressions. I do not try to say I screwed up because someone else made me. It is ALWAYS my own fault, and not His, for He does as He said He would do. And that is why Jesus tells us this in Matthew 4:4 **But he answered and said, It is written, Man shall not live by bread alone, but by every word that proceedeth out of the mouth of God.** And the starting point to learning and hearing every word that proceedeth out of the mouth of God is in our bible from Genesis 1:1 through Revelation 22:21.

In the last book, we showed how my dad died in 2003, then my mom passed in 2016. Then our Father joined these two souls as one and sent them back into captivity through my daughter. Yes, my granddaughter is my mon and dad as one. But here is what I feel I am being told to show you all. About two months before my mom passed, our Father had me on a load that conveniently through Columbia, Missouri at the very time my mom was in Columbia for a doctor's visit. She had cancer and was going to have it removed in a couple of months. While I was at the docs with her and my sister, I heard things being said in such a fashion, that I knew my mom was not coming home from the hospital. Then when she went in to have the surgery, I was sitting in Maine. I had been talking with my sister while mom was in the hospital to keep up on mom's status. I was going to move the truck about 15 miles south to a Walmart so I could send some money to my brother. He was staying with my mom and was going to install a new shower unit for mom when she came home. Just as I got ready to leave, I received a commandment, don't move. It was right then; I knew my mom was not going back to her house. Then come Monday morning, my sister called and said it has been touch and go but now they are starting to talk about sending mom home. I started to think maybe I understood things wrong. Which is not uncommon for me with me not being confident in my flesh. Then a couple more hours passed, and I received another call from my sister. Mom had a cardiac arrest while they were walking her in the hall and there was no way of saving her. I was shown two months before she passed that she was going to pass.

Now that we are bringing my mom up and how I was told in advance that she was going to pass, we need to look at something else. I found our shortly after my mom passed, that she refused to take blood. One of my three older brothers called me and asked me when mom became a Jew? Apparently while she was unconscious, they gave her some blood for she lost a lot in surgery. When she awoke, they were putting more blood in her and she told them to stop for she was a Jew. Now I do not ever recall my mom being anything of the sorts but I knew right then and there that this is a form of trying to save your life. This would also go with organ transplants. Genesis 9:4 **But flesh with the life thereof, which is the blood thereof, shall ye**

not eat. 5 And surely your blood of your lives will I require; at the hand of every beast will I require it, and at the hand of man; at the hand of every man's brother will I require the life of man. Leviticus 17:13 And whatsoever man there be of the children of Israel, or of the strangers that sojourn among you, which hunteth and catcheth any beast or fowl that may be eaten; he shall even pour out the blood thereof, and cover it with dust. 14 **For it is the life of all flesh; the blood of it is for the life thereof: therefore I said unto the children of Israel, Ye shall eat the blood of no manner of flesh: for the life of all flesh is the blood thereof: whosoever eateth it shall be cut off.** Acts 15:28 For it seemed good to the Holy Ghost, and to us, to lay upon you no greater burden than these necessary things; 29 **That ye abstain from meats offered to idols, and from blood, and from things strangled, and from fornication: from which if ye keep yourselves, ye shall do well. Fare ye well.** If we are truly listening to what we are being told, we can hear that we are not to consume any blood. If we are not to consume blood, then how could us receiving whole blood from another person in the flesh, be okay? We will be learning much more on the topic of saving our lives later in the book.

Now with our Father teaching me this obedience, He has brought me to a level that I believe or in my mind, know that there is no such thing as a coincidence. There is no such thing as good or bad luck. This will probably be hard for you all to understand, however there is no such thing as an accident. He has this timed to the very second and knows exactly what He is doing. It is up to us to just let go of our pride and trust Him.

Then it came to be January or so when I called Cathy and she said that my daughter needed to tell me something, but she wasn't ready to tell me. I told Cathy right then and there, she pregnant, she didn't comment. A couple weeks later, Erin told me she was pregnant. This will be explained better in the chapter of Reincarnation.

Ever heard the expression that everything happens for a reason? If you truly believe that everyone on the planet makes up the one son of God, or a servant and vessel of God, then you will know without a doubt that everything does happen for a reason. It does not matter whether it is something good, bad, wrong, or even evil. At the bare minimum, it could be our Father trying to get you to turn back to Him instead of man. This is what He wants all of us to do for He is the only one that can and does provide perfect instructions on how to live this life in the flesh so that we can and will obtain eternal life with Him. Zechariah 1:3 Therefore say thou unto them, **Thus saith the Lord of hosts; Turn ye unto me, saith the Lord of hosts, and I will turn unto you, saith the Lord of hosts.** 4 Be ye not as your fathers, unto whom the former prophets have cried, saying, Thus saith the Lord of hosts; Turn ye now from your evil ways, and from your evil doings: but they did not hear, nor hearken unto me, saith the Lord. 5 Your fathers, where are they? and the prophets, do they live for ever? And then listen to what we are told in Joel 2:12 Therefore also now, **saith the Lord, turn ye even to me with all your heart, and with fasting, and with weeping, and with mourning: 13 And rend your heart, and not your garments, and turn unto the Lord your God: for he is gracious and merciful, slow to anger, and of great kindness, and repenteth him of the evil.** 14 Who knoweth if he will return and repent, and leave a blessing behind him; even a meat offering and a drink offering unto the Lord your God?

Let us listen to Psalm 10 so that we can hear what makes a wicked man in our Father's eyes. Psalm 10 Why standest thou afar off, O Lord? why hidest thou thyself in times of trouble? 2 The wicked in his pride doth persecute the poor: let them be taken in the devices that they have imagined. 3 For the wicked boasteth of his heart's desire, and blesseth the covetous, whom the Lord abhorreth. 4 **The wicked, through the pride of his countenance, will not seek after God: God is not in all his thoughts.** 5 His ways are always grievous; thy judgments are far above out of his sight: as for all his enemies, he puffeth at them. 6 He hath said in his heart, I shall not be moved: for I shall never be in adversity. 7 His mouth is full of cursing and deceit and fraud: under his tongue is mischief and vanity. 8 He sitteth in the lurking places of the villages: in the secret places doth he murder the innocent: his eyes are privily set against the poor. 9 He lieth in wait secretly as a lion in his den: he lieth in wait to catch the poor: he doth catch the poor, when he draweth him into his net. 10 He croucheth, and humbleth himself, that the poor may fall by his strong ones. 11 He hath said in his heart, God hath forgotten: he hideth his face; he will never see it. 12 Arise, O Lord; O God, lift up thine hand: forget not the humble. 13 Wherefore doth the wicked contemn God? he hath said in his heart, Thou wilt not require it. 14 Thou hast seen it; for thou beholdest mischief and spite, to requite it with thy hand: the poor committeth himself unto thee; thou art the helper of the fatherless. 15 Break thou the arm of the wicked and the evil man: seek out his wickedness till thou find none. 16 The Lord is King for ever and ever: the heathen are perished out of his land. 17 Lord, thou hast heard the desire of the humble: thou wilt prepare their heart, thou wilt cause thine ear to hear: 18 To judge the fatherless and the oppressed, that the man of the earth may no more oppress.

Now we stated just a few minutes ago, that there is no such thing as an accident. What we are referring to is things like car accidents and such. Now I just told you all of a couple of times in which the globe fell of the porch light at my mom's house and the deer in which told my conscience to slow down a bit. If these were accidents, how did our Father know they were going to happen. How could He use these deer to slow me down if He didn't also command these deer to do exactly what they did, so that I would slow down a bit? Remember, God is in control of everything? Remember we are told that He takes care of the animals also. First let us look at Daniel and listen to how our Father closed the mouths of lions. Let us listen to Daniel 6:10 **Now when Daniel knew that the writing was signed, he went into his house; and his windows being open in his chamber toward Jerusalem, he kneeled upon his knees three times a day, and prayed, and gave thanks before his God, as he did aforetime.** 11 Then these men assembled, and found Daniel praying and making supplication before his God. 12 Then they came near, and spake before the king concerning the king's decree; **Hast thou not signed a decree, that every man that shall ask a petition of any God or man within thirty days, save of thee, O king, shall be cast into the den of lions?** The king answered and said, The thing is true, according to the law of the Medes and Persians, which altereth not. 13 Then answered they and said before the king, That Daniel, which is of the children of the captivity of Judah, regardeth not thee, O king, nor the decree that thou hast signed, but maketh his petition three times a day. 14 Then the king, when he heard these words, was sore displeased with himself, and set his heart on Daniel to deliver him: and he laboured till the going down of the sun to deliver him. 15 Then these men assembled unto the king, and said unto the king, Know, O king, that the law of the Medes and Persians is, That no decree nor statute which the king establisheth may be changed. 16 Then the king commanded, and they brought Daniel, **and cast him into the den of lions. Now the king spake and said unto Daniel, Thy God whom thou servest continually, he will deliver thee. 17 And a stone was brought, and laid upon the mouth of the den; and the king sealed it with his own signet, and with the signet of his lords; that the purpose might not be changed concerning Daniel.** 18 Then the king went to his palace, and passed the night fasting: neither were instruments of musick brought before him: and his sleep went from him. 19 **Then the king arose very early in the morning, and went in haste unto the den of lions. 20 And when he came to the den, he cried with a lamentable voice unto Daniel: and the king spake and said to Daniel, O Daniel, servant of the living God, is thy God, whom thou servest continually, able to deliver thee from the lions? 21 Then said Daniel unto the king, O king, live for ever. 22 My God hath sent his angel, and hath shut the lions' mouths, that they have not hurt me: forasmuch as before him innocency was found in me; and also before thee, O king, have I done no hurt.**

Without showing how Daniel believed, we will just show that it was our Father in which sent the angel to close the mouth of the lions while Daniel was in the den with them. Then listen to Matthew 6:26 **Behold the fowls of the air: for they sow not, neither do they reap, nor gather into barns; yet your heavenly Father feedeth them.** Are ye not much better than they?

Now how can our Father feed these fowls of the air, if He isn't telling them where to get their food? Now this has been leading to the big question. The car accident in which I had when I when I was 16, was on March 28th, Good Friday of 1986. How could this happen if it was what we call and accident? And then 30 years later, almost to the day, I got baptized by the Holy Ghost? Remember God is working a works that no man will believe. He caused it to happen. He dwells inside of me also and because of this, He is the one in which had me over steer when I swerved to miss the oncoming vehicle. I am going off of what the family told me and reading of the accident in the paper. I do not remember six or seven weeks of my life. I can remember about one week before the accident, and about five or six weeks after. The time in between, I have no recollection of. My family, and friends had told me that once I came out of the coma, I had to grow up again. I was reliving my live from the time I was three or four years old.

Now we are going to do the grand finale of this chapter and yes, it will take some explaining. On June 9th of this year, I was driving north on US highway 63, and all the sudden all these thoughts that are in this chapter, started flowing through my mind like a fountain of water. These thoughts were coming quick, but they were coming in a much better formation than I am sharing them with you all. It came to mind that I died, but yet I am alive. It came to mind that when I was sent to my brother's place in South Dakota. While I was there, I do remember that I would listen to the bible while playing free online poker tournaments. I wasn't really understanding what I was hearing, but just found comfort from hearing the word of God playing in the background. So, I was not being fed the spiritual meat, nor was I drinking of that spiritual water. 1 Corinthians 10:3 **and did all eat the same spiritual meat; 4 And did all drink the same spiritual drink: for they drank of that spiritual Rock that followed them:** and that Rock was Christ. I was not being fed with this meat nor drink. I was just there to help my brother because he was backed up in work. I was there about seven weeks, but we had a big argument about the bible. I remember this clearly for it was a Sunday. That day, my brother and his wife went to a man- made church and talked to the pastor about the unclean foods.

I want to note it was not my brother doing what he was doing, but rather our Father causing everything to happen just as it did, so that He could fulfill the scriptures. This was about a week before I left there. They came home from church and started telling me that we could eat of the unclean things now that Jesus died on the cross. No, I would not agree, and I showed them in my bible of what I could see. They in return, showed me what it said in a NIV version of the bible. I can't remember how it was worded in their bible but there was no way I was saying anything of our perfect Father has changed. We argued back and forth all day long and I would not back down. It got to the point that I remembered what the scriptures said. Matthew 10:13 And if the house be worthy, let your peace come upon it: but if it be not worthy, **let your peace return to you.** 14 And whosoever shall not receive you, nor hear your words, when ye depart out of that house or city, shake off the dust of your feet. I packed up my three pair of jeans, shirts, and undershorts. As I was doing this, my brother said just hold on. It was about 9 pm now. I told him that I have to leave for my peace had come back to me. Side note. I now had three pair of jeans and such for a friend of my mothers, bought them for me while I was with her. I had no money. I walked out of town a few miles before coming back. All along talking to our Father, telling Him that there is no way that I am going to say that it is okay to change Him. Then after taking about a week to find a job with a trucking company, I left my brothers. It was about six months ago when our Father showed me what a true fast is. So now I am starting to connect that I went to my brothers so that I could fast for 40 days and nights. Remember that the son of perdition sits in the temple of God and we are the temple of God. It was not my brother for I know my brother loves me, but rather is was Satan in which is in the temple of God. Satan is a son of God or the son of perdition.

Then I started thinking of how I understand the scriptures but yet I am not even 50 years old. This brought my mind to John 8:56 Your father Abraham rejoiced to see my day: and he saw it, and was glad. 57 Then said the Jews unto him, **Thou art not yet fifty years old, and hast thou seen Abraham?** 58 Jesus said unto them, Verily, verily, I say unto you, Before Abraham was, I am. Remember how we just showed you all how I was going to sacrifice my son and my brother was the ram in the bushes? **I have seen Abraham and have went through the same spiritual sacrifice that did not require an animal as we know them to be. And I am not yet 50 years of age.**

Up until June 9th of this year, I was thinking that I wouldn't ever be able to tell people of who I was. I was telling people I am being taught the same things as Jesus so that I can become him in my next life. Or that maybe our Father was not going to allow me to tell anyone and the He would just bring this world to an end and then everyone would be brought to shame once they found out. Most of all, I didn't really know it happened the way it did, or couldn't explain it as I can now. This is when I kept remembering Jesus saying no to tell anyone. Matthew 16:20 **Then charged he his disciples that they should tell no man that he was Jesus the Christ.** We will be doing a chapter on reincarnation later in the book. I was not connecting all that our Father was doing in my life. Then it started to connect. I had the accident on Good Friday, March 28th of 1986. Being in a coma for three days and three nights. 30 years later, almost to the day, I was baptized with the Holy Ghost. So, let us look at this in the scriptures. Matthew 10:38 Then certain of the scribes and of the Pharisees answered, saying, Master, we would see a sign from thee. 39 But he answered and said unto them, An evil and adulterous generation seeketh after a sign; and there shall no sign be given to it, but the sign of the prophet Jonas: 40 **For as Jonas was three days and three nights in the whale's belly; so shall the Son of man be three days and three nights in the heart of the earth.** Then let us look at when Jesus was baptized again. Luke 3:21 Now when all the people were baptized, it came to pass, that Jesus also being baptized, and praying, the heaven was opened, 22 And the Holy Ghost descended in a bodily shape like a dove upon him, and a voice came from heaven, which said, Thou art my beloved Son; in thee I am well pleased. 23 **And Jesus himself began to be about thirty years of age, being (as was supposed) the son of Joseph, which was the son of Heli,**

Then, after Jesus was baptized, he went into the fasted 40 days and nights. Matthew 4 Then was Jesus led up of the Spirit into the wilderness to be tempted of the devil. 2 And when he had fasted forty days and forty nights, he was afterward an hungred. 3 And when the tempter came to him, he said, If thou be the Son of God, command that these stones be made bread. 4 But he answered and said, It is written, Man shall not live by bread alone, but by every word that proceedeth out of the mouth of God. 5 Then the devil taketh him up into the holy city, and setteth him on a pinnacle of the temple, 6 And saith unto him, If thou be the Son of God, cast thyself down: for it is written, He shall give his angels charge concerning thee: and in their hands they shall bear thee up, lest at any time thou dash thy foot against a stone. 7 Jesus said unto him, It is written again, Thou shalt not tempt the Lord thy God. 8 Again, the devil taketh him up into an exceeding high mountain, and sheweth him all the kingdoms of the world, and the glory of them; 9 And saith unto him, All these things will I give thee, if thou wilt fall down and worship me. 10 Then saith Jesus unto him, Get thee hence, Satan: for it is written, Thou shalt worship the Lord thy God, and him only shalt thou serve. 11 Then the devil leaveth him, and, behold, angels came and ministered unto him.

Remember how I would not back down from the word of God and what I believed, not to change? The words that came out of our mouths were not the same as like what we read, but we need to remember of what we hear in Romans 8:26 Likewise the Spirit also helpeth our infirmities: for we know not what we should pray for as we ought: **but the Spirit itself maketh intercession for us with groanings which cannot be uttered.**

So here it goes, so now picture this entire chapter in your mind. Try to imagine all this going through your mind at once, as it did mine. I am putting all this together as I am driving and now it all made since. Now I knew how to explain what had happened to me. David Charles Jenkins II was born February 23, 1970. He died on March 8-9 of 2016. He willingly gave his life up of the flesh. When he did this out in the wilderness, the spirit of Jesus Christ took over his body. Remember Colossians 1:14 In whom we have redemption watch through his blood, even the forgiveness of sins: 15 **Who is the image of the invisible God, the firstborn of every creature:** I didn't even realize this is what happened when I went out in the wilderness to die. I now understand why I do not have anywhere to lay my head. I have no place to call home and everything I own is in my truck. Luke 9:58 And Jesus said unto him, Foxes have holes, and birds of the air have nests; **but the Son of man hath not where to lay his head.** I have told people this and they reply back with, you have a bed in your truck. To think like this is to think carnally. The scriptures teach that Jesus was a man and sleep is required for the human body to function. And to think carnal is enmity with our Father.

But now I can see it as plain as day. I now know who it was that told me I was just here to watch in the poker tournament. I now understand why I have such a desire to learn anything and everything of our Father. I now understood why this being the third book that our Father has had me write, why nobody seemed to be reading. Luke 9:22 Saying, The Son of man must suffer many things, **and be rejected of the elders and chief priests and scribes,** and be slain, and be raised the third day. These are spiritual elders, the same elders in which we showed in the last book. These elders and priest are above and have dominion over man. This is an addition after the initial manuscript was sent in. Our Father has reminded to show you all what is really going on when I am being rejected or in other words, people refuse to read the books that He has had me write. I have been asked by people as to why I continue to write books for nobody seems to be reading them. This is where our Father has let me know that it isn't me that is being rejected for, I only teach His doctrine and not mans. 1 Samuel 8:7 And the Lord said unto Samuel, Hearken unto the voice of the people in all that they say unto thee: for they have not rejected thee, but they have rejected me, that I should not reign over them.

Let us listen to a little of what we can hear in, **Hosea 4:6 My people are destroyed for lack of knowledge: because thou hast rejected knowledge, I will also reject thee, that thou shalt be no priest to me: seeing thou hast forgotten the law of thy God, I will also forget thy children.**

I now know why it caught my attention, the first time of listening to the bible, to say I am your sign. I now know what it means when our Father said He will raise a man for an ensign. Isaiah 11:10 And in day there shall be a root of Jesse, **which shall stand for an ensign of the people;** to it shall the Gentiles seek: and his rest shall be glorious. 11 And it shall come to pass in that day, that the Lord shall set his hand again the second time to recover the remnant of his people, which shall be left, from Assyria, and from Egypt, and from Pathros, and from Cush, and from Elam, and from Shinar, and from Hamath, and from the islands of the sea. 12 **And he shall set up an ensign for the nations,** and shall assemble the outcasts of Israel, and gather together the dispersed of Judah from the four corners of the earth.

So now let us do a little something with my age. I had the accident when I was 16 and in a coma for three days and three nights. I was baptized 30 years later. So, to line this up with the scriptures, I was 45 years old when I wrote the first book. This was preparing me for what was to come. I was 46 when I was baptized with the Holy Ghost. I am not fifty yet, but I showed you all how I have seen Abraham. Now we know Jesus was baptized when he was about 30 years of age. So, at age 46, I was 30 years old. Our Father had me write the second book when I was 48 years old, or 32 years after the being in the belly of the earth. I am now 49 years of age, or 33 years old. I have been and still do try to glorify our Father every chance I get. I will leave the rest of the math to you.

I now know why I was told to name the books with the names of them. The first book called Father, forgive us, we haven't been listening. Everything we need to know is in our bible and nowhere else. But because of the darkness of man's hearts, our Father will not allow us to see or hear what is right in front of us. Our Father has also brought something to my attention while writing this book. Actually, I was trying to fall asleep and it just came to mind last night. The first book, I wrote in 2015, before the baptism. I used to pass them out all the time. Not boasting on my alms, however I was excited to share this newfound knowledge that came to me. Then I started telling people that these books were the milk in which we needed to start out on. And about two months ago or so I heard Isaiah 28:9 **Whom shall he teach knowledge? and whom shall he make to understand doctrine? them that are weaned from the milk, and drawn from the breasts.** I had to believe what was in that 1st book before our Father would teach me all that He has and is. And I have to say it, if you want to be taught as I am, you need to believe of what is in the 1st book. Our Father does not respect or favor any man, so if I had to believe it before He taught me so will you. He is not going to say that I have to be weaned but others do not. But the beauty of it is you all will not have to go through everything that I am for He tells us that if you return back to Him, He will have mercy. Jeremiah 3:11 And the Lord said unto me, The backsliding Israel hath justified herself more than treacherous Judah. 12 Go and proclaim these words toward the north, and say, Return, thou backsliding Israel, saith the Lord; and I will not cause mine anger to fall upon you: for I am merciful, saith the Lord, and I will not keep anger for ever. 13 Only acknowledge thine iniquity, that thou hast transgressed against the Lord thy God, and hast scattered thy ways to the strangers under every green tree, and ye have not obeyed my voice, saith the Lord. 14 Turn, O backsliding children, saith the Lord; for I am married unto you: and I will take you one of a city, and two of a family, and I will bring you to Zion:

 The second book, I originally was going to call Judge not, less ye be judged. But I had this over whelming sensation to call it BEHOLD, A GREATER THAN JONAS IS HERE!!!. Now when I first sent this book to the publisher, they didn't like the name and they suggested I change it. But I just knew that had to be the name of it. I asked the Father why He would cause those servants to say that. I received the answer almost immediately, within two or three minutes, they do not believe. Now let us listen to where Jesus said this. Matthew 12:40 For as Jonas was three days and three nights in the whale's belly; so shall the Son of man be three days and three nights in the heart of the earth. 41 The men of Nineveh shall rise in judgment with this generation, and shall condemn it: because they repented at the preaching of Jonas; and, **behold, a greater than Jonas is here.**

Now I know the scriptures tell us that we all will see the son of man coming in the clouds. Mark 13:26 And then shall they see the Son of man coming in the clouds with great power and glory. Now I am thinking that there are not very many people that have gotten these books, however both books have clouds on the covers. I did not pick the covers and I always give our Father all credit for using me as a vessel to write these books. I say that He is the true author. Now I truly understand why this book is 316 pages long (John 3:16). When I first called and they told me that it was 316 pages, I thought it was because of how the book described how that everybody on the planet is part of the son of God. And now I truly understand how Jesus became the AUTHOR of our salvation. It is Jesus writing these books and not David. Hebrew 5:8 Though he were a Son, yet learned he obedience by the things which he suffered; 9 And being made perfect, **he became the author of eternal salvation unto all them that obey him;** It now made since as to why I couldn't get over this sensation that the world is getting ready to end. Hebrews 9:26 For then must he often have suffered since the foundation of the world: **but now once in the end of the world hath he appeared to put away sin by the sacrifice of himself.** And I will say this, David's life did end on March 8-9 of 2016. I kept telling people the world was going to end very soon, however I didn't realize that David's world did end and the spirit of Jesus Christ rose up in his body and took over and now I do nothing on my own.

Okay our Father has brought something to my attention that I didn't mention, and I am hoping that I am placing it in the right spot. We showed you all where Egypt is as water that covers the earth. In the last book, we showed how Jonas was a spirit that took about three days journey in the city of Nineveh. This city is actually the earth in which took three days to make in the very beginning. Now that we can see that Egypt is as water and covers the earth, **I can say I watch the Father part the sea all the time.** Have you ever heard the expression, sea of people? When I am driving and traffic is heavy, I watch how He just causes people to move so that it is a lot easier for me to get into the flow of traffic. Now this will bother a lot, but we all know that Jesus walked on water, right? Matthew 14:22 And straightway Jesus constrained his disciples to get into a ship, and to go before him unto the other side, while he sent the multitudes away. 23 And when he had sent the multitudes away, he went up into a mountain apart to pray: and when the evening was come, he was there alone. 24 But the ship was now in the midst of the sea, tossed with waves: for the wind was contrary. 25 **And in the fourth watch of the night Jesus went unto them, walking on the** sea. 26 And when the disciples saw him walking on the sea, they were troubled, saying, It is a spirit; and they cried out for fear. 27 But straightway Jesus spake unto them, saying, Be of good cheer; it is I; be not afraid. 28 And Peter answered him and said, Lord, if it be thou, bid me come unto thee on the water. 29 And he said, Come. And when Peter was come down out of the ship, he walked on the water, to go to Jesus. 30 But when he saw the wind boisterous, he was afraid; and beginning to sink, he cried, saying, Lord, save me. 31 And immediately Jesus stretched forth his hand, and caught him, and said unto him, O thou of little faith, wherefore didst thou doubt?

Now if you have read the last book, we showed that when we listen to the bible, it is like we are lifting ourselves above the clouds and listening to conversations going on in heaven. Philippians 3:20 **For our conversation is in heaven;** from whence also we look for the Saviour, the Lord Jesus Christ: Then remember that we are to meditate on the word of God all the time. 1 Timothy 4:13 Till I come, give attendance to reading, to exhortation, to doctrine. 14 Neglect not the gift that is in thee, which was given thee by prophecy, with the laying on of the hands of the presbytery. 15 **Meditate upon these things; give thyself wholly to them; that thy profiting may appear to all. 16 Take heed unto thyself, and unto the doctrine; continue in them: for in doing this thou shalt both save thyself, and them that hear thee.** I can't stop nor do I want to stop meditating on the word of God. I am talking with our Father when I wake, when I eat, when I go to the restroom, when I watch television, when I shower, when I am going to bed. It does not matter what I am doing, I cannot stop thinking about the bible. We showed in the last book it was like I was lifted up above the clouds and listening in.

Remember the hour cometh that the true worshippers of God must worship Him is spirit and truth. John 4:23 But the hour cometh, and now is, when the true worshippers shall worship the Father in spirit and in truth: for the Father seeketh such to worship him. 24 God is a Spirit: and they that worship him must worship him in spirit and in truth. Have you ever heard the expression of sea of people or the wave at sporting events and such? You have seen that Egypt is deep waters. Proverbs 18:4 **The words of a man's mouth are as** deep waters, and the wellspring of wisdom as a flowing brook. Then listen to James 1:6 But let him ask in faith, nothing wavering. For he that wavereth is like a wave of the sea driven with the wind and tossed. Jude 1:11 Woe unto them! for they have gone in the way of Cain, and ran greedily after the error of Balaam for reward, and perished in the gainsaying of Core. 12 These are spots in your feasts of charity, when they feast with you, feeding themselves without fear: clouds they are without water, carried about of winds; trees whose fruit withereth, without fruit, twice dead, plucked up by the roots; 13 Raging waves of the sea, foaming out their own shame; wandering stars, to whom is reserved the blackness of darkness for ever.

Now let us listen to when Jesus waked on water. Matthew 14:23 And when he had sent the multitudes away, he went up into a mountain apart to pray: and when the evening was come, he was there alone. **24 But the ship was now in the midst of the sea, tossed with waves: for the wind was contrary. 25 And in the fourth watch of the night Jesus went unto them, walking on the sea.** 26 And when the disciples saw him walking on the sea, they were troubled, saying, It is a spirit; and they cried out for fear. 27 But straightway Jesus spake unto them, saying, Be of good cheer; it is I; be not afraid. 28 And Peter answered him and said, Lord, if it be thou, bid me come unto thee on the water. 29 And he said, Come. And when Peter was come down out of the ship, **he walked on the water, to go to Jesus. 30 But when he saw the wind boisterous, he was afraid; and beginning to sink, he cried, saying, Lord, save me. 31 And immediately Jesus stretched forth**

his hand, and caught him, and said unto him, O thou of little faith, wherefore didst thou doubt? I will say I am walking on water and all the boisterous winds and waves do not startle me and I will not sink. Every time I am walking to or from my truck, I am walking on the water so that I can prepare to be shipped to where our Father needs me next.

I know we are getting a little sidetracked, but our Father has brought something to my attention in which needs to be brought up here. Okay we just read what I was saying about meditating on the word of God. We just mentioned that when we meditate, it is like we are being lifted about the clouds so that we can hear what they are saying in heaven. This is a level of heaven. This has to do with our conscience. When we meditate all the time on the scriptures we are being lifted up to a different level of heaven. We know there is levels of heaven just by listening to 2 Corinthians 12:2 I knew a man in Christ above fourteen years ago, (whether in the body, I cannot tell; or whether out of the body, I cannot tell: God knoweth;) **such an one caught up to the third heaven.** We can hear this in Psalm 139:8 **If I ascend up into heaven, thou art there: if I make my bed in hell, behold, thou art there.** That is how I can hear the things I hear and see the things I see. Matthew 13:17 For verily I say unto you, **That many prophets and righteous men have desired to see those things which ye see, and have not seen them; and to hear those things which ye hear, and have not heard them.** I will say that I have heard this a lot and knew it was about me, but I didn't understand how it worked exactly until today. This is why we hear what we hear in John 3:13 And no man hath ascended up to heaven, but he that came down from heaven, **even the Son of man which is in heaven.** I am in a level of heaven but still not in heaven with our Father.

Let us get back on the topic. Now I know that there must be others that think about the bible all the time as I do. So here is my question for those of you, do you ever have any doubts, within yourself, if what your hearing makes since to you, or do you still have doubts? Do you feel the love coming from our Father or does part of you still think of Him being cruel or vindictive? Do you truly believe that He is perfect, righteous, and justified in everything that He has done, doing, and will do? Do you feel like your sinking as shown in Psalm 69:2 I sink in deep mire, where there is no standing: **I am come into deep waters, where the floods overflow me.**

This is where I say all that came before me have been thieves and robbers for, they sought their own glory. With this being the third and final book of the trilogy our Father has had me write. I share everything to glorify our Father and not me. John 10:8 **All that ever came before me are thieves and robbers: but the sheep did not hear them.** 9 I am the door: by me if any man enter in, he shall be saved, and shall go in and out, and find pasture. 10 The thief cometh not, but for to steal, and to kill, and to destroy: I am come that they might have life, and that they might have it more abundantly. I gave up my life so that the people of this world could learn of what our Father wants from all mankind. These books shorten the bible. Because our Father has hidden everything within this 2,000 plus page book. I have taken the time to learn it and allowed our Father to show how people can do things in such a way that will bring this world out of darkness. I have not added, nor taking away from the word. As you will be able to tell when you read any or all of these books. I live by every word that proceedeth out of the mouth of God.

These books are somewhat of a shortcut to our Father. It does not change anything about Him. But without you having to go through all that I have, you get an easier, plain and simple way of understanding of what our Father has been saying since the beginning of the world. Now I am sure there are very many that are denying and refusing to hear what you are now hearing. I don't blame you for on the 9th when our Father first connected all of this in my mind, I too, totally freaked out. I lost a couple of days of sleep and am still having a hard time sleeping. My mind has bible verses bouncing around more than they ever have. I was and am still a little worried about putting this in here. Don't get me wrong, I had a pretty good idea, but I knew I couldn't say anything. Then on the 17th of June, I heard what the spirit was saying to me. I was told that I needed to get this book done. I was procrastinating, for this is huge. Then I heard the spirit tell me, make your name known and I was told twice. Yes, our Father did use a servant to tell me this and this servant didn't even realize what she had said, but she said it. Okay, I have heard it and I will do as I am commanded. Now, in closing of this chapter, we all know that it takes two or three witnesses to establish a matter, right? Here is the way our Father is making me feel I should do this. In this chapter alone, there is at least seven or eight witnesses. Now, all that came before me did not write any books showing an in depth understanding of the scriptures. So that makes me the vessel in which our Father is using to be the author of our salvation. Who is the author of our salvation? Hebrews 12:2 Looking unto Jesus the author and finisher of our faith; who for the joy that was set before him endured the cross, despising the shame, and is set down at the right hand of the throne of God.

If and when you read any of the three books our Father has had me write. You will see and hear a completely different doctrine, but this doctrine comes from the bible. It is our Father's doctrine and not mans. John 7:15 And the Jews marvelled, saying, How knoweth this man letters, having never learned? 16 Jesus answered them, and said, **My doctrine is not mine, but his that sent me.** 17 If any man will do his will, he shall know of the doctrine, whether it be of God, or whether I speak of myself. Now the three books, make three more witnesses. Now I realize that we have given a few witnesses but as we were eating dinner, I was reminded of the scripture asking if Jesus was the son of David. We all know that Joseph and Mary had Jesus. But, let us listen to Matthew 12:22 Then was brought unto him one possessed with a devil, blind, and dumb: and he healed him, insomuch that the blind and dumb both spake and saw. 23 **And all the people were amazed, and said, Is not this the son of David?** I know there are a lot of speculations on this. Here you go, my dad's name was David C. Jenkins. The David in which died March 8-9 of 2016 is David C Jenkins II. If this means anything or not, my dad was a carpenter by trade. He went to school and could gut a house and fancy it back up. He preferred factory work and did do this for a living; however, he just didn't like the hours carpenters put in. He liked being on a set schedule. I do not want any reward while hear on earth. If we ever meat and something that ever happens in which you feel the need to say thank you to me, I will tell you to thank our Father for He is my boss and I try to do what He tells me to do. Isaiah 45:13 **I have raised him up in righteousness, and I will direct all his ways: he shall build my city, and he shall let go my captives, not for price nor reward, saith the Lord of hosts.** And this is why I do not want anything on this planet for a reward. Isaiah 52:12 For ye shall not go out with haste, nor go by flight: for the Lord will go before you; **and the God of Israel will be your reward.** I trust Him and will wait for Him.

I feel our Father is telling me to share something else. It is kind of like He has told me to lay all my cards on the table, so to speak. We mentioned a bit ago that shortly after our Father called me to the bible, I made some videos and such. When I was making my channer, I wanted to use the screen name of THEJENKS. I have always just kind of like the sound of it, however YouTube would not let me use this name. They hey gave me a suggestion of THEJENKS1000. Okay I can live with that was what I was thinking, so that is what I named the channel. Our Father was telling me way back then of who I am and where we are at. I was making a few videos to help explain the book "BEHOLD, A GREATER THAN JONAS IS HERE!!!", when He brought to my attention. That was when He started to let me know that I needed to write another book. I do not know if He will allow me to make more videos or not, but I do know that it is up to Him and not me.

This does not make me any better than any other person on this planet. I am a fellow servant in which desires to obey our Father. We all have our own different rolls to fulfill as shown in the second book. Our Father did not choose me because of my works. He didn't choose me because I have always had more knowledge than others. He did not choose me because I am more or have ever been more deserving than others. Our Father chose me simply because He said He will choose whom He will choose and have mercy upon He will have mercy. Exodus 33:19 And he said, I will make all my goodness pass before thee, and I will proclaim the name of the Lord before thee; and will be gracious **to whom I will be gracious, and will shew mercy on**

whom I will shew mercy. Romans 9:15 For he saith to Moses, **I will have mercy on whom I will have mercy, and I will have compassion on whom I will have compassion.** 16 So then it is not of him that willeth, nor of him that runneth, but of God that sheweth mercy. Now I will make one last comment at the very end of this chapter. Before Abraham, I am. AND I AM NOT GOD THE FATHER. I did not create anyone, and I will be darned if I will even think of taking that away from our Father. I assure you though, He is sitting right next to me. I have aches and pains, I have tears, I have fears (only of God the Father), I smoke and cough a lot. (will not try to save my life), and most of all, I suffer just as the rest of mankind.

Now that we have brought all this up and showed you all that I have been learning obedience, there is something that needs to be known. I am very blessed in that our Father has chosen me to fulfill this roll. But at the same time, I want to make it known that it is not all fun and games learning this obedience. I love what He is doing with me and yes, I am extremely thankful. But there are days in which are very difficult. He recently reminded that I am still learning. He had me show this in the first book, Jesus was made perfect as the scriptures say. They do say that he was made perfect by learning obedience through the things in which he suffered. Hebrews 5:7 Who in the days of his flesh, when he had offered up prayers and supplications with strong crying and tears unto him that was able to save him from death, and was heard in that he feared; 8 **Though he were a Son, yet learned he obedience by the things which he suffered;** 9 And being made perfect, he became the author of eternal salvation unto all them that obey him;

There are some days in which I think it would be easier to just pull all of my teeth out at once. And yes, there are days in which I get very mad because, well because I get scared. Just like a little child does when they feel they have messed up or are not understanding what their parents want them to do. If Jesus is God, than I would not have days like I do. But I wouldn't trade it for the world.

Therefore, to this day I still give thanks in everything that happens to me whether it is go or bad. I hope that every step that I take is in the direction in which He wants. I thank Him for every breath for He can take it away at any time and I hope each time I blink my eyes; I want to be looking in the direction in which He needs me to be looking. And therefore, I do now feel it is robbery to think of myself as an equal to our Father for I seek His instruction in all that I do. Philippians 2:6 Who, being in the form of God, thought it not robbery to be equal with God:

THE THOUSAND-YEAR REIGN

We are going to be looking at a few spots in our bibles so we can hear that we are living in the reign with Christ now. Now as we showed in the last book, this is all a spiritual workings and not a physical workings. Excuse me for saying it this way, but if we know that God is spirit, then we should already be thinking that this is a spiritual workings. John 4:23 **But the hour cometh, and now is, when the true worshippers shall worship the Father in spirit and in truth: for the Father seeketh such to worship him. 24 God is a Spirit: and they that worship him must worship him in spirit and in truth.**

I know there are many that believe that 1,000-year reign with Christ is something that is coming after the world ends. Many believe this because of the way our bible is formatted. Many people think that we must start at the beginning of the bible and just chronologically go through it and the world ends in Revelation. But we need to remember what our Father tells us in Isaiah 46:10 **Declaring the end from the beginning, and from ancient times the things that are not yet done, saying, My counsel shall stand, and I will do all my pleasure:** by our Father telling us right here, we can be certain that the bible is not in chronical order.

If you remember, in the last book, we showed that when we read or listen to the bible, it is like we are lifting ourselves up and listening to the conversations going on in heaven. Let us listen to a few areas in which we are told to hear what is being said from heaven. Let us look at the second half of 2 Chronicles 6:21 Hearken therefore unto the supplications of thy servant, and of thy people Israel, which they shall make toward this place: hear thou from thy dwelling place, even from heaven; and when thou hearest, forgive. 22 If a man sin against his neighbour, and an oath be laid upon him to make him swear, and the oath come before thine altar in this house; 23 **Then hear thou from heaven, and do, and judge thy servants,** by requiting the wicked, by recompensing his way upon his own head; and by justifying the righteous, **by giving him according to his righteousness.** 24 And if thy people Israel be put to the worse before the enemy, because they have sinned against thee; and shall return and confess thy name, and pray and make supplication before thee in this house; 25 **Then hear thou from the heavens,** and forgive the sin of thy people Israel, **and bring them again unto the land which thou gavest to them and to their fathers.** 26 When the heaven is shut up, and there is no rain, because they have sinned against thee; yet if they pray toward this place, and confess thy name, and turn from their sin, when thou dost afflict them; 27 **Then hear thou from heaven, and forgive the sin of thy servants,** and of thy people Israel, when thou hast taught them the good way, wherein they should walk; and send rain upon thy land, which thou hast given unto thy people for an inheritance. 28 If there be dearth in the land, if there be pestilence, if there be blasting, or mildew, locusts, or caterpillers; if their enemies besiege them in the cities of their land; whatsoever sore or whatsoever sickness there be: 29 Then what prayer or what supplication soever shall be made of any man, or of all thy people Israel, when every one shall know his own sore and his own grief, and shall spread forth his hands in this house: 30 **Then hear thou from heaven thy dwelling place,** and forgive, and render unto every man according unto all his ways, whose heart thou knowest; (for thou only knowest the hearts of the children of men:) 31 That they may fear thee, to walk in thy ways, so long as they live in the land which thou gavest unto our fathers. 32 Moreover concerning the stranger, which is not of thy people Israel, but is come from a far country for thy great name's sake, and thy mighty hand, and thy stretched out arm; if they come and pray in this house; 33 **Then hear thou from the heavens,** even from thy dwelling place, and do according to all that the stranger calleth to thee for; that all people of the earth may know thy name, and fear thee, as doth thy people Israel, and may know that this house which I have built is called by thy name. 34 If thy people go out to war against their enemies by the way that thou shalt send them, and they pray unto thee toward this city which thou hast chosen, **and the house which I have built for thy name;** 35 **Then hear thou from the heavens** their prayer and their supplication, and maintain their cause. 36 If they sin against thee, (for there is no man which sinneth not,) and thou be angry with them, and deliver them over before their enemies, and they carry them away captives unto a land far off or near; 37 Yet if they bethink themselves in the land whither they are carried captive, and turn and pray unto thee in the land of their captivity, saying, We have sinned, we have done amiss, and have dealt wickedly; 38 If they return to thee with all their heart and with all their soul in the land of their captivity, whither they have carried them captives, and pray toward their land, which thou gavest unto their fathers, and toward the city which thou hast chosen, and toward the house which I have built for thy name: 39 **Then hear thou from the heavens,** even from thy dwelling place, their prayer and their supplications, and maintain their cause, and forgive thy people which have sinned against thee. 40 Now, my God, let, I beseech thee, thine eyes be open, and let thine ears be attent unto the prayer that is made in this place. 41 Now therefore arise, O Lord God, into thy resting place, thou, and the ark of thy strength: let thy priests, O Lord God, be clothed with salvation, and let thy saints rejoice in goodness. 42 O Lord God, turn not away the face of thine anointed: remember the mercies of David thy servant.

    Just to make a quick side note here. Let us listen to Genesis 1:26 And God said, Let us make man in our image, after our likeness: and let them have dominion over the fish of the sea, and over the fowl of the air, and over the cattle, and over all the earth, and over every creeping thing that creepeth upon the earth. Who is, us? He is talking to those in heaven and not man. He is showing us right here in the very beginning that we are hearing what is being said in heaven throughout the entire bible. Let us look at to when our Father created the sun, moon, and stars. Genesis 1:14 And God said, Let there be lights in the firmament of the heaven to divide the day from the night; and let them be for signs, and for seasons, and for days, and years: 15 And let them be for lights in the firmament of the heaven to give light upon the earth: and it was so. 16 And God made two great lights; the greater light to rule the day, and the lesser light to rule the night: he made the stars also. 17 And God set them in the firmament of the heaven to give light upon the earth, 18 And to rule over the day and over the night, and to divide the light from the darkness: and God saw that it was good. 19 And the evening and the morning were the fourth day.

This is on the 4th day of creation. Man wasn't created until the 6th day. So, once again, our Father is telling us right here that these are for signs, seasons, days, and years to the angels and spirits that are going to be creating man in their own image on the 6th day.

So, what we want to do now is just show a few spots in our bible that we can hear our Father say in that day. Remember a day is as a thousand years and thousand years is as a day. 2 Peter 3:8 But, beloved, be not ignorant of this one thing, that one day is with the Lord as a thousand years, and a thousand years as one day. Have you ever heard someone say something like back in the day when I was growing up, we didn't have that? Or back in the day, things didn't cost so much? Or back in the day, things were built to last but now not so much? Is this person talking about one day or are they talking about a time in which covers several days or even years? Well it is the same thing going on in the bible. Our Father is not talking just one day, but rather He is talking about a span of time being counted as one day. So now let us listen to a few times we can hear this.

Deuteronomy 31:16 And the Lord said unto Moses, Behold, thou shalt sleep with thy fathers; and this people will rise up, and go a whoring after the gods of the strangers of the land, whither they go to be among them, and will forsake me, and break my covenant which I have made with them. 17 **Then my anger shall be kindled against them in that day,** and I will forsake them, and I will hide my face from them, and they shall be devoured, and many evils and troubles shall befall them; so that they will say in that day, Are not these evils come upon us, because our God is not among us? 18 **And I will surely hide my face in that day for all the evils which they shall have wrought, in that they are turned unto other gods.** 1 Samuel 8 And it came to pass, when Samuel was old, that he made his sons judges over Israel. 2 Now the name of his firstborn was Joel; and the name of his second, Abiah: they were judges in Beersheba. 3 And his sons walked not in his ways, but turned aside after lucre, and took bribes, and perverted judgment. 4 Then all the elders of Israel gathered themselves together, and came to Samuel unto Ramah, 5 said unto him, Behold, thou art old, and thy sons walk not in thy ways: now make us a king to judge us like all the nations. 6 But the thing displeased Samuel, when they said, Give us a king to judge us. And Samuel prayed unto the Lord. 7 And the Lord said unto Samuel, Hearken unto the voice of the people in all that they say unto thee: for they have not rejected thee, but they have rejected me, that I should not reign over them. 8 According to all the works which they have done since the day that I brought them up out of Egypt even unto this day, wherewith they have forsaken me, and served other gods, so do they also unto thee. 9 Now therefore hearken unto their voice: howbeit yet protest solemnly unto them, and shew them the manner of the king that shall reign over them. 10 And Samuel told all the words of the Lord unto the people that asked of him a king. 11 And he said, This will be the manner of the king that shall reign over you: He will take your sons, and appoint them for himself, for his chariots, and to be his horsemen; and some shall run before his chariots. 12 And he will appoint him captains over thousands, and captains over fifties; and will set them to ear his ground, and to reap his harvest, and to make his instruments of war, and instruments of his chariots. 13 And he will take your daughters to be confectionaries, and to be cooks, and to be bakers. 14 And he will take your fields, and your vineyards, and your oliveyards, even the best of them, and give them to his servants. 15 And he will take the tenth of your seed, and of your vineyards, and give to his officers, and to his servants. 16 And he will take your menservants, and your maidservants, and your goodliest young men, and your asses, and put them to his work. 17 He will take the tenth of your sheep: and ye shall be his servants. 18 **And ye shall cry out in that day because of your king which ye shall have chosen you; and the Lord will not hear you in that day.**

Isaiah 10 Woe unto them that decree unrighteous decrees, and that write grievousness which they have prescribed; 2 To turn aside the needy from judgment, and to take away the right from the poor of my people, that widows may be their prey, and that they may rob the fatherless! 3 **And what will ye do in the day of visitation,** and in the desolation which shall come from far? to whom will ye flee for help? and where will ye leave your glory? 4 Without me they shall bow down under the prisoners, and they shall fall under the slain. For all this his anger is not turned away, but his hand is stretched out still. 5 O Assyrian, the rod of mine anger, and the staff in their hand is mine indignation. 6 I will send him against an hypocritical nation, and against the people of my wrath will I give him a charge, to take the spoil, and to take the prey, and to tread them down like the mire of the streets. 7 Howbeit he meaneth not so, neither doth his heart think so; but it is in his heart to destroy and cut off nations not a few. 8 For he saith, Are not my princes altogether kings? 9 Is not Calno as Carchemish? is not Hamath as Arpad? is not Samaria as Damascus? 10 As my hand hath found the kingdoms of the idols, and whose graven images did excel them of Jerusalem and of Samaria; 11 Shall I not, as I have done unto Samaria and her idols, so do to Jerusalem and her idols? 12 Wherefore it shall come to pass, that when the Lord hath performed his whole work upon mount Zion and on Jerusalem, I will punish the fruit of the stout heart of the king of Assyria, and the glory of his high looks. 13 For he saith, By the strength of my hand I have done it, and by my wisdom; for I am prudent: and I have removed the bounds of the people, and have robbed their treasures, and I have put down the inhabitants like a valiant man: 14 And my hand hath found as a nest the riches of the people: and as one gathereth eggs that are left, have I gathered all the earth; and there was none that moved the wing, or opened the mouth, or peeped. 15 Shall the axe boast itself against him that heweth therewith? or shall the saw magnify itself against him that shaketh it? as if the rod should shake itself against them that lift it up, or as if the staff should lift up itself, as if it were no wood. 16 Therefore shall the Lord, the Lord of hosts, send among his fat ones leanness; and under his glory he shall kindle a burning like the burning of a fire. 17 And the light of Israel shall be for a fire, and his Holy One for a flame: and it shall burn and devour his thorns and his briers in one day; 18 And shall consume the glory of his forest, and of his fruitful field, both soul and body: and they shall be as when a standard-bearer fainteth. 19 And the rest of the trees of his forest shall be few, that a child may write them. 20 And it shall come to pass in that day, that the remnant of Israel, and such as are escaped of the house of Jacob, shall no more again stay upon him that smote them; but shall stay upon the Lord, the Holy One of Israel, in truth.

Isaiah 11 And there shall come forth a rod out of the stem of Jesse, and a Branch shall grow out of his roots: 2 And the spirit of the Lord shall rest upon him, the spirit of wisdom and understanding, the spirit of counsel and might, the spirit of knowledge and of the fear of the Lord; 3 And shall make him of quick understanding in the fear of the Lord: and he shall not judge after the sight of his eyes, neither reprove after the hearing of his ears: 4 But with righteousness shall he judge the poor, and reprove with equity for the meek of the earth: and he shall smite the earth: with the rod of his mouth, and with the breath of his lips shall he slay the wicked. 5 And righteousness shall be the girdle of his loins, and faithfulness the girdle of his reins. 6 **The wolf also shall dwell with the lamb, and the leopard shall lie down with the kid; and the calf and the young lion and the fatling together; and a little child shall lead them. 7 And the cow and the bear shall feed; their young ones shall lie down together: and the lion shall eat straw like the ox.** 8 And the sucking child shall play on the hole of the asp, and the weaned child shall put his hand on the cockatrice' den. 9 They shall not hurt nor destroy in all my holy mountain: for the earth shall be full of the knowledge of the Lord, as the waters cover the sea. 10 **And in that day there shall be a root of Jesse,** which shall stand for an ensign of the people; to it shall the Gentiles seek: and his rest shall be glorious. 11 **And it shall come to pass in that day, that the Lord shall set his hand again the second**

time to recover the remnant of his people, which shall be left, from Assyria, and from Egypt, and from Pathros, and from Cush, and from Elam, and from Shinar, and from Hamath, and from the islands of the sea. 12 And he shall set up an ensign for the nations, and shall assemble the outcasts of Israel, and gather together the dispersed of Judah from the four corners of the earth.

This verse 11 automatically reminds me of John 12:28 Father, glorify thy name. **Then came there a voice from heaven, saying, I have both glorified it, and will glorify it again.** We are being told right here that Jesus has already been glorified once before. This is in the book of Isaiah, but yet so many people feel that Jesus died on the cross and we are now in the new testament. As we showed in the last book, Jesus is why we are here now and that includes all counties of the earth. This also brings to mind of the two witnesses. Revelation 11 And there was given me a reed like unto a rod: and the angel stood, saying, Rise, and measure the temple of God, and the altar, and them that worship therein. 2 But the court which is without the temple leave out, and measure it not; for it is given unto the Gentiles: and the holy city shall they tread under foot forty and two months. 3 And I will give power unto my two witnesses, and they shall prophesy a thousand two hundred and threescore days, clothed in sackcloth. 4 These are the two olive trees, and the two candlesticks standing before the God of the earth. 5 And if any man will hurt them, fire proceedeth out of their mouth, and devoureth their enemies: and if any man will hurt them, he must in this manner be killed. 6 These have power to shut heaven, that it rain not in the days of their prophecy: and have power over waters to turn them to blood, and to smite the earth with all plagues, as often as they will. 7 And when they shall have finished their testimony, the beast that ascendeth out of the bottomless pit shall make war against them, and shall overcome them, and kill them. 8 And their dead bodies shall lie in the street of the great city, which spiritually is called Sodom and Egypt, where also our Lord was crucified. 9 And they of the people and kindreds and tongues and nations shall see their dead bodies three days and an half, and shall not suffer their dead bodies to be put in graves. 10

And they that dwell upon the earth shall rejoice over them, and make merry, and shall send gifts one to another; because these two prophets tormented them that dwelt on the earth. 11 And after three days and an half the spirit of life from God entered into them, and they stood upon their feet; and great fear fell upon them which saw them. 12 And they heard a great voice from heaven saying unto them, Come up hither. And they ascended up to heaven in a cloud; and their enemies beheld them. 13 And the same hour was there a great earthquake, and the tenth part of the city fell, and in the earthquake were slain of men seven thousand: and the remnant were affrighted, and gave glory to the God of heaven. 14 The second woe is past; and, behold, the third woe cometh quickly.

Notice how God did not say that these two witnesses will be together, but rather He will give them power to prophecy a thousand two hundred and threescore days. We can hear our Father say that He will glorify His son the second time. Remember a day is as a thousand years and a thousand years is as a day. We have been hearing that we are in Egypt now. Notice how these bodies didn't get buried, Reincarnation. The last time Jesus was here, he was doing the same thing as I am. Then when the beast arose and killed him, this world rejoiced for they could do as they please and not have someone doing the same thing I am doing now. Then just over three and a half years ago is when our Father baptized me with the Holy Ghost. This fire that comes out of my mouth is not an actual fire, but when you all read these books, it is going to burn. Yes, I do believe that I am the second witness, so I will let you all do the rest of the math for those that just do not want to love in the same manner as our Father.

We could use several areas to show this, but we do not want to make this chapter that long for there are many areas to cover. Can you hear how our Father is using a space of time and calling it that day? And remember, Our Father is not just talking to us, but rather He is talking with gods, kings, and lords in which have dominion over our bodies. As you can hear from above, God said we have gone a whoring after other gods. I know many do not realize that there are many gods in which we use today. 1 Corinthians 8:5 **For though there**

be that are called gods, whether in heaven or in earth, (as there be gods many, and lords many,). As we showed in the last book, it is impossible not to have other gods, however we must put our Father first as the first commandment tells us. Notice how these kings and such were commanded to lead us to different areas? This is what we mean when we say they have dominion over us.

Because we just heard our Father say if they will pray towards this house, we need to cover a couple of things here. We need to remember that the laws, rules, judgements, testimonies, and commandments are for spirits, kings, lords, Satan or the son of perdition, and even Jesus in the last book. Remember that we are the house of God, as showed in the last book. We are the temple of God. God does not dwell in building build with hands. **1 Corinthians 3:16 Know ye not that ye are the temple of God, and that the Spirit of God dwelleth in you? Acts 7:48 Howbeit the most High dwelleth not in temples made with hands; as saith the prophet,** Now we are going to listen to when the house of God was being built in the old testament. We will not show all the details, however we will just show that where 1 Chronicles 28:26 And he said unto me, Solomon thy son, **he shall build my house and my courts:** for I have chosen him to be my son, and I will be his father. 1 Kings 6 And it came to pass in the four hundred and eightieth year after the children of Israel were come out of the land of Egypt, in the fourth year of Solomon's reign over Israel, in the month Zif, which is the second month, that he began to build the house of the Lord. 2 **And the house which king Solomon built for the Lord, the length thereof was threescore cubits,** and the breadth thereof twenty cubits, and the height thereof thirty cubits. But then listen to what we are being told in 1 Kings 8:27 **But will God indeed dwell on the earth? behold, the heaven and heaven of heavens cannot contain thee; how much less this house that I have builded?** And then again in 2 Chronicles 2:5 **And the house which I build is great: for great is our God above all gods. 6 But who is able to build him an house, seeing the heaven and heaven of heavens cannot contain him?** who am I then, that I should build him an house, save only to burn sacrifice before him? Now without showing all the details of the building of this house, we should be realizing that we are hearing how the human body was made. Remember man cannot figure out how to make a human body in which functions in the way that it does. They can make electric people, but man cannot duplicate the body.

Now in the process of building the house of God, there were tables set up. These table were placed on our hearts. Psalm 69:22 Let their table become a snare before them: and that which should have been for their welfare, let it become a trap. Proverbs 3:3 Let not mercy and truth forsake thee: bind them about thy neck; **write them upon the table of thine heart:** Jeremiah 17:1 The sin of Judah is written with a pen of iron, and with the point of a diamond: **it is graven upon the table of their heart, and upon the horns of your altars;** 2 Corinthians 3:3 Forasmuch as ye are manifestly declared to be the epistle of Christ ministered by us, written not with ink, but with the Spirit of the living God; **not in tables of stone, but in fleshy tables of the heart.** This is what we were showing in the last book, when Jesus comes into our own personal temple of God, he flips these tables so that we do not desire the merchandise of the money exchangers. We know that we are the temple of God, right? 1 Corinthians 3:16 **Know ye not that ye are the temple of God, and that the Spirit of God dwelleth in you?** Now listen to when Jesus flipped the tables. Matthew 21:12 **And Jesus went into the temple of God,** and cast out all them that sold and bought in the temple, and overthrew the tables of the moneychangers, and the seats of them that sold doves, 13 And said unto them, **It is written, My house shall be called the house of prayer; but ye have made it a den of thieves.** If you still feel you need to have more than just basic essentials to survive, your table has not been flipped. That is how most people do serve graven images and other gods. Our Father told us not to make anything in in the image or the likeness of anything in the heavens, earth or under the earth. Exodus 20:4 **Thou shalt not make unto thee any graven image, or any likeness of any thing that is in heaven above, or that is in the earth beneath, or that is in the water under the earth. 5 Thou shalt not bow down thyself to them, nor serve them: for I the Lord thy**

God am a jealous God, visiting the iniquity of the fathers upon the children unto the third and fourth generation of them that hate me; 6 And shewing mercy unto thousands of them that love me, and keep my commandments. Now I have talked with people that say they do not bow to these artifacts. Did our Father tell you to have them? NO, he said do not, so which god or spirit are you listening to? You are serving something other than our Father when you have more than you need. 1 Timothy 6:8 And having food and raiment let us be therewith content. So instead of allowing your house of God be a house of prayer, you ignore what He said and continue to buy and won things in which can and will be destroyed. The do not help you nor anyone else survive in this world. That is how you make the house of God a den of thieves.

Just listen to what we are told about having graven images. Deuteronomy 4:15 Take ye therefore good heed unto yourselves; for ye saw no manner of similitude on the day that the Lord spake unto you in Horeb out of the midst of the fire: 16 Lest ye corrupt yourselves, and make you a graven image, the similitude of any figure, the likeness of male or female, 17 The likeness of any beast that is on the earth, the likeness of any winged fowl that flieth in the air, 18 The likeness of any thing that creepeth on the ground, the likeness of any fish that is in the waters beneath the earth: 19 And lest thou lift up thine eyes unto heaven, and when thou seest the sun, and the moon, and the stars, even all the host of heaven, **shouldest be driven to worship them**, and serve them, which the Lord thy God hath divided unto all nations under the whole heaven. Remember they have dominion over us as we have dominion over the beast and fowls on earth.

By the way, this is also another way that most defile the temple of God. 1 Corinthian 3:17 If any man defile the temple of God, him shall God destroy; for the temple of God is holy, which temple ye are. If you are the house of God and houses of God is a house of payers, do not you defile this house when you ignore Him and don't give Him the attention in which He deserves?

If you can hear it, we have altars inside of us also. Remember what alters are for? Exodus 20:25 **An altar of earth thou shalt make unto** me, and shalt sacrifice thereon thy burnt offerings, and thy peace offerings, thy sheep, and thine oxen:** in all places where I record my name I will come unto thee, and I will bless thee. Deuteronomy 27:5 **And there shalt thou build an altar unto the Lord thy God, an altar of stones: thou shalt not lift up any iron tool upon them. 6 Thou shalt build the altar of the Lord thy God of whole stones: and thou shalt offer burnt offerings thereon unto the Lord thy God:** Remember how the sacrifices in which God enjoys are of a broken spirit. Psalm 51:16 **For thou desirest not sacrifice; else would I give it: thou delightest not in burnt offering. 17 The sacrifices of God are a broken spirit: a broken and a contrite heart, O God, thou wilt not despise.** We showed in the last book that our Father never commanded man to sacrifice animals. That was for those in heave in which have dominion over our bodies. Now we need to listen to how Jesus said everyone must be salted with fire. Mark 9:49 **For every one shall be salted with fire, and every sacrifice shall be salted with salt. 50 Salt is good: but if the salt have lost his saltness, wherewith will ye season it? Have salt in yourselves, and have peace one with another.** Then remember he said he didn't come to bring peace? Matthew 10:34 **Think not that I am come to send peace on earth: I came not to send peace, but a sword.**

These sacrifices in which we are to make, are actually upsetting somebody somehow. Let me use a real-life example. I know this woman that has been having marital problems for quite a while now. She has a daughter in which just turned 18 a few weeks ago. She is now looking for a place so that she can move out. They get along great; however, it is breaking the mom's heart. There is that sacrifice. She is moving out even though it is breaking her mom's heart. So, her mom is having her spirit broken. So now let me ask you this, what does salt do when you put it on an open wound? Oh, we all know it burns. There is that burnt sacrifice in which our Father is wanting, trying, and hoping will get her mom to turn back to Him. That is what He is trying to do with everybody. Now if there is someone that is always trying to please others and never offend, then their salt has lost it flavor.

Okay we are going to look at another area of the bible but will not show all that is involved for that would require a lot of scriptures to be shown. We will only show the areas that gets to the point of what we are showing. We are going to be looking at how Joseph's brothers sold him into slavery and how that turned out for Joseph. Genesis 37:20 Come now therefore, and let us slay him, and cast him into some pit, and we will say, Some evil beast hath devoured him: and we shall see what will become of his dreams. 21 And Reuben heard it, and he delivered him out of their hands; and said, Let us not kill him. 22 And Reuben said unto them, Shed no blood, but cast him into this pit that is in the wilderness, and lay no hand upon him; that he might rid him out of their hands, to deliver him to his father again. 23 And it came to pass, when Joseph was come unto his brethren, that they stript Joseph out of his coat, his coat of many colours that was on him; 24 And they took him, and cast him into a pit: and the pit was empty, there was no water in it. 25 And they sat down to eat bread: and they lifted up their eyes and looked, and, behold, a company of Ishmeelites came from Gilead with their camels bearing spicery and balm and myrrh, going to carry it down to Egypt. 26 And Judah said unto his brethren, What profit is it if we slay our brother, and conceal his blood? 27 Come, and let us sell him to the Ishmeelites, and let not our hand be upon him; for he is our brother and our flesh. And his brethren were content. 28 Then there passed by Midianites merchantmen; and they drew and lifted up Joseph out of the pit, and sold Joseph to the Ishmeelites for twenty pieces of silver: and they brought Joseph into Egypt. 29 And Reuben returned unto the pit; and, behold, Joseph was not in the pit; and he rent his clothes. 30 And he returned unto his brethren, and said, The child is not; and I, whither shall I go? 31 And they took Joseph's coat, and killed a kid of the goats, and dipped the coat in the blood; 32 And they sent the coat of many colours, and they brought it to their father; and said, This have we found: know now whether it be thy son's coat or no. 33 And he knew it, and said, It is my son's coat; an evil beast hath devoured him; Joseph is without doubt rent in pieces. 34 And Jacob rent his clothes, and put sackcloth upon his loins, and mourned for his son many days. 35 And all his sons and all his daughters rose up to comfort him; but he refused to be comforted; and he said, For I will go down into the grave unto my son mourning. Thus his father wept for him. 36 And the Midianites sold him into Egypt unto Potiphar, an officer of Pharaoh's, and captain of the guard.

Okay we just listened to the area in which his brother had sold him but now we are going to skip several years on Joseph's life so that we can hear how things turned out for him. Genesis 45 hen Joseph could not refrain himself before all them that stood by him; and he cried, Cause every man to go out from me. And there stood no man with him, while Joseph made himself known unto his brethren. 2 And he wept aloud: and the Egyptians and the house of Pharaoh heard. 3 And Joseph said unto his brethren, I am Joseph; doth my father yet live? And his brethren could not answer him; for they were troubled at his presence. 4 And Joseph said unto his brethren, Come near to me, I pray you. And they came near. And he said, I am Joseph your brother, whom ye sold into Egypt. 5 **Now therefore be not grieved, nor angry with yourselves, that ye sold me hither: for God did send me before you to preserve life. 6 For these two years hath the famine been in the land: and yet there are five years, in the which there shall neither be earing nor harvest. 7 And God sent me before you to preserve you a posterity in the earth, and to save your lives by a great deliverance. 8 So now it was not you that sent me hither, but God: and he hath made me a father to Pharaoh, and lord of all his house, and a ruler throughout all the land of Egypt.** 9 Haste ye, and go up to my father, and say unto him, Thus saith thy son Joseph, God hath made me lord of all Egypt: come down unto me, tarry not:

Can you hear how Joseph's brothers were salted with this fire? Do you think Joseph though it was a good thing happening when his brother sold him? Notice how Joseph, throughout his tribulations, kept believing in our Father and not some other God. Do you hear how Joseph knew that it was actually God our Father in which caused everything to happen the way that it did? Do you hear what our Father did for Joseph because of Joseph not losing His faith?

Now we mentioned in the last book, that I keep hearing things like in Psalm 104:2 Who coverest thyself with light as with a garment: **who stretchest out the heavens like a curtain:** Isaiah 40:22 It is he that sitteth upon the circle of the earth, and the inhabitants thereof are as grasshoppers; **that stretcheth out the heavens as a curtain, and spreadeth them out as a tent to dwell in:** So now let us listen to just a couple of spots as to when they were commanded to make the curtains. Exodus 26 **Moreover thou shalt make the tabernacle with ten curtains of fine twined linen, and blue, and purple, and scarlet: with cherubims of cunning work shalt thou make them. 2 The length of one curtain shall be eight and twenty cubits, and the breadth of one curtain four cubits: and every one of the curtains shall have one measure.** Exodus 36:8 **And every wise hearted man among them that wrought the work of the tabernacle made ten curtains of fine twined linen, and blue, and purple, and scarlet: with cherubims of cunning work made he them.** These are commandments for the spirits, kings, lords, and men in heaven. We can know that there are men in heaven and in earth. No, no man on earth has been to heaven as we can know by listening to John 3:13 **And no man hath ascended up to heaven, but he that came down from heaven, even the Son of man which is in heaven.** We can know this when we listen to Revelation 5:3 **And no man in heaven, nor in earth, neither under the earth,** was able to open the book, neither to look thereon. There is a lot of things in which we will not understand until the end. Yes, our Father is showing me a lot and I am showing you all a lot, but we will never (in the flesh) know everything about God the Father. This is the time of the end; however, it is not the end.

These curtains are our sky. We will not show all the details, but one can only imagine that most of the instruction and such in the books of Moses and the prophets are for those that were to build man, earth, and things in the heavens. Remember that a day is as a thousand years and a thousand years is as a day. When we read the bible, we normally do not think about how much time it took to make these curtains or make the house of God. This is why we are told the law is a shadow of things to come. Hebrew 10 **For the law**

having a shadow of good things to come, and not the very image of the things, can never with those sacrifices which they offered year by year continually make the comers thereunto perfect. This is what it will be for some after the end of this world. We can know this by listening to Matthew 12:32 And whosoever speaketh a word against the Son of man, it shall be forgiven him: but whosoever speaketh against the Holy Ghost, it shall not be forgiven him, **neither in this world, neither in the world to come.**

We could go in depth trying to understand how all the measurements and such could line up with the human body or try to figure out how maybe things could line up with how the sky was made. Without having to post several books of the bible, let us just think of how perfectly everything grows. How does the human body pump blood to every part of the body at the precise time in which the body needs? How does the nerves work throughout the entire body? Yes, doctors can show things on charts and such, but they cannot duplicate it. The same thing goes for animals of all sorts. Now just think about how the trees grow as they do. How food grows from the ground. We can now realize that when we listen to the bible, we can be certain that this is why man cannot understand it. Use my life for an example, I am a truck driver and have been for quite some while. Do you think I would know anything about doing a heart surgery on someone? Those above are from above and not earth.

Now that we have covered some of that we will get back on topic. There are very many people out here that believe that the book of Revelation is how that world is going to end. However, remember our Father has hidden this from the wise and prudent. Now we are going to show that the book of Revelation is how most of this got started and not how the world will end.

First thing we are going to show is the very end of the book. As we showed in the last book, our Father is the one that raises the spirit of Jesus in our own bodies. So, in reality, the first thing we need to be listening to is Revelation 22:17 And the Spirit and the bride say, Come. And let him that heareth say, Come. And let him that is athirst come. And whosoever will, let him take the water of life freely. 18

For I testify unto every man that heareth the words of the prophecy of this book, If any man shall add unto these things, God shall add unto him the plagues that are written in this book: 19 And if any man shall take away from the words of the book of this prophecy, God shall take away his part out of the book of life, and out of the holy city, and from the things which are written in this book. 20 He which testifieth these things saith, Surely I come quickly. Amen. **Even so, come, Lord Jesus.** 21 The grace of our Lord Jesus Christ be with you all. Amen.

We are going to show how this works again, just in case you're not sure of how it works. This world teaches that the only way to the Father is through Jesus. This is correct but that is not believing that he came and died on the cross and then your sealed. As we showed in the last book, every person on the planet makes up the one son of God, or Jesus. Acts 17:26 **And hath made of one blood all nations of men for to dwell on all the face of the earth, and hath determined the times before appointed, and the bounds of their habitation;** We are then told several times to love our neighbor as ourselves, so loving everyone on the planet is how we get to the Father. But that is just the tip of the ice burg, so to speak. Without showing all the verses again, we can know that everyone on the planet, is a servant and a vessel of God. Which means everyone on the planet is the one son of God. This is how Jesus taste death for every man. Hebrews 2:9 But we see Jesus, who was made a little lower than the angels for the suffering of death, crowned with glory and honour; **that he by the grace of God should taste death for every man.**

Now we need to listen to what Jesus tells us in John 5:43 I am come in my Father's name, and ye receive me not: if another shall come in his own name, him ye will receive. 44 How can ye believe, which receive honour one of another, and seek not the honour that cometh from God only? 45 Do not think that I will accuse you to the Father: there is one that accuseth you, even Moses, in whom ye trust. 46 **For had ye believed Moses, ye would have believed me; for he wrote of me. 47 But if ye believe not his writings, how shall ye believe my words?** John 6:43 Jesus therefore answered and said unto them, Murmur not among yourselves. 44 No man can come to me, except the Father which hath sent me draw him: and I will raise him up at the last day. 45 **It is written in the prophets, And they shall be all taught of God. Every man therefore that hath heard, and hath learned of the Father, cometh unto me.**

Remember our Father is the mastermind behind all of this, even His son. So now knowing this, we should be praying for the Lord Jesus to come before we even start to read Genesis. By doing this, it would be a start to showing our Father that we are willing to try and learn of Him and His ways so that He will raise His son of righteousness up inside of us. Remember Jesus is in the image of the invisible God. Colossians 1:14 In whom we have redemption through his blood, even the forgiveness of sins: 15 Who is the image of the invisible God, the firstborn of every creature:

This is where we need to remember that Jesus already died on the cross. Therefore, we are here. Now we need to listen to our Father what He tells us in Isaiah 46:10 **Declaring the end from the beginning, and from ancient times the things that are not yet done, saying, My counsel shall stand, and I will do all my pleasure:** So now we need to look at the very beginning of Genesis 1 In the beginning God created the heaven and the earth. 2 And the earth was without form, and void; and darkness was upon the face of the deep. And the Spirit of God moved upon the face of the waters. 3 And God said, Let there be light: and there was light. 4 And God saw the light, that it was good: and God divided the light from the darkness. 5 And God called the light Day, and the darkness he called Night. And the evening and the morning were the first day.

Now let us listen to a bit of Revelation 12:8 And prevailed not; neither was their place found any more in heaven. 9 And the great dragon was cast out, that old serpent, called the Devil, and Satan, which deceiveth the whole world: he was cast out into the earth, and his angels were cast out with him. 10 And I heard a loud voice saying in heaven, Now is come salvation, and strength, and the kingdom of our God, and the power of his Christ: for the accuser of our brethren is cast down, which accused them before our God day and night.

Notice how the earth was without form, and void, and darkness was upon the face of the deep? Now let us listen to Jesus when he tells us he is the light of this world. John 8:12 Then spake Jesus again unto them, saying, I am the light of the world: he that followeth me shall not walk in darkness, but shall have the light of life. Satan and his angels were cast here to earth and that is why the earth was without form, and void, and full of darkness. Now our Father is showing His mercy right here in the beginning. Satan and his angels were already cast here, but our Father is saying, without saying it directly, I will give you all another chance. Right here is where our Father could have just said you all have transgressed my law and I will not have anything to do with you again.

That light that our Father created on the very first day was not the sun for it was created on the 4th day as shown in the last book. This is where we learn that Adam was not just one man but rather many men as one man. And the same with Eve. Without having to show all the details shown in the last book, we all can know that many people make up the one son of God, right? Let us listen to a few other spots that we can hear this. Judges 20 Then all the children of Israel went out, **and the congregation was gathered together as one man,** from Dan even to Beersheba, with the land of Gilead, unto the Lord in Mizpeh. 2 And the chief of all the people, even of all the tribes of Israel, presented themselves in the assembly of the people of God, four hundred thousand footmen that drew sword. 3 (Now the children of Benjamin heard that the children of Israel were gone up to Mizpeh.) Then said the children of Israel, Tell us, how was this wickedness? 4 And the Levite, the husband of the woman that was slain, answered and said, I came into Gibeah that belongeth to Benjamin, I and my concubine, to lodge. 5 And the men of Gibeah rose against me, and beset the house round about upon me by night, and thought to have slain me: and my concubine have they forced, that she is dead. 6 And I took my concubine, and cut her in pieces, and sent her throughout all the country of the inheritance of Israel: for they have committed lewdness and folly in Israel. 7 Behold, ye are all children of Israel; give here your advice and counsel. 8 **And all the people arose as one man,** saying, We will not any of us go to his tent, neither will we any of us turn into his house. 9 But now this shall be the thing which we will do to Gibeah; we will go up by lot against it; 10 And we will take ten men of an hundred throughout all the tribes of Israel, and an hundred of a thousand, and a thousand out of ten thousand, to fetch victual for the people, that they may do, when they come to Gibeah of Benjamin, according to all the folly that they have wrought in Israel. 11 So all the men of Israel were gathered against the city, **knit together as one man.** Ezra 3:1 And when the seventh month was come, and the children of Israel were in the cities, the people gathered themselves together as one man to Jerusalem. Nehemiah 8:1 **And all the people gathered themselves together as one man into the street that was before the water gate;** and they spake unto Ezra the scribe to bring the book of the law of Moses, which the Lord had commanded to Israel.

Now if we will recall, the three sons of Noah, covered the entire earth. Genesis 9:19 These are the three sons of Noah: **and of them was the whole earth overspread.** Then remember when we are told that all men die in Adam. 1 Corinthians 15:22 **For as in Adam all die, even so in Christ shall all be made alive.** I believe that Adam is a spirit in which all men have within them. This is why we are told this in 1 Corinthians 15:45 And so it is written, The first man Adam was made a living soul; the last Adam was made a quickening spirit.

Now let us listen to when God created man. Genesis 2:7 And the Lord God formed man of the dust of the ground, and breathed into his nostrils the breath of life; and man became a living soul. Notice how man was man before he became a living soul? Man did not become a living soul until our Father breathed life into him. Now remember Jesus said he is the life. John 14:6 Jesus saith unto him, I am the way, the truth, and the life: no man cometh unto the Father, but by me. Philippians 2:5 Let this mind be in you, which was also in Christ Jesus: 6 Who, being in the form of God, thought it not robbery to be equal with God: 7 But made himself of no reputation, and took upon him the form of a servant, and was made in the likeness of men:

Now if we are truly believing the writings of Moses and the prophets than we can know that Adam must have represented many men as one man. And Eve would have represented many women as one woman. Just like the three sons of Noah overspread the whole earth. If this was not the case, then our Father would have been contradicting His own law. Let us listen to a little of Leviticus 18 And the Lord spake unto Moses, saying, 2 Speak unto the children of Israel, and say unto them, I am the Lord your God. 3 After the doings of the land of Egypt, wherein ye dwelt, shall ye not do: and after the doings of the land of Canaan, whither I bring you, shall ye not do: neither shall ye walk in their ordinances. 4 Ye shall do my judgments, and keep mine ordinances, to walk therein: I am the Lord your God. 5 Ye shall therefore keep my statutes, and my judgments: which if a man do, he shall live in them: I am the Lord. 6 None of you shall approach to any that is near of kin to him, to uncover their nakedness: I am the Lord. 7 The nakedness of thy father, or the nakedness of thy mother, shalt thou not uncover: she is thy mother; thou shalt not uncover her nakedness.8 The nakedness of thy father's wife shalt thou not uncover: it is thy father's nakedness. 9 The nakedness of thy sister, the daughter of thy father, or daughter of thy mother, whether she be born at home, or born abroad, even their nakedness thou shalt not uncover. 10 The nakedness of thy son's daughter, or of thy daughter's daughter, even their nakedness thou shalt not uncover: for theirs is thine own nakedness. 11 The nakedness of thy father's wife's daughter, begotten of thy father, she is thy sister, thou shalt not uncover her nakedness. 12 Thou shalt not uncover the nakedness of thy father's sister: she is thy father's near kinswoman. 13 Thou shalt not uncover the nakedness of thy mother's sister: for she is thy mother's near kinswoman. 14 Thou shalt not uncover the nakedness of thy father's brother, thou shalt not approach to his wife: she is thine aunt. 15 Thou shalt not uncover the nakedness of thy daughter in law: she is thy son's wife; thou shalt not uncover her nakedness. 16 Thou shalt not uncover the nakedness of thy brother's wife: it is thy brother's nakedness. 17 Thou shalt not uncover the nakedness of a woman and her daughter, neither shalt thou take her son's daughter, or her daughter's daughter, to uncover her nakedness; for they are her near kinswomen: it is wickedness. 18 Neither shalt thou take a wife to her sister, to vex her, to uncover her nakedness, beside the other in her life time. 19 Also thou shalt not approach unto a woman to uncover her nakedness, as long as she is put apart for her uncleanness. 20 Moreover thou shalt not lie carnally with thy neighbour's wife, to defile thyself with her.

Now if it started with just one of man of Adam, and one woman of Eve, then how could they be fruitful, multiply, and replenish the earth? Somebody would have to have sex with a relative of some sort in order to have children after Adam and Eve had children.

Now remember that we our listening to conversations going on in heaven when we listen to our bible. Philippians 3:20 **For our conversation is in heaven;** from whence also we look for the Saviour, the Lord Jesus Christ: So now let us listen to Revelation 20 And I saw an angel come down from heaven, having the key of the bottomless pit and a great chain in his hand. 2 **And he laid hold on the dragon, that old serpent, which is the Devil, and Satan, and bound him a thousand years,** 3 And cast him into the bottomless pit, and shut him up, and set a seal upon him, that he should deceive the nations no more, **till the thousand years should be fulfilled:** and after that he must be loosed a little season. Notice how we can hear that Satan, that old serpent, which is the Devil was bound up, but not the angels that came with him. Or one third of the stars as noted in Revelation 12:4 And his tail drew the third part of the stars of heaven, and did cast them to the earth: and the dragon stood before the woman which was ready to be delivered, for to devour her child as soon as it was born.

I feel as if I am not getting the picture painted in your minds as well as I see it. Therefore, I ask you as a reader, to ask our Father to help you understand for He is the ultimate teacher and I am just a man in the flesh trying to teach what He has been teaching me. Now we know that Satan is locked up, we can hear that very well. That darkness that covered the entire earth on the first day was all that had been kicked out of heaven and that was now in hell. Remember in the last book, we showed that this is hell? Then that light that our Father created on the first day is what He gave to everyman when

He breathed life into them so that man became a living soul. This is when our Father translated us into the kingdom of God. Colossians 1:12 Giving thanks unto the Father, which hath made us meet to be partakers of the inheritance of the saints in light: 13 Who hath delivered us from the power of darkness, **and hath translated us into the kingdom of his dear Son:** Revelation 20:4 And I saw thrones, and they sat upon them, and judgment was given unto them: and I saw the souls of them that were beheaded for the witness of Jesus, and for the word of God, and which had not worshipped the beast, neither his image, neither had received his mark upon their foreheads, or in their hands; and they lived and reigned with Christ a thousand years. 5 But the rest of the dead lived not again until the thousand years were finished. This is the first resurrection. 6 Blessed and holy is he that hath part in the first resurrection: on such the second death hath no power, but they shall be priests of God and of Christ, and shall reign with him a thousand years.

Now to understand where our bibles explain this we need to listen to a couple of different things. Deuteronomy 4 Now therefore hearken, O Israel, unto the statutes and unto the judgments, which I teach you, for to do them, that ye may live, and go in and possess the land which the Lord God of your fathers giveth you. 2 Ye shall not add unto the word which I command you, neither shall ye diminish ought from it, that ye may keep the commandments of the Lord your God which I command you. 3 Your eyes have seen what the Lord did because of Baalpeor: for all the men that followed Baalpeor, the Lord thy God hath destroyed them from among you. 4 **But ye that did cleave unto the Lord your God are alive every one of you this day.** 5 Behold, I have taught you statutes and judgments, even as the Lord my God commanded me, that ye should do so in the land whither ye go to possess it.

Now we need to reflect to Ecclesiastes 1:10 Is there any thing whereof it may be said, See, this is new? it hath been already of old time, which was before us. 11 There is no remembrance of former things; neither shall there be any remembrance of things that are to come with those that shall come after. Now with us knowing that we do not remember things from the past, or of things to come thereafter, we can start to understand that we have been delivered from the lowest hell. In the last book I stated that I wasn't sure what level of hell we are in, however we showed that we are in some level of hell. But when we listen to Deuteronomy 32:21 They have moved me to jealousy with that which is not God; they have provoked me to anger with their vanities: and I will move them to jealousy with those which are not a people; I will provoke them to anger with a foolish nation. 22 For a fire is kindled in mine anger, and shall burn unto the lowest hell, and shall consume the earth with her increase, and set on fire the foundations of the mountains. Let us listen to what we are told in Psalm 86:13 For great is thy mercy toward me: **and thou hast delivered my soul from the lowest hell.** When we were in the lowest hell, we all cleaved to our Father one way or another. Therefore, we all are now here in the thousand years of reigning with Christ.

To understand this better, we need to listen to Colossians 3:11 Where there is neither Greek nor Jew, circumcision nor uncircumcision, Barbarian, Scythian, **bond nor free: but Christ is all, and in all.** We are being told right here; we are reigning with Christ. If Christ dwells inside of you, you are with him and he is with you. Remember Christ died on the cross, so now it is his spirit that dwells inside of us.

Now we need to listen to what Jesus said in Mathew 5:17 Think not that I am come to destroy the law, or the prophets: I am not come to destroy, but to fulfil. 18 For verily I say unto you, Till heaven and earth pass, one jot or one tittle shall in no wise pass from the law, till all be fulfilled. 19 Whosoever therefore shall break one of these least commandments, and shall teach men so, he shall be called the least in the kingdom of heaven: but whosoever shall do and teach them, the same shall be called great in the kingdom of heaven.

Now note the similarities to what we hear in the old testament. Deuteronomy 28 And it shall come to pass, if thou shalt hearken diligently unto the voice of the Lord thy God, to observe and to do all his commandments which I command thee this day, that the Lord thy God will set thee on high above all nations of the earth: 2 And all these blessings shall come on thee, and overtake thee, if thou shalt hearken unto the voice of the Lord thy God. 3 Blessed shalt thou be in the city, and blessed shalt thou be in the field. 4 Blessed shall be the fruit of thy body, and the fruit of thy ground, and the fruit of thy cattle, the increase of thy kine, and the flocks of thy sheep. 5 Blessed shall be thy basket and thy store. 6 Blessed shalt thou be when thou comest in, and blessed shalt thou be when thou goest out. 7 The Lord shall cause thine enemies that rise up against thee to be smitten before thy face: they shall come out against thee one way, and flee before thee seven ways. 8 The Lord shall command the blessing upon thee in thy storehouses, and in all that thou settest thine hand unto; and he shall bless thee in the land which the Lord thy God giveth thee. 9 The Lord shall establish thee an holy people unto himself, as he hath sworn unto thee, if thou shalt keep the commandments of the Lord thy God, and walk in his ways. 10 And all people of the earth shall see that thou art called by the name of the Lord; and they shall be afraid of thee. 11 And the Lord shall make thee plenteous in goods, in the fruit of thy body, and in the fruit of thy cattle, and in the fruit of thy ground, in the land which the Lord sware unto thy fathers to give thee. 12 The Lord shall open unto thee his good treasure, the heaven to give the rain unto thy land in his season, and to bless all the work of thine hand: and thou shalt lend unto many nations, and thou shalt not borrow. 13 **And the Lord shall make thee the head, and not the tail; and thou shalt be above only, and thou shalt not be beneath; if that thou hearken unto the commandments of the Lord thy God, which I command thee this day, to observe and to do them:** 14 And thou shalt not go aside from any of the words which I command thee this day, to the right hand, or to the left, to go after other gods to serve them. 15 But it shall come to pass, if thou wilt not hearken unto the voice of the Lord thy God, to observe to do all his commandments and his statutes which I command thee this day; that all these curses shall come upon thee, and overtake thee: 16 Cursed shalt thou be in the city, and cursed shalt thou be in the field. 17 Cursed shall be thy basket and thy store. 18 Cursed shall be the fruit of thy body, and the fruit of thy land, the increase of thy kine, and the flocks of thy sheep. 19 Cursed shalt thou be when thou comest in, and cursed shalt thou be when thou goest out. 20 The Lord shall send upon thee cursing, vexation, and rebuke, in all that thou settest thine hand unto for to do, until thou be destroyed, and until thou perish quickly; because of the wickedness of thy doings, whereby thou hast forsaken me. 21 The Lord shall make the pestilence cleave unto thee, until he have consumed thee from off the land, whither thou goest to possess it. 22 The Lord shall smite thee with a consumption, and with a fever, and with an inflammation, and with an extreme burning, and with the sword, and with blasting, and with mildew; and they shall pursue thee until thou perish. 23 And thy heaven that is over thy head shall be brass, and the earth that is under thee shall be iron. 24 The Lord shall make the rain of thy land powder and dust: from heaven shall it come down upon thee, until thou be destroyed. 25 The Lord shall cause thee to be smitten before thine enemies: thou shalt go out one way against them, and flee seven ways before them: and shalt be removed into all the kingdoms of the earth. 26 And thy carcase shall be meat unto all fowls of the air, and unto the beasts of the earth, and no man shall fray them away. 27 The Lord will smite thee with the botch of Egypt, and with the emerods, and with the scab, and with the itch, whereof thou canst not be healed. 28 The Lord shall smite thee with madness, and blindness, and astonishment of heart:

29 And thou shalt grope at noonday, as the blind gropeth in darkness, and thou shalt not prosper in thy ways: and thou shalt be only oppressed and spoiled evermore, and no man shall save thee. 30 Thou shalt betroth a wife, and another man shall lie with her: thou shalt build an house, and thou shalt not dwell therein: thou shalt plant a vineyard, and shalt not gather the grapes thereof. 31 Thine ox shall be slain before thine eyes, and thou shalt not eat thereof: thine ass shall be violently taken away from before thy face, and shall not be restored to thee: thy sheep shall be given unto thine enemies, and thou shalt have none to rescue them. 32 Thy sons and thy daughters shall be given unto another people, and thine eyes shall look, and fail with longing for them all the day long; and there shall be no might in thine hand. 33 The fruit of thy land, and all thy labours, shall a nation which thou knowest not eat up; and thou shalt be only oppressed and

crushed alway: 34 So that thou shalt be mad for the sight of thine eyes which thou shalt see. 35 The Lord shall smite thee in the knees, and in the legs, with a sore botch that cannot be healed, from the sole of thy foot unto the top of thy head. 36 The Lord shall bring thee, and thy king which thou shalt set over thee, unto a nation which neither thou nor thy fathers have known; and there shalt thou serve other gods, wood and stone. 37 And thou shalt become an astonishment, a proverb, and a byword, among all nations whither the Lord shall lead thee. 38 Thou shalt carry much seed out into the field, and shalt gather but little in; for the locust shall consume it. 39 Thou shalt plant vineyards, and dress them, but shalt neither drink of the wine, nor gather the grapes; for the worms shall eat them. 40 Thou shalt have olive trees throughout all thy coasts, but thou shalt not anoint thyself with the oil; for thine olive shall cast his fruit. 41 Thou shalt beget sons and daughters, but thou shalt not enjoy them; for they shall go into captivity. 42 All thy trees and fruit of thy land shall the locust consume. 43 The stranger that is within thee shall get up above thee very high; and thou shalt come down very low. 44 **He shall lend to thee, and thou shalt not lend to him: he shall be the head, and thou shalt be the tail.** Notice how we are hearing the same thing Jesus said in Matthew 5:17-19. It is just said in more detail in the old testament than in the new testament.

Now we need to remember that this earth or this world was and is here for the son of God. Colossians 1:10 That ye might walk worthy of the Lord unto all pleasing, being fruitful in every good work, and increasing in the knowledge of God; 11 Strengthened with all might, according to his glorious power, unto all patience and longsuffering with joyfulness; 12 Giving thanks unto the Father, which hath made us meet to be partakers of the inheritance of the saints in light: 13 Who hath delivered us from the power of darkness, and hath translated us into the kingdom of his dear Son: 14 **In whom we have redemption through his blood, even the forgiveness of sins: 15 Who is the image of the invisible God, the firstborn of every creature: 16 For by him were all things created, that are in heaven, and that are in earth, visible and invisible, whether they be thrones,**

or dominions, or principalities, or powers: all things were created by him, and for him: 17 And he is before all things, and by him all things consist. 18 And he is the head of the body, the church: who is the beginning, the firstborn from the dead; that in all things he might have the preeminence. 19 For it pleased the Father that in him should all fulness dwell;20 And, having made peace through the blood of his cross, by him to reconcile all things unto himself; by him, I say, whether they be things in earth, or things in heaven.

Now let us venture back to the very beginning of the bible again. Genesis 1 In the beginning God created the heaven and the earth. 2 And the earth was without form, and void; and darkness was upon the face of the deep. And the Spirit of God moved upon the face of the waters. 3 And God said, Let there be light: and there was light. 4 And God saw the light, that it was good: and God divided the light from the darkness. 5 And God called the light Day, and the darkness he called Night. And the evening and the morning were the first day. As we showed everyone in the last book, we really have no idea of what time period we are in. When Satan and the angels were kicked out of heaven, there was no longer any light within them. So now our Father is locking Satan up right here. This is where our Father divided the darkness and made light. He is now showing His love for us for He is giving us another chance to learn how to love in the same manner as He does in which is not about your own life. If He made it about His own life, then He would have never said or brought forth the earth so that we could still have a chance to get back into heaven. 1 John 4:19 **We love him, because he first loved us.**

1 Thessalonians 5 But of the times and the seasons, brethren, ye have no need that I write unto you. 2 For yourselves know perfectly that the day of the Lord so cometh as a thief in the night. 3 For when they shall say, Peace and safety; then sudden destruction cometh upon them, as travail upon a woman with child; and they shall not escape. 4 **But ye, brethren, are not in darkness, that that day should overtake you as a thief. 5 Ye are all the children of light, and the children of the day: we are not of the night, nor of darkness.** This is the light

that our Father created on the first day. Notice how we are not of the night, nor of the darkness. This darkness covered the entire earth.

Now with Jesus being the light of the world and that light is within us, we need to understand why many can't see this light. John 3:16 For God so loved the world, that he gave his only begotten Son, that whosoever believeth in him should not perish, but have everlasting life. 17 For God sent not his Son into the world to condemn the world; but that the world through him might be saved. 18 He that believeth on him is not condemned: but he that believeth not is condemned already, because he hath not believed in the name of the only begotten Son of God. 19 **And this is the condemnation, that light is come into the world, and men loved darkness rather than light, because their deeds were evil. 20 For every one that doeth evil hateth the light, neither cometh to the light, lest his deeds should be reproved. 21 But he that doeth truth cometh to the light, that his deeds may be made manifest, that they are wrought in God.** Proverbs 20:27 The spirit of man is the candle of the Lord, searching all the inward parts of the belly. Remember how Jesus is holding seven candle sticks in the book of Revelation 1:20 The mystery of the seven stars which thou sawest in my right hand, **and the seven golden candlesticks.** The seven stars are the angels of the seven churches: and the seven candlesticks which thou sawest are the seven churches. The church is within each person and not in a building. This darkness thinks of himself or herself before others. Now quick, because we mentioned herself, we need to listen to what helps a woman. 1 Timothy 2:13 For Adam was first formed, then Eve. 14 And Adam was not deceived, but the woman being deceived was in the transgression. 15 **Notwithstanding she shall be saved in childbearing, if they continue in faith and charity and holiness with sobriety.** Now let us just think of a woman giving birth. She usually bears the pain and anguish with childbirth. When the child is born, she neglects herself so she can fulfill the needs of the baby. She will go without sleep, without food, and without bathing before the child's needs are met. That is what Jesus did, he gave up his own desires of the flesh so that he could learn of our Father so that he could leave us an example. He even commanded us to do the same.

However, most would rather judge others, condemn others, think of themselves before they think of others. And this is because each person chooses not to learn of our Father so that our Father can teach them how to love others as they love themselves. This world teaches that I must be happy before I can make anyone else happy. This world teaches that my needs must to be met before I can help you with your needs. Now let is listen to 1 Corinthians 6:6 But brother goeth to law with brother, and that before the unbelievers. 7 Now therefore there is utterly a fault among you, because ye go to law one with another. Why do ye not rather take wrong? why do ye not rather suffer yourselves to be defrauded? 8 Nay, ye do wrong, and defraud, and that your brethren. 9 Know ye not that the unrighteous shall not inherit the kingdom of God? Be not deceived: neither fornicators, nor idolaters, nor adulterers, nor effeminate, nor abusers of themselves with mankind, 10 Nor thieves, nor covetous, nor drunkards, nor revilers, nor extortioners, shall inherit the kingdom of God. This is because our Father is all light and men hate light. 1 John 1:5 This then is the message which we have heard of him, and declare unto you, that God is light, and in him is no darkness at all.

Remember Jesus said he is the light of the world. Remember Jesus said the kingdom of God does not come with observation. Luke 17:20 And when he was demanded of the Pharisees, when the kingdom of God should come, he answered them and said, **The kingdom of God cometh not with observation: 21 Neither shall they say, Lo here! or, lo there! for, behold, the kingdom of God is within you.** There is that light that our Father created on the very first day. This is the reason our Father created the earth, so that His son could live on it and be the king as we showed in the last book.

This is when our Father locked up Satan and we will be explaining where he is locked up, later in the book. We showed in the last book, that Jesus dwelled in Adam. Jesus is that life that God breathed into man so that man became a living soul. Then we showed that we live 70 to 80 years and then we die as shown in Psalm 90:10 The days of our years are threescore years and ten; and if by reason of strength they be fourscore years, yet is their strength labour and sorrow; for it is soon cut off, and we fly away. Our Father said the covenant is for 1000 generations. I think I did the math incorrectly in the last book, however if we live 70 years for one generation and then we must live 1000 lives, that comes out to be 70-80,000 years. Now we know that a day is like a thousand years and a thousand years are as a day, how many days are there in a year? Would not that be 365,000 years. I am not saying that this is exactly how it is, but when we truly think about this, we do not have any idea of where we are at in history. Are souls never die so a million years in our Father's world could only be a month or so in our world.

Just another quick note here, in the last book we showed how when the earth began, the day was just four hours long. Could that be why the people in the very beginning of the bible, lived so long. If we do the math, how many times does four go into 24. That would make six days in one of our days. Wouldn't that be 60 of our days to complete a year? In God's calendar, there are 360 days to a year. So, in one of our years today, they would have been six years old. Methuselah lived to be 969 years old. Divide that by six and it comes out to 161.5 years old in our years today. Definitely not saying this is the case but it gives you something to think about.

This is what is going to lead us into what was truly being said when we hear what is said in Genesis 1:26 And God said, Let us make man in our image, after our likeness: and let them have dominion over the fish of the sea, and over the fowl of the air, and over the cattle, and over all the earth, and over every creeping thing that creepeth upon the earth. 27 So God created man in his own image, in the image of God created he him; male and female created he them. In the first book our Father had me show how we are to learn to love everybody with unwritten laws. He had me use examples of how we use unwritten laws all day long, every day of our life. We will just give an example of a little child in this book to help with a quick illustration. When we have a child, this child does not know how to do anything. Yes, they know how to drink milk, however they do not know how to chew, eat, craw, walk, etcetera. As they get older, they must learn how to do all these things. Now we are going to ask you as a reader something. How much do you think about how to do these things now? You don't, it just comes naturally. That is how we are to learn to love everybody as one. Just a quick side note, many think that we look like them is what being in their image is all about. Wouldn't that mean we would be invisible? Colossians 1:15 Who is the image of the invisible God, the firstborn of every creature:

Then in the second book in which we wrote, we showed that being in their image is us being in like on a model or something. What I mean is that they have an Israel in heaven, they have countries in heaven, they have nations, they have different worlds, they have priest, kings, and such all in heaven, We have all of the same but all of it is on this one little rock or planet. They have a Jerusalem in heaven and that is the mother of all. Galatians 4:26 But Jerusalem which is above is free, which is the mother of us all. Are Father which is in heaven is the Father in which we are to honor. We can know this when we listen to Malachi 1 The burden of the word of the Lord to Israel by Malachi. 2 I have loved you, saith the Lord. Yet ye say, Wherein hast thou loved us? Was not Esau Jacob's brother? saith the Lord: yet I loved Jacob, 3 And I hated Esau, and laid his mountains and his heritage waste for the dragons of the wilderness. 4 Whereas Edom saith, We are impoverished, but we will return and build the desolate places; thus saith the Lord of hosts, They shall build, but I will throw down; and they shall call them, The border of wickedness, and, The people against whom the Lord hath indignation for ever. 5 And your eyes shall see, and ye shall say, The Lord will be magnified from the border of Israel. 6 **A son honoureth his father, and a servant his master: if then I be a father, where is mine honour? and if I be a master, where is my fear? saith the Lord of hosts unto you, O priests, that despise my name. And ye say, Wherein have we despised thy name?**

In the last book we showed that we are counted as beast in the bible. Job 18:3 **Wherefore are we counted as beasts,** and reputed vile in your sight? We showed that our Father never commanded man to sacrifice animals. Isaiah 1:10 Hear the word of the Lord, ye rulers of

Sodom; give ear unto the law of our God, ye people of Gomorrah. 11 To what purpose is the multitude of your sacrifices unto me? saith the Lord: I am full of the burnt offerings of rams, and the fat of fed beasts; and I delight not in the blood of bullocks, or of lambs, or of he goats. 12 When ye come to appear before me, **who hath required this at your hand, to tread my courts?** We introduced that the kings, lords, and spirits of the have dominion over our bodies. Nehemiah 9:37 And it yieldeth much increase unto the kings whom thou hast set over us because of our sins: **also they have dominion over our bodies,** and over our cattle, at their pleasure, and we are in great distress. Isaiah 26:13 O Lord our God, **other lords beside thee have had dominion over us: but by thee only will we make mention of thy name.**

This is where we need to realize how this really works. I had the car accident on March 28th 1986, Good Friday. 30 years later almost to the day, I was led out into the wilderness to baptized by the Holy Ghost. Do you think I planned either of these? When I played the poker tournament, who shuffled those cards so that I could actually win eight hours after being told I was just there to watch? Who was it that told my brother that he was not going to pay me for the help I was going to give him before I went to his place to help? I had no money whatsoever but yet I refused to get paid.

Now let us go back to Genesis 1:27 So God created man in his own image, in the image of God created he him; male and female created he them. 28 And God blessed them, and God said unto them, Be fruitful, and multiply, and replenish the earth, and subdue it: and have dominion over the fish of the sea, and over the fowl of the air, and over every living thing that moveth upon the earth. Now we need to reflect to Matthew 6:9 After this manner therefore pray ye: Our Father which art in heaven, Hallowed be thy name. 10 Thy kingdom come, Thy will be done in earth, as it is in heaven. 11 Give us this day our daily bread. 12 And forgive us our debts, as we forgive our debtors. 13 And lead us not into temptation, but deliver us from evil: For thine is the kingdom, and the power, and the glory, for ever. Amen.

We have dominion over the animals, and they have dominion over us. Thy will be done in earth as it is in heaven. Hebrew 2:6 But one in a certain place testified, saying, What is man, that thou art mindful of him? or the son of man that thou visitest him? 7 Thou madest him a little lower than the angels; thou crownedst him with glory and honour, and didst set him over the works of thy hands: 8 Thou hast put all things in subjection under his feet. For in that he put all in subjection under him, he left nothing that is not put under him. But now we see not yet all things put under him. 9 But we see Jesus, who was made a little lower than the angels for the suffering of death, crowned with glory and honour; that he by the grace of God should taste death for every man. Notice that man and or the son of man is what was made a little lower than the angels. Notice how at the end of verse 9, that Jesus tasted death for every man. Is not Adam one of these men? Jesus tasted death for him also.

Remember Jesus did say that nothing of the law would pass until all be fulfilled. Matthew 5:17 Think not that I am come to destroy the law, or the prophets: I am not come to destroy, but to fulfil. 18 For verily I say unto you, Till heaven and earth pass, one jot or one tittle shall in no wise pass from the law, till all be fulfilled. Then remember that Jesus is the head of man. 1 Corinthians 11:3 But I would have you know, that the head of every man is Christ; and the head of the woman is the man; and the head of Christ is God. Since the beginning of the world, Christ has been the head of every man.

This is where we need to realize that it is up to each one of us as to which king or spirit has dominion over our bodies. Jesus is doing what he must in order to fulfill whatever needs to be fulfilled. This was explained very well in the last book that we wrote. Our Father is the head of Christ and Christ does everything in which our Father commands of him. Which is causing us to do what needs to be done. It is the attitude or personality in which we do what we do. Just by refusing to read all of the bible and trying to understand all of it, is spiritually telling our Father that you do not want Him having dominion over you. And because He is a loving Father, He will not force Himself on you. It is your choice. Joshua 24:14 Now therefore fear the Lord, and serve him in sincerity and in truth: and put away the gods which your fathers served on the other side of the flood, and in Egypt; and serve ye the Lord. 15 And if it seem evil unto you to serve the Lord, **choose you this day whom ye will serve; whether the gods which your fathers served that were on the other side of the flood, or the gods of the Amorites, in whose land ye dwell: but as for me and my house, we will serve the Lord.** Notice what our Father will do just because we choose not to listen to all that Moses commands. 2 Kings 18:10 And at the end of three years they took it: even in the sixth year of Hezekiah, that is in the ninth year of Hoshea king of Israel, Samaria was taken. 11 And the king of Assyria did carry away Israel unto Assyria, and put them in Halah and in Habor by the river of Gozan, and in the cities of the Medes: 12 Because they obeyed not the voice of the Lord their God, but transgressed his covenant, and all that Moses the servant of the Lord commanded, and would not hear them, nor do them. We should be realizing that these places in which people were taken are not here on earth, however they are above in heaven. We are only in their image.

This is where we need to remember that this is a spiritual workings. We need to reflect to when Jesus was taken to heaven. Luke 24:49 And, behold, I send the promise of my Father upon you: but tarry ye in the city of Jerusalem, until ye be endued with power from on high. 50 And he led them out as far as to Bethany, and he lifted up his hands, and blessed them. 51 And it came to pass, while he blessed them, he was parted from them, and carried up into heaven.

Now we are going to venture back into the book of Ezekiel so that we can hear where Jesus is at. This is also where we need to realize that Jesus is in heaven, and dwells in each one of us. This is also where I believe there is some sort of each one of us also in heaven. It is a spiritual form of us and obviously I have no idea of what we look like. Let us just start to show this so that we can see how it is working the same in heaven as it is in or on earth. I am going to post 6 chapters of Ezekiel as our Father had me show in the first book. First, we need to realize that Jesus is the prince that reports to our Father in heaven. Revelation 1:5 And from Jesus Christ, who is the faithful witness, and the first begotten of the dead, and the prince of the kings of the earth. Unto him that loved us, and washed us from our sins in his own blood,

Now I know there are a lot of people in which think the battle has already been won. Yes, this is correct, but this battle that has been won is the battle in which Satan got locked up. Now we still battle unseen powers. Ephesians 6:12 **For we wrestle not against flesh and blood, but against principalities, against powers, against the rulers of the darkness of this world, against spiritual wickedness in high places.**

This is where we should be paying attention to what Jesus said in Matthew 16:18 And I will give unto thee the keys of the kingdom of heaven: **and whatsoever thou shalt bind on earth shall be bound in heaven: and whatsoever thou shalt loose on earth shall be loosed in heaven.** This is when we really need to thinking of how we think of and treat others. Then remember that we are here because our Father forgave us and gave us a chance to learn how love in the same matter He does. Then listen to this and just think of how important is to forgive anyone that you feel has done you wrong. Matthew 18:21 **Then came Peter to him, and said, Lord, how oft shall my brother sin against me, and I forgive him? till seven times? 22 Jesus saith unto him, I say not unto thee, Until seven times: but, Until seventy times seven.** 23 Therefore is the kingdom of heaven likened unto a certain king, which would take account of his servants. 24 And when he had begun to reckon, one was brought unto him, which owed him ten thousand talents. 25 But forasmuch as he had not to pay, his lord commanded him to be sold, and his wife, and children, and all that he had, and payment to be made. 26 The servant therefore fell down, and worshipped him, saying, Lord, have patience with me, and I will pay thee all. 27 Then the lord of that servant was moved with compassion, and loosed him, and forgave him the debt. 28 But the same servant went out, and found one of his fellowservants, which owed him an hundred pence: and he laid hands on him, and took him by the throat, saying, Pay me that thou owest. 29 And his fellowservant fell down at his feet, and besought him, saying, Have patience with me, and I will pay thee all. 30 And he would not: but went and cast him into prison, till he should pay the debt. 31 So when his fellowservants saw what was done, they were very sorry, and came and told unto their lord all that was done. 32 Then his lord, after that he had called him, said unto him, O thou wicked servant, I forgave thee all that debt, because thou desiredst me: 33 Shouldest not thou also have had compassion on thy fellowservant, even as I had pity on thee? 34 And his lord was wroth, and delivered him to the tormentors, till he should pay all that was due unto him. 35 **So likewise shall my heavenly Father do also unto you, if ye from your hearts forgive not every one his brother their trespasses.**

Now think about this as you read through this next section, then realize that our Father already forgave you, as the servant, and brought you here. But at the same time, realize that HE has also brought all other servants just as He brought you. Then remember Matthew 18:23 Therefore is the kingdom of heaven likened unto a certain king, which would take account of his servants. 24 And when he had begun to reckon, one was brought unto him, which owed him ten thousand talents. 25 But forasmuch as he had not to pay, his lord commanded him to be sold, and his wife, and children, and all that he had, and payment to be made. 26 The servant therefore fell down, and worshipped him, saying, Lord, have patience with me, and I will pay thee all. 27 Then the lord of that servant was moved with compassion, and loosed him, and forgave him the debt. 28 But the same servant went out, and found one of his fellowservants, which owed him an hundred pence: and he laid hands on him, and took him by the throat, saying, Pay me that thou owest. 29 And his fellowservant fell down at his feet, and besought him, saying, Have patience with me, and I will pay thee all. 30 And he would not: but went and cast him into prison, till he should pay the debt. 31 So when his fellowservants saw what was done, they were very sorry, and came and told unto their lord all that was done. 32 Then his lord, after that he had called him, said unto him, O thou wicked servant, I forgave thee all that debt, because thou desiredst me: 33 Shouldest not thou also have had compassion on thy fellowservant, even as I had pity on thee? 34 And his lord was wroth, and delivered him to the tormentors, till he should pay all that was due unto him. 35 So likewise shall my heavenly Father do also unto you, if ye from your hearts forgive not every one his brother their trespasses.

Ezekiel 40 In the five and twentieth year of our captivity, in the beginning of the year, in the tenth day of the month, in the fourteenth year after that the city was smitten, in the selfsame day the hand of the Lord was upon me, and brought me thither. 2 In the visions of God brought he me into the land of Israel, and set me upon a very high mountain, by which was as the frame of a city on the south. 3 And he brought me thither, and, behold, there was a man, whose appearance was like the appearance of brass, with a line of flax in his hand, and a measuring reed; and he stood in the gate. 4 And the man said unto me, Son of man, behold with thine eyes, and hear with thine ears, and set thine heart upon all that I shall shew thee; for to the intent that I might shew them unto thee art thou brought hither: declare all that thou seest to the house of Israel. 5 And behold a wall on the outside of the house round about, and in the man's hand a measuring reed of six cubits long by the cubit and an hand breadth: so he measured the breadth of the building, one reed; and the height, one reed. 6 Then came he unto the gate which looketh toward the east, and went up the stairs thereof, and measured the threshold of the gate, which was one reed broad; and the other threshold of the gate, which was one reed broad. 7 And every little chamber was one reed long, and one reed broad; and between the little chambers were five cubits; and the threshold of the gate by the porch of the gate within was one reed. 8 He measured also the porch of the gate within, one reed. 9 Then measured he the porch of the gate, eight cubits; and the posts thereof, two cubits; and the porch of the gate was inward. 10 And the little chambers of the gate eastward were three on this side, and three on that side; they three were of one measure: and the posts had one measure on this side and on that side. 11 And he measured the breadth of the entry of the gate, ten cubits; and the length of the gate, thirteen cubits. 12 The space also before the little chambers was one cubit on this side, and the space was one cubit on that side: and the little chambers were six cubits on this side, and six cubits on that side. 13 He measured then the gate from the roof of one little chamber to the roof of another: the breadth was five and twenty cubits, door against door. 14 He made also posts of threescore cubits, even unto the post of the court round about the gate. 15 And from the face of the gate of the entrance unto the face of the porch of the inner gate were fifty cubits. 16 And there were narrow windows to the little chambers, and to their posts within the gate round about, and likewise to the arches: and windows were round about inward: and upon each post were palm trees. 17 Then brought he me into the outward court, and, lo, there were chambers, and a pavement made for the court round about: thirty chambers were upon the pavement. 18 And the pavement by the side of the gates over against the length of the gates was the lower pavement. 19 Then he measured the breadth from the forefront of the lower gate unto the forefront of the inner court without, an hundred cubits eastward and northward. 20 And the gate of the outward court that looked toward the north, he measured the length thereof, and the breadth thereof. 21 And the little chambers thereof were three on this side and three on that side; and the posts thereof and the arches thereof were after the measure of the first gate: the length thereof was fifty cubits, and the breadth five and twenty cubits. 22 And their windows, and their arches, and their palm trees, were after the measure of the gate that looketh toward the east; and they went up unto it by seven steps; and the arches thereof were before them. 23 And the gate of the inner court was over against the gate toward the north, and toward the east; and he measured from gate to gate an hundred cubits. 24 After that he brought me toward the south, and behold a gate toward the south: and he measured the posts thereof and the arches thereof according to these measures. 25 And there were windows in it and in the arches thereof round about, like those windows: the length was fifty cubits, and the breadth five and twenty cubits. 26 And there were seven steps to go up to it, and the arches thereof were before them: and it had palm trees, one on this side, and another on that side, upon the posts thereof. 27 And there was a gate in the inner court toward the south: and he measured from gate to gate toward the south an hundred cubits. 28 And he brought me to the inner court by the south gate: and he measured the south gate according to these measures; 29 And the little chambers thereof, and the posts thereof, and the arches thereof, according to these measures: and there were windows in it and in the arches thereof round about: it was fifty cubits long, and five and twenty cubits broad. 30 And the arches round about were five and twenty cubits long, and five cubits broad. 31 And the arches thereof were toward the utter court; and palm trees were upon the posts thereof: and the going up to it had eight steps. 32 And he brought me into the inner court toward the east: and he measured the gate according to these measures. 33 And the little chambers thereof, and the posts thereof, and the arches thereof, were according to these measures: and there were windows therein and in the arches thereof round about: it was fifty cubits long, and five and twenty cubits broad. 34 And the arches thereof were toward the outward court; and palm trees were upon the posts thereof, on this side, and on that side: and the going up to it had eight steps. 35 And he brought me to the north gate, and measured it according to these measures; 36 The little chambers thereof, the posts thereof, and the arches thereof, and the windows to it round about: the length was fifty cubits, and the breadth five and twenty cubits. 37 And the posts thereof were toward the utter court; and palm trees were upon the posts thereof, on this side, and on that side: and the going up to it had eight steps. 38 And the chambers and the entries thereof were by the posts of the gates, where they washed the burnt offering. 39 And in the porch of the gate were two tables on this side, and two tables on that side, to slay thereon the burnt offering and the sin offering and the trespass offering. 40 And at the side without, as one goeth up to the entry of the north gate, were two tables; and on the other side, which was at the porch of the gate, were two tables. 41 Four tables were on this side, and four tables on that side, by the side of the gate; eight tables, whereupon they slew their sacrifices. 42 And the four tables were of hewn stone for the burnt offering, of a cubit and an half long, and a cubit and an half broad, and one cubit high: whereupon also they laid the instruments wherewith they slew the burnt offering and the sacrifice. 43 And within were hooks, an hand broad, fastened round about: and upon the tables was the flesh of the offering. 44 And without the inner gate were the chambers of the singers in the inner court, which was at the side of the north gate; and their prospect was toward the south: one at the side of the east gate having the prospect toward the north. 45 And he said unto me, This chamber, whose prospect is toward the south, is for the priests, the keepers of the charge of the house. 46 And the chamber whose prospect is toward the north is for the priests, the keepers of the charge of the altar: these are the sons of Zadok among the sons of Levi, which come near to the Lord to minister unto him. 47 So he measured the court, an hundred cubits long, and an hundred cubits broad, foursquare; and the altar that was before the house. 48 And he brought me to the porch of the house, and measured each post of the porch, five cubits on this side, and five cubits on that side: and the breadth of the gate was three cubits on this side, and three cubits on that side. 49 The length of the porch was twenty cubits, and the breadth eleven cubits, and he brought me by the steps whereby they went up to it: and there were pillars by the posts, one on this side, and another on that side.

What we are seeing now is the holy mountain that our Father talks about. This is the mountain in which our Father is on top of. It is a spiritual mountain in which cannot be seen in with our eyes here on earth. Notice how each of the gates face to each direction. Now as you read this, imagine this picture in your mind. Try to see this with another form of us that isn't us, being within sight of the top of the mountain. Then try to realizes that we here on earth cannot phantom the measurements used in our Father's world for we try to measure things on earth in small amounts. And our Father's world consist of everything in the earth, heavens, and under the earth.

Ezekiel 41 Afterward he brought me to the temple, and measured the posts, six cubits broad on the one side, and six cubits broad on the other side, which was the breadth of the tabernacle. 2 And the breadth of the door was ten cubits; and the sides of the door were five cubits on the one side, and five cubits on the other side: and he measured the length thereof, forty cubits: and the breadth, twenty cubits. 3 Then went he inward, and measured the post of the door, two cubits; and the door, six cubits; and the breadth of the door, seven cubits. 4 So he measured the length thereof, twenty cubits; and the breadth, twenty cubits, before the temple: and he said unto me, This is the most holy place. 5 After he measured the wall of the house, six cubits; and the breadth of every side chamber, four cubits, round about the house on every side. 6 And the side chambers were three, one over another, and thirty in order; and they entered into the wall which was of the house for the side chambers round about, that they might have hold, but they had not hold in the wall of the house. 7 And there was an enlarging, and a winding about still upward to the side chambers: for the winding about of the house went still upward round about the house: therefore the breadth of the house was still upward, and so increased from the lowest chamber to the highest by the midst. 8 I saw also the height of the house round about: the foundations of the side chambers were a full reed of six great cubits. 9 The thickness of the wall, which was for the side chamber without, was five cubits: and that which was left was the place of the side chambers that were within. 10 And between the chambers was the wideness of twenty cubits round about the house on every side. 11 And the doors of the side chambers were toward the place that was left, one door toward the north, and another door toward the south: and the breadth of the place that was left was five cubits round about. 12 Now the building that was before the separate place at the end toward the west was seventy cubits broad; and the wall of the building was five cubits thick round about, and the length thereof ninety cubits. 13 So he measured the house, an hundred cubits long; and the separate place, and the building, with the walls thereof, an hundred cubits long; 14 Also the breadth of the face of the house, and of the separate place toward the east, an hundred cubits. 15 And he measured the length of the building over against the separate place which was behind it, and the galleries thereof on the one side and on the other side, an hundred cubits, with the inner temple, and the porches of the court; 16 The door posts, and the narrow windows, and the galleries round about on their three stories, over against the door, cieled with wood round about, and from the ground up to the windows, and the windows were covered; 17 To that above the door, even unto the inner house, and without, and by all the wall round about within and without, by measure. 18 And it was made with cherubims and palm trees, so that a palm tree was between a cherub and a cherub; and every cherub had two faces; 19 So that the face of a man was toward the palm tree on the one side, and the face of a young lion toward the palm tree on the other side: it was made through all the house round about. 20 From the ground unto above the door were cherubims and palm trees made, and on the wall of the temple. 21 The posts of the temple were squared, and the face of the sanctuary; the appearance of the one as the appearance of the other. 22 The altar of wood was three cubits high, and the length thereof two cubits; and the corners thereof, and the length thereof, and the walls thereof, were of wood: and he said unto me, This is the table that is before the Lord. 23 And the temple and the sanctuary had two doors. 24 And the doors had two leaves apiece, two turning leaves; two leaves for the one door, and two leaves for the other door. 25 And there were made on them, on the doors of the temple, cherubims and palm trees, like as were made upon the walls; and there were thick planks upon the face of the porch without. 26 And there were narrow windows and palm trees on the one side and on the other side, on the sides of the porch, and upon the side chambers of the house, and thick planks.

Ezekiel 42 Then he brought me forth into the utter court, the way toward the north: and he brought me into the chamber that was over against the separate place, and which was before the building toward the north. 2 Before the length of an hundred cubits was the north door, and the breadth was fifty cubits. 3 Over against the twenty cubits which were for the inner court, and over against the pavement which was for the utter court, was gallery against gallery in three stories. 4 And before the chambers was a walk to ten cubits breadth inward, a way of one cubit; and their doors toward the north.

5 Now the upper chambers were shorter: for the galleries were higher than these, than the lower, and than the middlemost of the building. 6 For they were in three stories, but had not pillars as the pillars of the courts: therefore the building was straitened more than the lowest and the middlemost from the ground. 7 And the wall that was without over against the chambers, toward the utter court on

the forepart of the chambers, the length thereof was fifty cubits. 8 For the length of the chambers that were in the utter court was fifty cubits: and, lo, before the temple were an hundred cubits. 9 And from under these chambers was the entry on the east side, as one goeth into them from the utter court. 10 The chambers were in the thickness of the wall of the court toward the east, over against the separate place, and over against the building. 11 And the way before them was like the appearance of the chambers which were toward the north, as long as they, and as broad as they: and all their goings out were both according to their fashions, and according to their doors. 12 And according to the doors of the chambers that were toward the south was a door in the head of the way, even the way directly before the wall toward the east, as one entereth into them. 13 Then said he unto me, The north chambers and the south chambers, which are before the separate place, they be holy chambers, where the priests that approach unto the Lord shall eat the most holy things: there shall they lay the most holy things, and the meat offering, and the sin offering, and the trespass offering; for the place is holy. 14 When the priests enter therein, then shall they not go out of the holy place into the utter court, but there they shall lay their garments wherein they minister; for they are holy; and shall put on other garments, and shall approach to those things which are for the people. 15 Now when he had made an end of measuring the inner house, he brought me forth toward the gate whose prospect is toward the east, and measured it round about. 16 He measured the east side with the measuring reed, five hundred reeds, with the measuring reed round about. 17 He measured the north side, five hundred reeds, with the measuring reed round about. 18 He measured the south side, five hundred reeds, with the measuring reed. 19 He turned about to the west side, and measured five hundred reeds with the measuring reed. 20 He measured it by the four sides: it had a wall round about, five hundred reeds long, and five hundred broad, to make a separation between the sanctuary and the profane place.

    Now if we are remembering from the last book, we showed that we are counted as the beast of the earth and we are what is sacrificed in a spiritual manner. Let me use a quick example of my life. We know that a broken spirit is a sacrifice of God. Psalm 51:17 The sacrifices of God are a broken spirit: a broken and a contrite heart, O God, thou wilt not despise. I spoke of a nine-year relationship I had just before I tried to take my life in 2009 in the last book. At the time I just lost my 5th child in my mind and was completely tired of failing everything that I had tried in my life. Now these priests we are reading about, are on this holy mountain making these things happen. By doing this, they were breaking my spirit in which was the start to leading me the bible.

Ezekiel 43 Afterward he brought me to the gate, even the gate that looketh toward the east: 2 And, behold, the glory of the God of Israel came from the way of the east: and his voice was like a noise of many waters: and the earth shined with his glory. 3 And it was according to the appearance of the vision which I saw, even according to the vision that I saw when I came to destroy the city: and the visions were like the vision that I saw by the river Chebar; and I fell upon my face. 4 And the glory of the Lord came into the house by the way of the gate whose prospect is toward the east. 5 So the spirit took me up, and brought me into the inner court; and, behold, the glory of the Lord filled the house. 6 And I heard him speaking unto me out of the house; and the man stood by me. 7 And he said unto me, Son of man, the place of my throne, and the place of the soles of my feet, where I will dwell in the midst of the children of Israel for ever, and my holy name, shall the house of Israel no more defile, neither they, nor their kings, by their whoredom, nor by the carcases of their kings in their high places. 8 In their setting of their threshold by my thresholds, and their post by my posts, and the wall between me and them, they have even defiled my holy name by their abominations that they have committed: wherefore I have consumed them in mine anger. 9 Now let them put away their whoredom, and the carcases of their kings, far from me, and I will dwell in the midst of them for ever. 10 Thou son of man, shew the house to the house of Israel, that they may be ashamed of their iniquities: and let them measure the pattern. 11 And if they be ashamed of all that they have done, shew them the form of the house, and the fashion thereof, and the goings out thereof, and the comings in thereof, and all the forms thereof, and all the ordinances thereof, and all the forms thereof, and all the laws thereof: and write it in their sight, that they may keep the whole form thereof, and all the ordinances thereof, and do them. 12 This is the law of the house; Upon the top of the mountain the whole limit thereof round about shall be most holy. Behold, this is the law of the house. 13 And these are the measures of the altar after the cubits: The cubit is a cubit and an hand breadth; even the bottom shall be a cubit, and the breadth a cubit, and the border thereof by the edge thereof round about shall be a span: and this shall be the higher place of the altar. 14 And from the bottom upon the ground even to the lower settle shall be two cubits, and the breadth one cubit; and from the lesser settle even to the greater settle shall be four cubits, and the breadth one cubit. 15 So the altar shall be four cubits; and from the altar and upward shall be four horns. 16 And the altar shall be twelve cubits long, twelve broad, square in the four squares thereof. 17 And the settle shall be fourteen cubits long and fourteen broad in the four squares thereof; and the border about it shall be half a cubit; and the bottom thereof shall be a cubit about; and his stairs shall look toward the east. 18 And he said unto me, Son of man, thus saith the Lord God; These are the ordinances of the altar in the day when they shall make it, to offer burnt offerings thereon, and to sprinkle blood thereon. 19 And thou shalt give to the priests the Levites that be of the seed of Zadok, which approach unto me, to minister unto me, saith the Lord God, a young bullock for a sin offering. 20 And thou shalt take of the blood thereof, and put it on the four horns of it, and on the four corners of the settle, and upon the border round about: thus shalt thou cleanse and purge it. 21 Thou shalt take the bullock also of the sin offering, and he shall burn it in the appointed place of the house, without the sanctuary. 22 And on the second day thou shalt offer a kid of the goats without blemish for a sin offering; and they shall cleanse the altar, as they did cleanse it with the bullock. 23 When thou hast made an end of cleansing it, thou shalt offer a young bullock without blemish, and a ram out of the flock without blemish. 24 And thou shalt offer them before the Lord, and the priests shall cast salt upon them, and they shall offer them up for a burnt offering unto the Lord. 25 Seven days shalt thou prepare every day a goat for a sin offering: they shall also prepare a young bullock, and a ram out of the flock, without blemish. 26 Seven days shall they purge the altar and purify it; and they shall consecrate themselves. 27 And when these days are expired, it shall be, that upon the eighth day, and so forward, the priests shall make your burnt offerings upon the altar, and your peace offerings; and I will accept you, saith the Lord God.

Now using the example of my life, we just used a little while ago. Let us listen to how this sacrifice was a sweet aroma for our Father. Leviticus 1 And the Lord called unto Moses, and spake unto him out of the tabernacle of the congregation, saying, 2 Speak unto the children of Israel, and say unto them, If any man of you bring an offering unto the Lord, ye shall bring your offering of the cattle, even of the herd, and of the flock. 3 If his offering be a burnt sacrifice of the herd, let him offer a male without blemish: he shall offer it of his own voluntary will at the door of the tabernacle of the congregation before the Lord. 4 And he shall put his hand upon the head of the burnt offering; and it shall be accepted for him to make atonement for him. 5 And he shall kill the bullock before the Lord: and the priests, Aaron's sons, shall bring the blood, and sprinkle the blood round about upon the altar that is by the door of the tabernacle of the congregation. 6 And he shall flay the burnt offering, and cut it into his pieces. 7 And the sons of Aaron the priest shall put fire upon the altar, and lay the wood in order upon the fire: 8 And the priests, Aaron's sons, shall lay the parts, the head, and the fat, in order upon the wood that is on the fire which is upon the altar: 9 But his inwards and his legs shall he wash in water: and the priest shall burn all on the altar, to be a burnt sacrifice, an offering made by fire, of a sweet savour unto the Lord.

Now some might ask, why would this be a sweet savour unto our Father. Imagine the emotions I was going through before I tried to take my life. If things wouldn't have happened the way they did, I would have kept on living as I was. Yes, I prayed regularly to myself, but I would not even talk about the bible, rather even read it. Now with the two books that our Father has had me write, and now this one, can you see where that sacrifice took my life? That sacrifice they made hurt me back then but started to get me on the path our Father needed me to be on so now He is seeing His son do what He needed him to do.

Ezekiel 44 Then he brought me back the way of the gate of the outward sanctuary which looketh toward the east; and it was shut. 2 Then said the Lord unto me; This gate shall be shut, it shall not be opened, and no man shall enter in by it; because the Lord, the God of Israel, hath entered in by it, therefore it shall be shut. 3 It is for the prince; the prince, he shall sit in it to eat bread before the Lord; he shall enter by the way of the porch of that gate, and shall go out by the way of the same. 4 Then brought he me the way of the north gate before the house: and I looked, and, behold, the glory of the Lord filled the house of the Lord: and I fell upon my face. 5 And the Lord said unto me, Son of man, mark well, and behold with thine eyes, and hear with thine ears all that I say unto thee concerning all the ordinances of the house of the Lord, and all the laws thereof; and mark well the entering in of the house, with every going forth of the sanctuary. 6 And thou shalt say to the rebellious, even to the house of Israel, Thus saith the Lord God; O ye house of Israel, let it suffice you of all your abominations, 7 In that ye have brought into my sanctuary strangers, **uncircumcised in heart, and uncircumcised in flesh, to be in my sanctuary, to pollute it, even my house, when ye offer my bread, the fat and the blood, and they have broken my covenant because of all your abominations.** 8 And ye have not kept the charge of mine holy things: but ye have set keepers of my charge in my sanctuary for yourselves. 9 Thus saith the Lord God; **No stranger, uncircumcised in heart, nor uncircumcised in flesh, shall enter into my sanctuary, of any stranger that is among the children of Israel. 10 And the Levites that are gone away far from me, when Israel went astray, which went astray away from me after their idols; they shall even bear their iniquity.** 11 Yet they shall be ministers in my sanctuary, having charge at the gates of the house, and ministering to the house: they shall slay the burnt offering and the sacrifice for the people, and they shall stand before them to minister unto them. 12 Because they ministered unto them before their idols, and caused the house of Israel to fall into iniquity; therefore have I lifted up mine hand against them, saith the Lord God, and they shall bear their iniquity. 13 And they shall not come near unto me, to do the office of a priest unto me, nor to come near to any of my holy things, in the most holy place: but they shall bear their shame, and their abominations which they have committed. 14 But I will make them keepers of the charge of the house, for all the service thereof, and for all that shall be done therein. 15 But the priests the Levites, the sons of Zadok, that kept the charge of my sanctuary when the children of Israel went astray from me, they shall come near to me to minister unto me, and they shall stand before me to offer unto me the fat and the blood, saith the Lord God: 16 They shall enter into my sanctuary, and they shall come near to my table, to minister unto me, and they shall keep my charge. 17 And it shall come to pass, that when they enter in at the gates of the inner court, they shall be clothed with linen garments; and no wool shall come upon them, whiles they minister in the gates of the inner court, and within. 18 They shall have linen bonnets upon their heads, and shall have linen breeches upon their loins; they shall not gird themselves with any thing that causeth sweat. 19 And when they go forth into the utter court, even into the utter court to the people, they shall put off their garments wherein they ministered, and lay them in the holy chambers, and they shall put on other garments; and they shall not sanctify the people with their garments. 20 Neither shall they shave their heads, nor suffer their locks to grow long; they shall only poll their heads. 21 Neither shall any priest drink wine, when they enter into the inner court. 22 Neither shall they take for their wives a widow, nor her that is put away: but they shall take maidens of the seed of the house of Israel, or a widow that had a priest before. 23 And they shall teach my people the difference between the holy and profane, and cause them to discern between the unclean and the clean. 24 And in controversy they shall stand in judgment; and they shall judge it according to my judgments: and they shall keep my laws and my statutes in all mine assemblies; and they shall hallow my sabbaths.

25 And they shall come at no dead person to defile themselves: but for father, or for mother, or for son, or for daughter, for brother, or for sister that hath had no husband, they may defile themselves. 26 And after he is cleansed, they shall reckon unto him seven days. 27 And in the day that he goeth into the sanctuary, unto the inner court, to minister in the sanctuary, he shall offer his sin offering, saith the Lord God. 28 And it shall be unto them for an inheritance: I am their inheritance: and ye shall give them no possession in Israel: I am their possession. 29 They shall eat the meat offering, and the sin offering, and the trespass offering: and every dedicated thing in Israel shall be theirs. 30 And the first of all the firstfruits of all things, and every oblation of all, of every sort of your oblations, shall be the priest's: ye shall also give unto the priest the first of your dough, that he may cause the blessing to rest in thine house. 31 The priests shall not eat of any thing that is dead of itself, or torn, whether it be fowl or beast.

This is the very top of the mountain if you will. Notice the prince sitting outside of the door to where the Father is. This is where Jesus is sitting and nobody is getting to the Father, but through him. Now we are going to start to visualize, if you will, the part of us in which is in heaven now. We can see where our Father is, and we can see where Jesus is. We have been noticing where the priests are, but they only report to Jesus or the prince. Then Jesus reports to the Father. Now this mountain, we can only imagine must be humongous. Remember our Father's world is a lot larger than just this little rock we call earth.

I think this is a good spot of this. In the last book, I stated that my dad passed in 2003. I said he went up to the next level of hell to await my mom to finish fulfilling what she needed to fulfill. Then when she passed their souls were joined as one and sent back into captivity. Okay, we have everything here on earth as they do in heaven, as shown in the last book, so we are going to visualize this from and earthly perspective. We have been cast out of heaven and sent to hell as shown in the last book, this is hell. We have prisons here on earth as they do in heaven. In fact, the earth is a prison. We are kept here until the end of the world. Psalm 69:33 For the Lord heareth the poor, **and despiseth not his prisoners.** Psalm 146:7 Which executeth judgment for the oppressed: which giveth food to the hungry. **The Lord looseth the prisoners:** Psalm 142:7 **Bring my soul out of prison, that I may praise thy name:** the righteous shall compass me about; for thou shalt deal bountifully with me. It is not an actual prison as we know it but it is a prison in which keeps us out of heaven with our Father. This mountain that we are reading about is where my dad went to be with Christ to await his and mom's sentencing after they were joined as one. Then they were judged as one and sentenced back into captivity. Now I do not know that much about the court system other than what I see on television. Or have heard on some news channels and such. Some people get sentenced right away. Some do not get sentenced until sometime after the trial. It is just like that in our life. Of course, I do not know the judgement system our Father uses, but I am sure this is where we go when we await our sentencing. Remember we all have transgressed our Father's law.

This is what people are seeing when they have these near-death experiences. Christ is the head at the top of the mountain just before our Father in which no one can talk to but Christ. Our Father is the ultimate judge and He decides where each soul goes and not Christ. But this mountain is still full of love and peace. Up there and not here!

Ezeliel 45 Moreover, when ye shall divide by lot the land for inheritance, ye shall offer an oblation unto the Lord, an holy portion of the land: the length shall be the length of five and twenty thousand reeds, and the breadth shall be ten thousand. This shall be holy in all the borders thereof round about. 2 Of this there shall be for the sanctuary five hundred in length, with five hundred in breadth, square round about; and fifty cubits round about for the suburbs thereof. 3 And of this measure shalt thou measure the length of five and twenty thousand, and the breadth of ten thousand: and in it shall be the sanctuary and the most holy place. 4 The holy portion of the land shall be for the priests the ministers of the sanctuary, which shall come near to minister unto the Lord: and it shall be a place for their houses, and an holy place for the sanctuary. 5 And the five and twenty thousand of length, and the ten thousand of breadth shall also the Levites, the ministers of the house, have for themselves, for a possession for twenty chambers. 6 And ye shall appoint the possession of the city five thousand broad, and five and twenty thousand long, over against the oblation of the holy portion: it shall be for the whole house of Israel. 7 And a portion shall be for the prince on the one side and on the other side of the oblation of the holy portion, and of the possession of the city, before the oblation of the holy portion, and before the possession of the city, from the west side westward, and from the east side eastward: and the length shall be over against one of the portions, from the west border unto the east border. 8 In the land shall be his possession in Israel: and my princes shall no more oppress my people; and the rest of the land shall they give to the house of Israel according to their tribes. 9 Thus saith the Lord God; Let it suffice you, O princes of Israel: remove violence and spoil, and execute judgment and justice, take away your exactions from my people, saith the Lord God. 10 Ye shall have just balances, and a just ephah, and a just bath. 11 The ephah and the bath shall be of one measure, that the bath may contain the tenth part of an homer, and the ephah the tenth part of an homer: the measure thereof shall be after the homer. 12 And the shekel shall be twenty gerahs: twenty shekels, five and twenty shekels, fifteen shekels, shall be your maneh. 13 This is the oblation that ye shall offer; the sixth part of an ephah of an homer of wheat, and ye shall give the sixth part of an ephah of an homer of barley: 14 Concerning the ordinance of oil, the bath of oil, ye shall offer the tenth part of a bath out of the cor, which is an homer of ten baths; for ten baths are an homer: 15 And one lamb out of the flock, out of two hundred, out of the fat pastures of Israel; for a meat offering, and for a burnt offering, and for peace offerings, to make reconciliation for them, saith the Lord God. 16 All the people of the land shall give this oblation for the prince in Israel. 17 And it shall be the prince's part to give burnt offerings, and meat offerings, and drink offerings, in the feasts, and in the new moons, and in the sabbaths, in all solemnities of the house of Israel: he shall prepare the sin offering, and the meat offering, and the burnt offering, and the peace offerings, to make reconciliation for the house of Israel. 18 Thus saith the Lord God; In the first month, in the first day of the month, thou shalt take a young bullock without blemish, and cleanse the sanctuary: 19 And the priest shall take of the blood of the sin offering, and put it upon the posts of the house, and upon the four corners of the settle of the altar, and upon the posts of the gate of the inner court. 20 And so thou shalt do the seventh day of the month for every one that erreth, and for him that is simple: so shall ye reconcile the house. 21 In the first month, in the fourteenth day of the month, ye shall have the passover, a feast of seven days; unleavened bread shall be eaten. 22 And upon that day shall the prince prepare for himself and for all the people of the land a bullock for a sin offering. 23 And seven days of the feast he shall prepare a burnt offering to the Lord, seven bullocks and seven rams without blemish daily the seven days; and a kid of the goats daily for a sin offering. 24 And he shall prepare a meat offering of an ephah for a bullock, and an ephah for a ram, and an hin of oil for an ephah. 25 In the seventh month, in the fifteenth day of the month, shall he do the like in the feast of the seven days, according to the sin offering, according to the burnt offering, and according to the meat offering, and according to the oil.

Now we are hearing the lands in which we are in. Try and picture this mountain and try to see the very top. Then try to picture yourself above this mountain as seeing all these sections of land going out in every direction. Now with your imagination, press this mountain down to where it is one humongous flat area so that you can see all of the souls kept in different parts of this area. There are fences, as we call them, to separate some from others. Also try to picture us as the beast of the earth. Look at it as it is one great big farm with all kinds of different animals on it. Or people counted as beast.

Ezekiel 46 Thus saith the Lord God; The gate of the inner court that looketh toward the east shall be shut the six working days; but on the sabbath it shall be opened, and in the day of the new moon it shall be opened. 2 And the prince shall enter by the way of the porch of that gate without, and shall stand by the post of the gate, and the priests shall prepare his burnt offering and his peace offerings, and he shall worship at the threshold of the gate: then he shall go forth; but the gate shall not be shut until the evening. 3 Likewise the people of the land shall worship at the door of this gate before the Lord in the sabbaths and in the new moons. 4 And the burnt offering that the prince shall offer unto the Lord in the sabbath day shall be six lambs without blemish, and a ram without blemish. 5 And the meat offering shall be an ephah for a ram, and the meat offering for the lambs as he shall be able to give, and an hin of oil to an ephah. 6 And in the day of the new moon it shall be a young bullock without blemish, and six lambs, and a ram: they shall be without blemish. 7 And he shall prepare a meat offering, an ephah for a bullock, and an ephah for a ram, and for the lambs according as his hand shall attain unto, and an hin of oil to an ephah. 8 And when the prince shall enter, he shall go in by the way of the porch of that gate, and he shall go forth by the way thereof. 9 But when the people of the land shall come before the Lord in the solemn feasts, he that entereth in by the way of the north gate to worship shall go out by the way of the south gate; and he that entereth by the way of the south gate shall go forth by the way of the north gate: he shall not return by the way of the gate whereby he came in, but shall go forth over against it. 10 And the prince in the midst of them, when they go in, shall go in; and when they go forth, shall go forth. 11 And in the feasts and in the solemnities the meat offering shall be an ephah to a bullock, and an ephah to a ram, and to the lambs as he is able to give, and an hin of oil to an ephah. 12 Now when the prince shall prepare a voluntary burnt offering or peace offerings voluntarily unto the Lord, one shall then open him the gate that looketh toward the east, and he shall prepare his burnt offering and his peace offerings, as he did on the sabbath day: then he shall go forth; and after his going forth one shall shut the gate. 13 Thou shalt daily prepare a burnt offering unto the Lord of a lamb of the first year without blemish: thou shalt prepare it every morning. 14 And thou shalt prepare a meat offering for it every morning, the sixth part of an ephah, and the third part of an hin of oil, to temper with the fine flour; a meat offering continually by a perpetual ordinance unto the Lord. 15 Thus shall they prepare the lamb, and the meat offering, and the oil, every morning for a continual burnt offering. 16 Thus saith the Lord God; If the prince give a gift unto any of his sons, the inheritance thereof shall be his sons'; it shall be their possession by inheritance. 17 But if he give a gift of his inheritance to one of his servants, then it shall be his to the year of liberty; after it shall return to the prince: but his inheritance shall be his sons' for them. 18 Moreover the prince shall not take of the people's inheritance by oppression, to thrust them out of their possession; but he shall give his sons inheritance out of his own possession: that my people be not scattered every man from his possession. 19 After he brought me through the entry, which was at the side of the gate, into the holy chambers of the priests, which looked toward the north: and, behold, there was a place on the two sides westward. 20 Then said he unto me, This is the place where the priests shall boil the trespass offering and the sin offering, where they shall bake the meat offering; that they bear them not out into the utter court, to sanctify the people. 21 Then he brought me forth into the utter court, and caused me to pass by the four corners of the court; and, behold, in every corner of the court there was a court. 22 In the four corners of the court there were courts joined of forty cubits long and thirty broad: these four corners were of one measure. 23 And there was a row of building round about in them, round about them four, and it was made with boiling places under the rows round about. 24 Then said he unto me, These are the places of them that boil, where the ministers of the house shall boil the sacrifice of the people.

These courts or fenced off areas furthest out from our Father, are the areas that people that are assigned to be disobedient are kept. This furthest out areas are the areas are where people go when they are cast out into outer darkness. Matthew 8:12 But the children of the kingdom shall be cast out into outer darkness: there shall be weeping and gnashing of teeth.

Now there seems to be more in the book of Ezekiel, but I am only using the six chapters our Father had me put in the first book. Now listen to what we are being told in Exodus 19:12 And thou shalt set bounds unto the people round about, saying, Take heed to yourselves, that ye go not up into the mount, or touch the border of it: whosoever toucheth the mount shall be surely put to death: This is where we start to understand what it means when we hear that they will be cast into out darkness. We saw where Jesus is, right? In the last book, we showed how everybody has their own laws, rulings, statues, and commandments. We all have different rolls to fulfill. We are being held in these different areas so that we can hopefully fulfill whatever roll we have. This is why I said in the last chapter I will not give details on how I receive commandments as to which lane to be in when driving. When to stop, when there is a traffic jam coming up. If I am hooking a different trailer, I am told before I hook to it, if it needs some sort of repairs.

As we showed in the last book, I have been in school with our Father, one on one, hands on training. If you are someone that is being kept in the outer courts, and you try to do what I know how to do now, without being taught precept upon precept, then you would be spiritually put to death. Or put further out in the sections of the mountain so that you would be further out from Jesus and our Father. Remember Jesus is the light of the world. If you're doing what you are supposed to be doing, you are closer to Jesus and there will be a lot of light within you. But if you're not doing what you supposed to be doing you will be cast further out away from this light. Try to picture yourself in this square mile building, if you will. Let us just think of one light bulb in the very center of the building. You just walked in the door so obviously you are far away from the light. Now you must find your way to this light, but you must go through a maze. If you make a wrong turn, you could very well end up on the other side of the building without ever finding the light in the center.

Now we can start to understand what Jesus was saying in Matthew 8:12 But the children of the kingdom shall be cast out into outer darkness: there shall be weeping and gnashing of teeth. So, this is where we start picturing ourselves there and here at the same time. If the part of us there does something other than what is commanded, they will be cast into outer darkness or taken further away from the light. And this effects how our conscience is going to be able to hear what the spirit is saying. Luke 11 And it came to pass, that, as he was praying in a certain place, when he ceased, one of his disciples said unto him, Lord, teach us to pray, as John also taught his disciples. 2

And he said unto them, When ye pray, say, Our Father which art in heaven, Hallowed be thy name. Thy kingdom come. Thy will be done, as in heaven, so in earth. 3 Give us day by day our daily bread. 4 And forgive us our sins; for we also forgive every one that is indebted to us. And lead us not into temptation; but deliver us from evil.

In the last book we showed that a person becomes a bastard when they refuse to listen to our Father when He is chastises them. Hebrew 12:7 If ye endure chastening, God dealeth with you as with sons; for what son is he whom the father chasteneth not? 8 But if ye be without chastisement, whereof all are partakers, then are ye bastards, and not sons. 9 Furthermore we have had fathers of our flesh which corrected us, and we gave them reverence: shall we not much rather be in subjection unto the Father of spirits, and live? When this happens, this soul is cast out into the courts furthest from our Father and they must remain there for their next 10 lives or generations.

Now we are going to be looking at more of the book of Revelation so that can hear for certain that Revelations is a book aimed more toward the beginning, rather than the end of the world. The first thing we need to listen to are the first two chapters of the book. As we showed in the last book, each person is the house of God. This is always where we should be praying. God dwells in every person, Jesus dwells in every person, that holy ghost dwells in every person. The seven spirits of God dwell in very person, the son of perdition dwells in every person or the temple of God. If all these dwells in every person, then every person must be the house of God. So, we can know also that the church of God is within man also and not some building. So, when we listen to these two chapters, hear what the spirit says to you personally. We say it this way because you are the only one responsible for you. You are the only one that truly knows you. Your spouse may know you but he or she does not know your every thought. Let your conscience hear what the spirit says to you.

Revelation 2 Unto the angel of the church of Ephesus write; These things saith he that holdeth the seven stars in his right hand, who walketh in the midst of the seven golden candlesticks; 2 I know thy works, and thy labour, and thy patience, and how thou canst not bear them which are evil: and thou hast tried them which say they are apostles, and are not, and hast found them liars: 3 And hast borne, and hast patience, and for my name's sake hast laboured, and hast not fainted. 4 Nevertheless I have somewhat against thee, because thou hast left thy first love. 5 Remember therefore from whence thou art fallen, and repent, and do the first works; or else I will come unto thee quickly, and will remove thy candlestick out of his place, except thou repent. 6 But this thou hast, that thou hatest the deeds of the Nicolaitanes, which I also hate. 7 He that hath an ear, let him hear what the Spirit saith unto the churches; To him that overcometh will I give to eat of the tree of life, which is in the midst of the paradise of God. 8 And unto the angel of the church in Smyrna write; These things saith the first and the last, which was dead, and is alive; 9 I know thy works, and tribulation, and poverty, (but thou art rich) and I know the blasphemy of them which say they are Jews, and are not, but are the synagogue of Satan.

We must take a side note here. This world thinks that you must go to the country of Israel here on earth. Jerusalem is above as we showed in Galatians 4. We now know that we have everything here on earth as they do in heaven. So, in reality nobody knows whether or not they are a Jew. Remember in the last book that we showed how we live 1,000 different lives. We all have been Jew, Russian, Chinese, Korean, American, black white, male, female, etc. We all are here just to learn to love in the same manner as our Father. 10 Fear none of those things which thou shalt suffer: behold, the devil shall cast some of you into prison, that ye may be tried; and ye shall have tribulation ten days: be thou faithful unto death, and I will give thee a crown of life.

We want to make a side note here. Notice how Jesus is saying some will be in prison for ten days. I believe he is talking to our souls for we are stuck here on earth. We are in prison. Now a day is as a thousand years and a thousand years is as a day. So, I believe that he is saying that some of our souls will be here in prison for 10,000 years.

11 He that hath an ear, let him hear what the Spirit saith unto the churches; He that overcometh shall not be hurt of the second death. 12 And to the angel of the church in Pergamos write; These things

saith he which hath the sharp sword with two edges; 13 I know thy works, and where thou dwellest, even where Satan's seat is: and thou holdest fast my name, and hast not denied my faith, even in those days wherein Antipas was my faithful martyr, who was slain among you, where Satan dwelleth. 14 But I have a few things against thee, because thou hast there them that hold the doctrine of Balaam, who taught Balac to cast a stumblingblock before the children of Israel, to eat things sacrificed unto idols, and to commit fornication. 15 **So hast thou also them that hold the doctrine of the Nicolaitanes, which thing I hate.**

We need to be paying attention to what we are hearing here. This is not the only time we can hear Jesus say that he hates the doctrine of the Nicolaitanes, so we need to be looking at to what and who these people are. Let us look up the name on the online bible concordance and listen. G3531 Νικολαΐτης Nikolaitēs nik-ol-ah-ee'- tace From G3532; a Nicolaite, that is, adherent of **Nicolaus:–** Nicolaitane. We showed you all in the last book that Jeremiah 10 is talking about Christmas. Yes, if you go out and find books on man's opinion, they will say no it isn't, but when you just listen to what is being said, you can know it is about Christmas. What is Christmas based on? Most will say it is about Jesus's birthday. As we showed in the last book, everybody makes up part of the son of God, so his birthday is every day of the year. By celebrating birthdays, you are adding to the word of God. You are spiritually telling our Father, you need more than His perfection. So, what is Nicolaitane, and who is this fictional character? **St. Nicholas or Santa Clause.** A fictional character in which people lie to their children and tell them that this character is going to bring gifts. First, you are teaching your children to lie. Then you give them gifts in which are Father hates man receiving gifts from man. You waste money on these gifts in which could go to a neighbor that is in need. The poor and needy will always be in the land. Then celebrating this holiday or any other day, you teach your children to love more at certain times of the year and that they should be loved more at certain times of the year. That is not loving as our Father, for He loves equally every day of the year.

16 Repent; or else I will come unto thee quickly, and will fight against them with the sword of my mouth. 17 He that hath an ear, let him hear what the Spirit saith unto the churches; To him that overcometh will I give to eat of the hidden manna, and will give him a white stone, and in the stone a new name written, which no man knoweth saving he that receiveth it. 18 And unto the angel of the church in Thyatira write; These things saith the Son of God, who hath his eyes like unto a flame of fire, and his feet are like fine brass; 19 I know thy works, and charity, and service, and faith, and thy patience, and thy works; and the last to be more than the first. 20 Notwithstanding I have a few things against thee, because thou sufferest that woman Jezebel, which calleth herself a prophetess, to teach and to seduce my servants to commit fornication, and to eat things sacrificed unto idols. 21 And I gave her space to repent of her fornication; and she repented not. 22 Behold, I will cast her into a bed, and them that commit adultery with her into great tribulation, except they repent of their deeds. 23 And I will kill her children with death; and all the churches shall know that I am he which searcheth the reins and hearts: and I will give unto every one of you according to your works. 24 But unto you I say, and unto the rest in Thyatira, as many as have not this doctrine, and which have not known the depths of Satan, as they speak; I will put upon you none other burden. 25 But that which ye have already hold fast till I come. 26 And he that overcometh, and keepeth my works unto the end, to him will I give power over the nations: 27 And he shall rule them with a rod of iron; as the vessels of a potter shall they be broken to shivers: even as I received of my Father. 28 And I will give him the morning star. 29 He that hath an ear, let him hear what the Spirit saith unto the churches.

Revelation 3 And unto the angel of the church in Sardis write; These things saith he that hath the seven Spirits of God, and the seven stars; I know thy works, that thou hast a name that thou livest, and art dead. 2 Be watchful, and strengthen the things which remain, that are ready to die: for I have not found thy works perfect before God. Note here that we are being told that there are some that hast a name that livest, but art dead. Remember how Jesus said let the dead burry the dead in Matthew 8:21 And another of his disciples said unto him, Lord, suffer me first to go and bury my father. 22 But Jesus said unto him, Follow me; and let the dead bury their dead. Just because you have a heartbeat and are breathing does not make you alive in our Father's eyes. If you do not want anything to do with our Father, there is no light in you. You are completely full of darkness in which is the same thing as being dead. This is how the dead can bury the dead.

3 Remember therefore how thou hast received and heard, and hold fast, and repent. If therefore thou shalt not watch, I will come on thee as a thief, and thou shalt not know what hour I will come upon thee. 4 Thou hast a few names even in Sardis which have not defiled their garments; and they shall walk with me in white: for they are worthy. 5 He that overcometh, the same shall be clothed in white raiment; and I will not blot out his name out of the book of life, but I will confess his name before my Father, and before his angels. 6 He that hath an ear, let him hear what the Spirit saith unto the churches. 7 And to the angel of the church in Philadelphia write; These things saith he that is holy, he that is true, he that hath the key of David, he that openeth, and no man shutteth; and shutteth, and no man openeth; 8 I know thy works: behold, I have set before thee an open door, and no man can shut it: for thou hast a little strength, and hast kept my word, and hast not denied my name. 9 Behold, I will make them of the synagogue of Satan, which say they are Jews, and are not, but do lie; behold, I will make them to come and worship before thy feet, and to know that I have loved thee. 10 Because thou hast kept the word of my patience, I also will keep thee from the hour of temptation, which shall come upon all the world, to try them that dwell upon the earth. 11 Behold, I come quickly: hold that fast which thou hast, that no man take thy crown. 12 Him that overcometh will I make a pillar in the temple of my God, and he shall go no more out: and I will write upon him the name of my God, and the name of the city of my God, which is new Jerusalem, which cometh down out of heaven from my God: and I will write upon him my new name. 13 He that hath an ear, let him hear what the Spirit saith unto the churches. 14 And unto the angel of the church of the Laodiceans write; These things saith the Amen,

the faithful and true witness, the beginning of the creation of God; 15 I know thy works, that thou art neither cold nor hot: I would thou wert cold or hot. 16 So then because thou art lukewarm, and neither cold nor hot, I will spue thee out of my mouth. 17 Because thou sayest, I am rich, and increased with goods, and have need of nothing; and knowest not that thou art wretched, and miserable, and poor, and blind, and naked: 18 I counsel thee to buy of me gold tried in the fire, that thou mayest be rich; and white raiment, that thou mayest be clothed, and that the shame of thy nakedness do not appear; and anoint thine eyes with eyesalve, that thou mayest see. 19 As many as I love, I rebuke and chasten: be zealous therefore, and repent. 20 Behold, I stand at the door, and knock: if any man hear my voice, and open the door, I will come in to him, and will sup with him, and he with me. 21 To him that overcometh will I grant to sit with me in my throne, even as I also overcame, and am set down with my Father in his throne. 22 He that hath an ear, let him hear what the Spirit saith unto the churches.

Now we need to be looking at Revelation 6 And I saw when the Lamb opened one of the seals, and I heard, as it were the noise of thunder, one of the four beasts saying, Come and see. 2 And I saw, and behold a white horse: and he that sat on him had a bow; and a crown was given unto him: and he went forth conquering, and to conquer. Now we all have heard that these are the four horses of the apocalypse. So, what we are going to do is hear how these were sent out in the very beginning and not going to be sent out to be a sign of the end. So, the white horse went forth conquering. Now if anybody has ever read the old testament, they know that it is full of wars. In fact, many people say that we live in the new testament now. They think that now. If that was the case, why is there so many wars in the world now.? Someone must win or conquer a war. This all stems off what Jesus said when he said he did not come to bring peace into the world, but diversity. Luke 12:51 Suppose ye that I am come to give peace on earth? I tell you, Nay; but rather division: 52 For from henceforth there shall be five in one house divided, three against two, and two against three. Now we need to remember that our Father separated us Genesis 11:6 And the Lord said, Behold, the people is one, and they have all one language; and this they begin to do: and now nothing will be restrained from them, which they have imagined to do. 7 Go to, let us go down, and there confound their language, that they may not understand one another's speech. 8 So the Lord scattered them abroad from thence upon the face of all the earth: and they left off to build the city. 9 Therefore is the name of it called Babel; because the Lord did there confound the language of all the earth: and from thence did the Lord scatter them abroad upon the face of all the earth.

Now that our Father had separated the people and gave them different languages, is when the countries of the world started to grow. Listen to what we are being told in Job 8:11 Can the rush grow up without mire? **can the flag grow without water?** A flag does not grow, however the country that the flag represents, does. Remember in the last book that Jesus is living water, and we are living waters. Then we should be remembering that Jesus is the manna in which are Father feeds us without us knowing about it. That water is basic knowledge in which allows the country to grow. Once a country grows, they have disagreements with other countries and the wars began. 3 And when he had opened the second seal, I heard the second beast say, Come and see. 4 And there went out another horse that was red: and power was given to him that sat thereon to take peace from the earth, and that they should kill one another: and there was given unto him a great sword. Now this horse goes along with the first. Remember we spiritually kill with our tongues. If we didn't, then nobody would ever turn back to our Father. Everything happens for a reason. And of course, we need to remember that our Father told us that there is a season for everything. Ecclesiastes 3 To every thing there is a season, and a time to every purpose under the heaven: 2 A time to be born, and a time to die; a time to plant, and a time to pluck up that which is planted; 3 A time to kill, and a time to heal; a time to break down, and a time to build up; 4 A time to weep, and a time to laugh; a time to mourn, and a time to dance; 5 A time to cast away stones, and a time to gather stones together; a time to embrace, and a time to refrain from embracing; 6 A time to get, and a time to lose; a time to keep, and a time to cast away; 7 A time to rend, and a time to sew; a time to keep silence, and a time to speak; 8 A time to love, and a time to hate; a time of war, and a time of peace.

5 And when he had opened the third seal, I heard the third beast say, Come and see. And I beheld, and lo a black horse; and he that sat on him had a pair of balances in his hand.6 And I heard a voice in the midst of the four beasts say, A measure of wheat for a penny, and three measures of barley for a penny; and see thou hurt not the oil and the wine. This horse was sent out to keep things fair in the world. What I mean by that is it keeps the cost of things within range of pay. I do not know what percentage of farms only grow wheat in the states but let us say around 10%. Just figures, but if these farmers wanted to charge so much that it cost a hundred dollars for a loaf of bread, hardly anyone would ever buy bread or better said, could afford to buy bread. This keeps a fair balance in the world. And yes, this country we live in needs the rest of the world as well as they need us.

7 And when he had opened the fourth seal, I heard the voice of the fourth beast say, Come and see. 8 And I looked, and behold a pale horse: and his name that sat on him was Death, and Hell followed with him. And power was given unto them over the fourth part of the earth, to kill with sword, and with hunger, and with death, and with the beasts of the earth. Now we to think about this for a minute. This death is a spiritual death. It is not a physical death. Remember in the last book, we showed that we are in hell now? We are constantly walking in the fire. That fire is chastisement coming from our Father, but most do not understand that and it causes all kinds of pains in which can be related to burning.

9 And when he had opened the fifth seal, I saw under the altar the souls of them that were slain for the word of God, and for the testimony which they held: 10 And they cried with a loud voice, saying, How long, O Lord, holy and true, dost thou not judge and avenge our blood on them that dwell on the earth? 11 And white robes were given unto every one of them; and it was said unto them, that they should rest yet for a little season, until their fellowservants also and their brethren, that should be killed as they were, should be

fulfilled. This here is where need to remember we are hearing what they are saying in heaven. Remember we just showed that Jesus did this once before. That was at the very beginning. I believe these are the souls in which are on that mountain we showed in Ezekiel 40-46. 12 And I beheld when he had opened the sixth seal, and, lo, there was a great earthquake; and the sun became black as sackcloth of hair, and the moon became as blood; 13 And the stars of heaven fell unto the earth, even as a fig tree casteth her untimely figs, when she is shaken of a mighty wind. 14 And the heaven departed as a scroll when it is rolled together; and every mountain and island were moved out of their places.

Remember the stars in which came to the earth when Satan was cast out of heaven? Revelation 12:4 **And his tail drew the third part of the stars of heaven, and did cast them to the earth:** and the dragon stood before the woman which was ready to be delivered, for to devour her child as soon as it was born. This is how it began.

Yes; I have shown you all that I am Jesus Christ that appeared once in the earth in the end of the world. But we need to remember it is happening in earth as it is in heaven. I am a man in the flesh still and have not been made perfect yet. I took part in the first resurrection, and I am not sure of how many more has or will be, for only a remnant will be saved. This is where we need to realize that this entire earth is covered with the walking dead. I was dead but still alive. Then I died and am still alive. Let us just listen to a few times of when we can hear this. Ephesians 2 And you hath he quickened, who were dead in trespasses and sins; 2 **Wherein in time past ye walked according to the course of this world, according to the prince of the power of the air, the spirit that now worketh in the children of disobedience:** 3 Among whom also we all had our conversation in times past in the lusts of our flesh, fulfilling the desires of the flesh and of the mind; and were by nature the children of wrath, even as others. 4 But God, who is rich in mercy, for his great love wherewith he loved us, 5 **Even when we were dead in sins, hath quickened us together with Christ, (by grace ye are saved;) 6 And hath raised us up together, and made us sit together in heavenly places in Christ Jesus:**

This is where a lot of people think they will be raptured. No, I wasn't raptured, nor do I want to be. I resurrected out of Egypt, the spiritual waters that cover the entire earth. Remember God is working a works that no man will believe. This world reads the bible carnally and thinks that God physically put his son to death. I described how I gave up living in this world, but yet stayed alive. That is why Jesus said what he did in John 4:23 But the hour cometh, and now is, when the true worshippers shall worship the Father in spirit and in truth: for the Father seeketh such to worship him. 24 God is a Spirit: and they that worship him must worship him in spirit and in truth.

We need to be looking at some areas Revelation that are talking about when this was all set up. Now remember we are hearing what they are saying in heaven. So, I ask that you try to imagine yourself to be up in heaven, looking down on the earth as you hear this. Revelation 13 And I stood upon the sand of the sea, and saw a beast rise up out of the sea, having seven heads and ten horns, and upon his horns ten crowns, and upon his heads the name of blasphemy. 2 And the beast which I saw was like unto a leopard, and his feet were as the feet of a bear, and his mouth as the mouth of a lion: and the dragon gave him his power, and his seat, and great authority. How many continents are on this planet? Seven continents, or seven heads.

Now let us venture to the book of Genesis 1 In the beginning God created the heaven and the earth. 2 And the earth was without form, and void; and darkness was upon the face of the deep. And the Spirit of God moved upon the face of the waters. 3 And God said, Let there be light: and there was light. 4 And God saw the light, that it was good: and God divided the light from the darkness. 5 And God called the light Day, and the darkness he called Night. And the evening and the morning were the first day. 6 And God said, Let there be a firmament in the midst of the waters, and let it divide the waters from the waters. 7 And God made the firmament, and divided the waters which were under the firmament from the waters which were above the firmament: and it was so. 8 And God called the firmament Heaven. And the evening and the morning were the second day. 9 And God said, Let the waters under the heaven be gathered together unto one place, **and let the dry land appear: and it was so. 10 And God called the dry land Earth; and the gathering together of the waters called he Seas:** and God saw that it was good. 11 And God said, Let the earth bring forth grass, the herb yielding seed, and the fruit tree yielding fruit after his kind, whose seed is in itself, upon the earth: and it was so. 12 And the earth brought forth grass, and herb yielding seed after his kind, and the tree yielding fruit, whose seed was in itself, after his kind: and God saw that it was good. 13 And the evening and the morning were the third day.

Notice how the earth was without form and nothing but water in the very beginning. Then the seven continents divided the waters? Obviously, we cannot see these heads for they are spiritual. 3 And I saw one of his heads as it were wounded to death; and his deadly wound was healed: and all the world wondered after the beast. 4 And they worshipped the dragon which gave power unto the beast: and they worshipped the beast, saying, Who is like unto the beast? who is able to make war with him? 5 And there was given unto him a mouth speaking great things and blasphemies; and power was given unto him to continue forty and two months. 6 And he opened his mouth in blasphemy against God, to blaspheme his name, and his tabernacle, and them that dwell in heaven. 7 And it was given unto him to make war with the saints, and to overcome them: and power was given him over all kindreds, and tongues, and nations. 8 And all that dwell upon the earth shall worship him, whose names are not written in the book of life of the Lamb slain from the foundation of the world. 9 If any man have an ear, let him hear.

Now I have been sitting here and looking over everything and trying to figure out how to get this all in here and I feel I was just told not to worry about getting all of it in. Just show that some of your understanding so that is what I am going to do. There is no way I will understand everything perfectly, but it is the desire I have to keep learning. So, now we need to look at Revelation 8:7 The first angel sounded, and there followed hail and fire mingled with blood, and they were cast upon the earth: and the third part of trees was burnt up, and all green grass was burnt up. At this time we are going to show a google search to see how much the earths land mass is desert. Most of the world's surface is covered in water, in the form of oceans. The remaining landmass of Earth amounts to approximately 29 percent of the surface. Of this remaining 29 percent, deserts of all types constitute an estimated 33 percent, or one-third, of the Earth's total landmass. This has already been done.

Now let us look at the flood in Revelation 12:15 And the serpent cast out of his mouth water as a flood after the woman, that he might cause her to be carried away of the flood. 16 And the earth helped the woman, and the earth opened her mouth, and swallowed up the flood which the dragon cast out of his mouth. I believe that this is the same flood as the flood of Noah. Remember our Father is the creator of the serpent also. This is not me saying that our Father is Satan but rather saying that our Father told the serpent to do this just like He told Satan he could do bad things unto Job except take his life. Job 1 There was a man in the land of Uz, whose name was Job; and that man was perfect and upright, and one that feared God, and eschewed evil. 2 And there were born unto him seven sons and three daughters. 3 His substance also was seven thousand sheep, and three thousand camels, and five hundred yoke of oxen, and five hundred she asses, and a very great household; so that this man was the greatest of all the men of the east. 4 And his sons went and feasted in their houses, every one his day; and sent and called for their three sisters to eat and to drink with them. 5 And it was so, when the days of their feasting were gone about, that Job sent and sanctified them, and rose up early in the morning, and offered burnt offerings according to the number of them all: for Job said, It may be that my sons have sinned, and cursed God in their hearts. Thus did Job continually. 6 Now there was a day when the sons of God came to present themselves before the Lord, and Satan came also among them. 7 And the Lord said unto Satan, Whence comest thou? Then Satan answered the Lord, and said, From going to and fro in the earth, and from walking up and down in it. 8 And the Lord said unto Satan, Hast thou considered my servant Job, that there is none like him in the earth, a perfect and an upright man, one that feareth God, and escheweth evil? 9 Then Satan answered the Lord, and said, Doth Job fear God for nought? 10 Hast not thou made an hedge about him, and about his house, and about all that he hath on every side? thou hast blessed the work of his hands, and his substance is increased in the land. 11 But put forth thine hand now, and touch all that he hath, and he will curse thee to thy face. 12 And the Lord said unto Satan, Behold, **all that he hath is in thy power; only upon himself put not forth thine hand.** So Satan went forth from the presence of the Lord. 13 And there was a day when his sons and his daughters were eating and drinking wine in their eldest brother's house: 14 And there came a messenger unto Job, and said, The oxen were plowing, and the asses feeding beside them: 15 And the Sabeans fell upon them, and took them away; yea, they have slain the servants with the edge of the sword; and I only am escaped alone to tell thee. 16 While he was yet speaking, there came also another, and said, The fire of God is fallen from heaven, and hath burned up the sheep, and the servants, and consumed them; and I only am escaped alone to tell thee. 17 While he was yet speaking, there came also another, and said, The Chaldeans made out three bands, and fell upon the camels, and have carried them away, yea, and slain the servants with the edge of the sword; and I only am escaped alone to tell thee. 18 While he was yet speaking, there came also another, and said, Thy sons and thy daughters were eating and drinking wine in their eldest brother's house: 19 And, behold, there came a great wind from the wilderness, and smote the four corners of the house, and it fell upon the young men, and they are dead; and I only am escaped alone to tell thee. 20 Then Job arose, and rent his mantle, and shaved his head, and fell down upon the ground, and worshipped, 21 And said, Naked came I out of my mother's womb, and naked shall I return thither: the Lord gave, and the Lord hath taken away; blessed be the name of the Lord. 22 In all this Job sinned not, nor charged God foolishly. Job 2 Again there was a day when the sons of God came to present themselves before the Lord, and Satan came also among them to present himself before the Lord. 2 And the Lord said unto Satan, From whence comest thou? And Satan answered the Lord, and said, From going to and fro in the earth, and from walking up and down in it. 3 And the Lord said unto Satan, Hast thou considered my servant Job, that there is none like him in the earth, a perfect and an upright man, one that feareth God, and escheweth evil? and still he holdeth fast his integrity, although thou movedst me against him, to destroy him without cause. 4 And Satan answered the Lord, and said, Skin for skin, yea, all that a man hath will he give for his life. 5 But put forth thine hand now, and touch his bone and his flesh, and he will curse thee to thy face. 6 **And the Lord said unto Satan, Behold, he is in thine hand; but save his life.** 7 So went Satan forth from the presence of the Lord, and smote Job with sore boils from the sole of his foot unto his crown. 8 And he took him a potsherd to scrape himself withal; and he sat down among the ashes. 9 Then said his wife unto him, Dost thou still retain thine integrity? curse God, and die. 10 But he said unto her, Thou speakest as one of the foolish women speaketh. What? shall we receive good at the hand of God, and shall we not receive evil? In all this did not Job sin with his lips. 11 Now when Job's three friends heard of all this evil that was come upon him, they came every one from his own place; Eliphaz the Temanite, and Bildad the Shuhite, and Zophar the Naamathite: for they had made an appointment together to come to mourn with him and to comfort him. 12 And when they lifted up their eyes afar off, and knew him not, they lifted up their voice, and wept; and they rent every one his mantle, and sprinkled dust upon their heads toward heaven. 13 So they sat down with him upon the ground seven days and seven nights, and none spake a word unto him: for they saw that his grief was very great.

I would have to place the entire book of Job for you all to get the full understanding, but you can surely see that our Father is the boss of Satan as well. Our Father is the king of all kings and has the utmost authority to do what He pleases to do, so that we will turn back to Him.

This is something our Father showed me as I am writing this book so I probably will not be painting the picture as clear as I should. So, please ask our Father for help in understanding this better as you read, for He is the ultimate teacher. This is why it is so important that we listen to all of the bible and not just bits and pieces. We all know how the Jesus told the disciples that he would make them fishermen to men, right? Matthew 4:18 And Jesus, walking by the sea of Galilee, saw two brethren, Simon called Peter, and Andrew his brother, **casting a net into the sea:** for they were fishers. 19 **And he saith unto them, Follow me, and I will make you fishers of men.** This is exactly what has been done. In the last book, we showed that I believe the disciples are spirits. Just showing one area for more will covered later. Luke 9:54 And when his disciples James and John saw this, they said, Lord, wilt thou that we command fire to come down from heaven, and consume them, even as Elias did? 55 **But he turned, and rebuked them, and said, Ye know not what manner of spirit ye are of.** We have seen that we are in deep waters, right? Jeremiah 46:8 **Egypt riseth up like a flood, and his waters are moved like the rivers; and he saith, I will go up, and will cover the earth;** I will destroy the city and the inhabitants thereof.

Now lifting yourself up into the clouds again looking down on the earth, try to visualize the earth being one great big sea. We are all just fish of some sort in a spiritual realm. Remember in the last book how we lifted ourselves up and seen the body of the son of God covering the entire earth with almost 8 billion functioning body parts? Now try to look into this water and see all the kinds of fish swimming around. Remember we are in their image. These fish are all kinds of colors, shapes, sizes, and they all have different attitudes. You know like a shark is always looking for its next meal, but a dolphin is always playing. Then you have the fish that are very colorful and beautiful, but yet there are some that are just plain and simple. But for the better part they all get along.

Now let us listen to a few times that our Father talks about the nets that are catching people. 19 Isaiah The burden of Egypt. Behold, the Lord rideth upon a swift cloud, and shall come into Egypt: and the idols of Egypt shall be moved at his presence, and the heart of Egypt shall melt in the midst of it. 2 And I will set the Egyptians against the Egyptians: and they shall fight every one against his brother, and every one against his neighbour; city against city, and kingdom against kingdom. 3 And the spirit of Egypt shall fail in the midst thereof; and I will destroy the counsel thereof: **and they shall seek to the idols, and to the charmers, and to them that have familiar spirits, and to the wizards.** 4 And the Egyptians will I give over into the hand of a cruel lord; and a fierce king shall rule over them, saith the Lord, the Lord of hosts. 5 And the waters shall fail from the sea, and the river shall be wasted and dried up. 6 And they shall turn the rivers far away; and the brooks of defence shall be emptied and dried up: the reeds and flags shall wither. 7 The paper reeds by the brooks, by the mouth of the brooks, and every thing sown by the brooks, shall wither, be driven away, and be no more. 8 The fishers also shall mourn, **and all they that cast angle into the brooks shall lament, and they that spread nets upon the waters shall languish.** Remember how Egypt is as waters that cover the earth? Why would our Father do this with those that have familiar spirits and wizards? Because they do not turn to Him with their whole heart, soul, and mind.

Ezekiel 26 And it came to pass in the eleventh year, in the first day of the month, that the word of the Lord came unto me, saying, 2 Son of man, because that Tyrus hath said against Jerusalem, Aha, she is broken that was the gates of the people: she is turned unto me: I shall be replenished, now she is laid waste: 3 Therefore thus saith the Lord God; Behold, I am against thee, O Tyrus, and will cause many nations to come up against thee, as the sea causeth his waves to come up. 4 And they shall destroy the walls of Tyrus, and break down her towers: I will also scrape her dust from her, and make her like the top of a rock. 5 **It shall be a place for the spreading of nets in the midst of the sea: for I have spoken it, saith the Lord God: and it shall become a spoil to the nations.** When we are listening here, we can hear that this not actually water, but yet shall be a place for spreading of nets in the midst of the sea. This is where I believe people cast their own nets of a sorts. What I mean is like when you go to a big gathering of some sorts, we can usually see people in their own little groups, why? Are not we all made by the same Father? Do we not we all have the same blood? Do not we all breath the same air? Do not we all walk on the same dry earth? But yet people tend to only hang with people that dress alike, act alike, and look alike. Is your net going to become a snare?

Now let us listen to when our Father tells us that He will put hooks in the jaws of some. Ezekiel 29 In the tenth year, in the tenth month, in the twelfth day of the month, the word of the Lord came unto me, saying, 2 Son of man, set thy face against Pharaoh king of Egypt, and prophesy against him, and against all Egypt: 3 Speak, and say, Thus saith the Lord God; Behold, I am against thee, Pharaoh king of Egypt, the great dragon that lieth in the midst of his rivers, which hath said, My river is mine own, and I have made it for myself. 4 **But I will put hooks in thy jaws, and I will cause the fish of thy rivers to stick unto thy scales, and I will bring thee up out of the midst of thy rivers, and all the fish of thy rivers shall stick unto thy scales.** 5 And I will leave thee thrown into the wilderness, thee and all the fish of thy rivers: thou shalt fall upon the open fields; thou shalt not be brought together, nor gathered: I have given thee for meat to the beasts of the field and to the fowls of the heaven. Ezekiel 38 And the word of the Lord came unto me, saying, 2 Son of man, set thy face against Gog, the land of Magog, the chief prince of Meshech and Tubal, and prophesy against him, 3 And say, Thus saith the Lord God; Behold, I am against thee, O Gog, the chief prince of Meshech and Tubal: 4 **And I will turn thee back, and put hooks into thy jaws, and I will bring thee forth, and all thine army, horses and horsemen, all of them clothed with all sorts of armour, even a great company with bucklers and shields, all of them handling swords:** These are spiritual hooks, and we are spiritual fish being fished for. As we heard, we even cast our own nets and get stuck in our own nets. It is all on how we treat our Father and other people.

Notice how there is 153 fish in this net? I believe we are being told of how many the remnant is. Remember we are fish, and this is the only time the bible mentions the number of how many fish are in the net. These fish are also called as great fish. At the same time, we need to remember that one man can represent a group of people so this could be 153 groups of people as one. But mainly focus on how Judas is there. He hanged himself, if we will recall. Matthew 27 When the morning was come, all the chief priests and elders of the people took counsel against Jesus to put him to death: 2 And when they had bound him, they led him away, and delivered him to Pontius Pilate the governor. 3 Then Judas, which had betrayed him, when he saw that he was condemned, repented himself, and brought again the thirty pieces of silver to the chief priests and elders, 4 Saying, I have sinned in that I have betrayed the innocent blood. And they said, What is that to us? see thou to that. 5 **And he cast down the pieces of silver in the temple, and departed, and went and hanged himself.**

Now we know that Jesus told the other disciples that he was going to make them fishermen of men. Our bible does not tell us what profession Judas had but we can know that he was a disciple, so we can figure he too, is a fisherman of men. And he is casting his net just as the others are. So now let us listen to a couple times that our Father tells us that He has made the wicked man for the evil day. Proverbs 16 The preparations of the heart in man, and the answer of the tongue, is from the Lord. 2 All the ways of a man are clean in his own eyes; but the Lord weigheth the spirits. 3 Commit thy works unto the Lord, and thy thoughts shall be established. 4 **The Lord hath made all things for himself: yea, even the wicked for the day of evil.** 5 Every one that is proud in heart is an abomination to the Lord: though hand join in hand, he shall not be unpunished. Job 21:30 **That the wicked is reserved to the day of destruction? they shall be brought forth to the day of wrath.** Notice how Jesus said it shouldn't matter to the other disciples if Judas was there till the end? How big is his net?

Now this is where we need to be listening to Revelation 8:10 And the third angel sounded, and there fell a great star from heaven, burning as it were a lamp, and it fell upon the third part of the rivers, and upon the fountains of waters; 11 **And the name of the star is called Wormwood: and the third part of the waters became wormwood; and many men died of the waters, because they were made bitter.** These waters are the waters in which we are in. These waters have already been turned into blood. Revelation 16 And I heard a great voice out of the temple saying to the seven angels, Go your ways, and pour out the vials of the wrath of God upon the earth.

2 And the first went, and poured out his vial upon the earth; and there fell a noisome and grievous sore upon the men which had the mark of the beast, and upon them which worshipped his image. 3 And the second angel poured out his vial upon the sea; and it became as the blood of a dead man: and every living soul died in the sea.

Remember how Jesus said we cannot be his disciple if we do not eat his flesh and drink his blood? John 6:53 Then Jesus said unto them, Verily, verily, I say unto you, Except ye eat the flesh of the Son of man, and drink his blood, ye have no life in you. 54 Whoso eateth my flesh, and drinketh my blood, hath eternal life; and I will raise him up at the last day. 55 For my flesh is meat indeed, and my blood is drink indeed. 56 He that eateth my flesh, and drinketh my blood, dwelleth in me, and I in him. 57 As the living Father hath sent me, and I live by the Father: so he that eateth me, even he shall live by me. That is a spiritual flesh consuming our minds and a spiritual blood of love for all of mankind. Now when we don't seek God with all of our heart, soul, and mind and or love our neighbor as ourselves, we are eating of flesh and drinking of blood in which will not save us.

Remember the water that Jesus said if we drink of, we will never thirst again? John 4:13 Jesus answered and said unto her, Whosoever drinketh of this water shall thirst again: 14 But whosoever drinketh of the water that I shall give him shall never thirst; but the water that I shall give him shall be in him a well of water springing up into everlasting life. 15 The woman saith unto him, Sir, give me this water, that I thirst not, neither come hither to draw.

Now one last thing to bring this chapter to and end, we are told that the end of all things is at hand. 1 Peter 4:7 But the end of all things is at hand: be ye therefore sober, and watch unto prayer. If the end of all things is at hand, wouldn't that also mean the end of the thousand year rein? It is not something that is coming at the end for we are living in the reign now and that too, is getting ready to end. Now that you are learning that you are reigning with Christ and have been here for some time now, we ask how are you doing your part of being a priest of God and Christ? Remember Christ never even thought about changing anything of God, our Father.

We are told that God is not the author of confusion, but man has taken it upon himself to seek other books other than the bible to find out what God is saying. Everything we need to know about our Father is in our bible and nowhere else. Man confuses himself by seeking what others think He is saying. 1 Corinthians 14:33 For God is not the author of confusion, but of peace, as in all churches of the saints. For everything that I teach comes from the King James bible only, well and our Father.

REINCARNATION

This chapter will be rather short, however there are a few things that need to be shown in a short chapter so that everyone can realize that this is something that is very real. This was covered in the last book, in the chapter The Son Of God, but I feel our Father is telling me to do a chapter just on this topic There are many that have told me that they are not sure if this is real. I have been taught by our Father, that this is very real and is something that really needs to be understood.

The first thing we need to realize is that our Father said that the covenant is good for a thousand generations. There are many that believe that we are in the new covenant now but that is far from what our bibles teach us. So, let us look at a couple of times that we are told that the old covenant is for a thousand generations. Exodus 20:6 And shewing mercy unto thousands of them that love me, and keep my commandments. Deuteronomy 7:9 **Know therefore that the Lord thy God, he is God, the faithful God, which keepeth covenant and mercy with them that love him and keep his commandments to a thousand generations;** Notice how we are being told that God keepeth covenant and mercy with them that love Him and keep His commandments. He is no saying He will keep the covenant and mercy if you do not keep His commandments.

Now before diving into this to deep, we need to understand that this covenant is not flawed or done wrong. Many thinks this because yes, our bible does say this. So now let us listen to what we are being told. Hebrews 8:6 But now hath he obtained a more excellent ministry, by how much also he is the mediator of a better covenant, which was established upon better promises. 7 For if that first covenant had been faultless, then should no place have been sought for the second. 8 For finding fault with them, he saith, Behold, the days come, saith the Lord, when I will make a new covenant with the house of Israel and with the house of Judah: 9 Not according to the covenant that I made with their fathers in the day when I took them by the hand to lead them out of the land of Egypt; because they continued not in my covenant, and I regarded them not, saith the Lord. 10 For this is the covenant that I will make with the house of Israel after those days, saith the Lord; I will put my laws into their mind, and write them in their hearts: and I will be to them a God, and they shall be to me a people: 11 And they shall not teach every man his neighbour, and every man his brother, saying, Know the Lord: for all shall know me, from the least to the greatest. 12 For I will be merciful to their unrighteousness, and their sins and their iniquities will I remember no more. 13 In that he saith, A new covenant, he hath made the first old. Now that which decayeth and waxeth old is ready to vanish away.

First thing we are noticing is that the old covenant did have a fault. However, notice in verse eight how it starts out for finding fault with them? Right away we should be realizing that our Father is perfect in everything He has done, doing, and will do. There is absolutely no way this fault is with Him. As we can hear, the fault is with them. Remember we are hearing conversations being held in heaven. The fault is mankind. That is the "them" that we are hearing. Our Father's perfection is so much more profound than man will ever imagine. His righteousness exceeds the comprehension of man. The fault of the covenant is with man and not with the covenant itself, nor our Father. Then we need to realize that we are not in the new covenant for we are still learning and still teaching. Notice how in verse 11 that all will know the Father, and no one will have to ask anyone of our Father.

Now that we should be having a much better understanding about that, we need to look at how long a generation is. But before we do that let us understand that when our Father said the covenant is good for a thousand generations, that means no one is getting out of here before this time span is finished. If there are some that are thinking that our Father will allow some out early, then you need to realize that our Father cannot lie and He will not change.

Malachi 3:6 **For I am the Lord, I change not;** therefore ye sons of Jacob are not consumed. Psalm 90:10 The days of our years are threescore years and ten; and if by reason of strength they be fourscore years, yet is their strength labour and sorrow; for it is soon cut off, and we fly away. This is telling us right here that we live to be 70 to 80 years of age. Then we fly away. This is our soul going somewhere else, back into captivity.

Now we need to adventure into this for a minute. This is where we need to realize that there are many planets in our Father's world. There are many people that believe that mankind is the only for but this too, is because people do not take the time to try and get to know who our Father is and what He is all about. Hebrews 1:2 Hath in these last days spoken unto us by his Son, whom he hath appointed heir of all things, **by whom also he made the worlds;** We are being told right here that there are more worlds than just the one we are on. But to understand this fully we need to be listening to what Jesus said. John 10:16 And other sheep I have, which are not of this fold: them also I must bring, and they shall hear my voice; and there shall be one fold, and one shepherd. This fold is a different world. These are souls that have been brought here from some other world. They haven't been here for the full thousand generations. They were in some other world, heard the same voice that I hear and came here.

This is what Jesus was talking about in the parable about the workers who worked all day and got paid the same for people that worked just a couple of hours or so. Now wording to be exact so let us listen to the parable. Matthew 20 For the kingdom of heaven is like unto a man that is an householder, which went out early in the morning to hire labourers into his vineyard. 2 And when he had agreed with the labourers for a penny a day, he sent them into his vineyard. 3 And he went out about the third hour, and saw others standing idle in the marketplace, 4 And said unto them; Go ye also into the vineyard, and whatsoever is right I will give you. And they went their way. 5 Again he went out about the sixth and ninth hour, and did likewise. 6 And about the eleventh hour he went out, and found others standing idle, and saith unto them, Why stand ye here all the day idle? 7 They say unto him, Because no man hath hired us. He saith unto them, Go ye also into the vineyard; and whatsoever is right, that shall ye receive. 8 So when even was come, the lord of the vineyard saith unto his steward, Call the labourers, and give them their hire, beginning from the last unto the first. 9 And when they came that were hired about the eleventh hour, they received every man a penny. 10 But when the first came, they supposed that they should have received more; and they likewise received every man a penny. 11 And when they had received it, they murmured against the goodman of the house, 12 Saying, These last have wrought but one hour, and thou hast made them equal unto us, which have borne the burden and heat of the day. 13 But he answered one of them, and said, Friend, I do thee no wrong: didst not thou agree with me for a penny? 14 Take that thine is, and go thy way: I will give unto this last, even as unto thee. 15 Is it not lawful for me to do what I will with mine own? Is thine eye evil, because I am good?

We are be told that it does not matter how long or how many generations some are here for. If some have only been here for three generation or 1000 generations, everyone will be rewarded for his or her spiritual works. If some have been here for the entire 1000 generations or more and some have been brought here from another world to serve a couple of generations, then they are still treated equally. If they do right, they will be rewarded the same, but if they do wrong, they will suffer just the same. Our Father respects or favors no one. This is why I believe we are told not to seek other spirits Leviticus 19:31 **Regard not them that have familiar spirits, neither seek after wizards, to be defiled by them: I am the Lord your God.** I believe that these are souls that have clang on to our Father somehow or another and have been brought here. I believe the world in which they came from is ahead of us or something in time. I know that I will not under any circumstances try to seek anyone or anything other than our Father for He brings me more than I could ever ask for. And

I know for sure that when He teaches me, I can't go wrong as long as I am listening to Him.

Now let us listen to what Jesus said about the regeneration of the son of man. Matthew 19:27 Then answered Peter and said unto him, Behold, we have forsaken all, and followed thee; what shall we have therefore? 28 And Jesus said unto them, Verily I say unto you, That ye which have followed me, **in the regeneration when the Son of man shall sit in the throne of his glory, ye also shall sit upon twelve thrones, judging the twelve tribes of Israel.** Then listen to what Jesus tells the disciples about bringing things back to memory. 14:26 But the Comforter, which is the Holy Ghost, whom the Father will send in my name, he shall teach you all things, and bring all things to your remembrance, whatsoever I have said unto you. Now do we really think that Jesus was referring to how they needed to remember in just a few weeks? Now let us listen to how our Father is talking about the regeneration of all. Titus 3:4 But after that the kindness and love of God our Saviour toward man appeared, 5 Not by works of righteousness which we have done, but according to his mercy he saved us, But after that the kindness and love of God our Saviour toward man appeared, 5 Not by works of righteousness which we have done, but according to his mercy he saved us, by the washing of regeneration, and renewing of the Holy Ghost; Now if we only live one life, then why would we be being told that there is going to a washing of regeneration and renewing of the Holy Ghost? Once you receive the Holy Ghost, it is not like it goes away and comes back in a week or two. This was explained in the last book. We will be learning of how my mom and dad are now one flesh in the body of my granddaughter.

This is where we want to show that Jesus was saying himself, that there are going to be souls in which will not die until they see the son of man coming into his kingdom. Matthew 16:26 For what is a man profited, if he shall gain the whole world, and lose his own soul? or what shall a man give in exchange for his soul? 27 For the Son of man shall come in the glory of his Father with his angels; and then he shall reward every man according to his works. 28 Verily I say unto you, **There be some standing here, which shall not taste of death, till they see the Son of man coming in his kingdom.** So here is where we ask you this, do you realize he was telling these people of how things would be then, or at the time of the end of the world?

Now we need to be listening to a bit in the book of Job, but before we do, I want to point out something. I do not pay attention to genealogy. I do not worry about anything in the past. What is done in the past is already done and can't be changed. I do not to try and figure what heritage I come from for I know without a doubt that we all came from our Father. 1 Timothy 1:4 Neither give heed to fables and endless genealogies, which minister questions, rather than godly edifying which is in faith: so do. I do not know exactly when the King James bible was written. I think sometime around the 15 or 16 hundred. That is all really need to know for this next illustration. Okay, I just did a google search and I guess the King James bible was originally written in 1611. So, we know without a doubt that the life of Job was at least some time before that, right?

So now let us listen to a part of Job 19:22 Why do ye persecute me as God, and are not satisfied with my flesh? 23 Oh that my words were now written! oh that they were printed in a book! 24 That they were graven with an iron pen and lead in the rock for ever! 25 For I know that my redeemer liveth, **and that he shall stand at the latter day upon the earth: 26 And though after my skin worms destroy this body, yet in my flesh shall I sees God: 27 Whom I shall see for myself, and mine eyes shall behold, and not another; though my reins be consumed within me.** 28 But ye should say, Why persecute we him, seeing the root of the matter is found in me? 29 Be ye afraid of the sword: for wrath bringeth the punishments of the sword, that ye may know there is a judgment. Now we all can know for certain that Job's life was written about a long time ago. We know for certain that it had to some time before 1611. But yet, Job states that after his body is will be buried and eaten by the worms, He tells us that he will see his redeemer in his flesh. He is telling us that he knows that even though he will die and be buried, he will be alive when Jesus is back at the latter days. So, to this I will say that I have seen him and even maybe talked with him. Neither I or he knows or remember anything from our last lives.

This is where we need to take a look at Ecclesiastes 1:8 All things are full of labour; man cannot utter it: the eye is not satisfied with seeing, nor the ear filled with hearing. 9 The thing that hath been, it is that which shall be; and that which is done is that which shall be done: and there is no new thing under the sun. 10 Is there any thing whereof it may be said, See, this is new? it hath been already of old time, which was before us. 11 There is no remembrance of former things; neither shall there be any remembrance of things that are to come with those that shall come after. Our Father is telling us right here that we cannot remember things from our past lives. Neither will we remember of what is to come. Now how can we remember of what is to come, if we haven't already lived the future in some way or another.

Now if anyone does a web search to see cave drawing from 10,000 years ago, you will find out that there are pictures well over a few thousand years old showing airplanes and such. This is because they have had them here before. Remember our Father told us there is no remembrance of things. There is nothing new under the sun. this is telling us that at sometime in the past, there were planes and such. We have no idea of what time in history we are in. Remember we have showed that we are in the thousand year reign now. As we showed in the last book, the so called lost books of the bible are from a different 1,000 generation cycle. Our sous were made by our Father and our Father never dies. So, neither do or souls. This is just a humongous revolving circle. We will keep coming and going into and from other worlds until each person learn how to love in the same manner that our Father loves us.

Now there is something that I want to bring up that is talked about in our bibles, but yet it is not talked about in our bibles. What I am talking about is the internet. Notice how we are told that there is no new thing under the sun? If there is no new thing, wouldn't have to mean that the internet is not new. They must have had it sometime in the past. Now we are going to show something in the bible in which

I myself, can relate to the internet. Genesis 11 And the whole earth was of one language, and of one speech. 2 And it came to pass, as they journeyed from the east, that they found a plain in the land of Shinar; and they dwelt there. 3 And they said one to another, Go to, let us make brick, and burn them thoroughly. And they had brick for stone, and slime had they for morter. 4 And they said, Go to, let us build us a city and a tower, whose top may reach unto heaven; and let us make us a name, lest we be scattered abroad upon the face of the whole earth. 5 And the Lord came down to see the city and the tower, which the children of men builded. 6 And the Lord said, Behold, the people is one, and they have all one language; and this they begin to do: and now nothing will be restrained from them, which they have imagined to do. 7 Go to, let us go down, and there confound their language, that they may not understand one another's speech. 8 So the Lord scattered them abroad from thence upon the face of all the earth: and they left off to build the city. 9 Therefore is the name of it called Babel; because the Lord did there confound the language of all the earth: and from thence did the Lord scatter them abroad upon the face of all the earth.

Now I realize that we are not all of one language, however we can communicate with other countries pretty easy. I have even shown you all how I use google and web searches on here. Whatever I want to know, or research is at my fingertips. My belief is that this is pretty much as it was then. Then when it gets to the day our Father says it is enough, that is when He will scatter all of our souls again and we start over. This is the end of the world. Or the end of the thousand generations.

Now we are going to be learning of how I know without a shadow of a doubt, that my granddaughter is my mom and dad as one person now. To understand that we need to remember that our Father said that the covenant is for a thousand generations. We know that not one person has ever lived that long and will never live that long so what could He mean? This is where we start to connect the washing away and the regeneration. My Dad passed in 2003. My mom passed in 2016. My dad, after he passed he went to a level just above us in which he was at some kind of rest. My mom, however, didn't pass until Oct 2016. Now our bibles tell us that when a man and woman twain together, they become one flesh. Let us look at Genesis 2:24 Therefore shall a man leave his father and his mother, and shall cleave unto his wife: and they shall be one flesh. Now when they were both alive and together, they were being judged for how they loved one another and all the people they came in contact with as one. They paid the bills as one, they took care of the house as one, they raised the children as one. The two of them together, became one flesh.

Because our Father did not count them as separate people, they both had to finish whatever rolls they needed to fulfill while yet on earth. Now my dad passed when he was in his early 60's. Now I am thinking this was his 2nd or 3rd generation of being in captivity from whatever sin he may have committed against our Father two or three lives ago. We are told that our Father will visit our iniquities to the 3rd and 4th generation. Deuteronomy 5:9 Thou shalt not bow down thyself unto them, nor serve them: for I the Lord thy God am a jealous God, visiting the iniquity of the fathers upon the children unto the third and fourth generation of them that hate me, Now I will not show all the details for I really have a pet peeve about repeating myself. But we are told that if we despise some people, that our Father will send us to the land of those we despise. So if my dad really despised a certain kind of person, this is where our Father will send his soul. Then we just learned that a generation is 70-80 years long. Then we listen to Psalm 55:23 But thou, O God, shalt bring them down into the pit of destruction: bloody and deceitful men shall not live out half their days; but I will trust in thee. Now my dad only lived to be 63 so, I am thinking he was living out his 3rd generation because he did not make it till the full minimum of 70 years. His first generation after he did this transgression against our Father, he only lived to be 30 or 40 years of age. Then a little longer the next life and so on. He died of cancer in which is brought on by our Father. He had me show how all that in the first book he had me write so I will not show it here.

Now my mom lived to be 73 so, now that dad had already passed, our Father joined these two souls back together because they were one flesh. This is what Ephesians 5:31 For this cause shall a man leave his father and mother, and shall be joined unto his wife, and they two shall be one flesh. 32 This is a great mystery: but I speak concerning Christ and the church. Once my mom was finished fulfilling whatever roll she was needed for she passed. Ince this happened, our Father rejoined their souls as one. Now shortly after my mom passed, my 15-year-old daughter got pregnant. Do not cast that stone for that will be held against you. It was around the beginning of June 2017, I started getting this overwhelming sensation that my granddaughter was going to be born on August 4th. I called my daughter and told her and she insisted that the doctors say August 15th and no earlier. I called several more time before August insisting that this child would be born on the 4th. I got a call on the 2nd of August, telling me that my daughter went to the hospital for contractions, and then sent home. It happened again on the 3rd, then on the 4th I got a call stating that my granddaughter had been born.

This was my dad's birthday. He was born on August 4th 1941, I think 41 is the correct year. My dad passed in 2003. My mom passed in 2016. Once both of them were finished with whatever rolls they had to complete while here, they were joined back together and sent back into captivity as one flesh. This is no longer a mystery and explained better in the last book. Now that they are both back into captivity, my granddaughter will be done unto as mom and dad did unto others in their last life as one. This is what Jesus was talking about in Matthew 7:12 Therefore all things whatsoever ye would that men should do to you, do ye even so to them: for this is the law and the prophets. Our Father will lead her or feed her that invisible manna in which will lead her to live wherever that soul is needed to fulfill whatever needs to be fulfilled. Can you start to understand why I stated in the last book, that I marvel on what He is doing every day. He is so smart and powerful. Man can't even begin to imagine how brilliant He is. Ephesians 5:31 For this cause shall a man leave his father and mother, and shall be joined unto his wife, and they two shall be one flesh.32 This is a great mystery: but I speak concerning Christ and the church.

Because I am in the flesh and do not understand everything to the fullest, I must mention my other granddaughter in which is sister to the one born on August 4th. I mentioned in the last book that my daughter was pregnant again and that I was thinking the baby might be born on January 7th for that was my mom's birthday. However, she was born on the 8th of January at 2:35 am. Some days I still wonder if that is my mom. I do know that dad was not judged until my mom passed. Then they were judged as one and sent back into captivity. I sometimes think that maybe the two granddaughters are my parents. Now they will be treated as they did unto their children. I am still more convinced that the first is mom and dad as one, but I am not the Father and it is not for me to say that is a fact. I can and will say without a doubt, my mom and dad's mother, is my daughter.

This leads us to what has been happening with us and what happens to us in the future. This is where we need to realize that each of us have been white, black Chinese, Japanese, Korean, and so forth. We all have been male and female. We have been here for, well a thousand generations or lives. Our Father said this covenant is for a thousand generations and that is exactly what He meant. This is very well explained in the last book so we will not cover it all again. This is how our Father is justified. In the last book, we showed that we are in hell now and that we walk through fire daily. When we despise others, our Father sends us to that land so that our soul can learn what it feels like to be treated just the same as you treated them in your last life.

Now I want to show something that our bible does not come out and outright say. If we live these many lives, and have several different wives or husbands, doesn't that mean that several souls will be joined as one? Let me use my life for example. I know that I have been with a few women in my life. If I die tomorrow, and all of my wives do not die for another five years. When we are all joined as one and we come back into captivity as one. Wouldn't this explain why we have some people with multiple personalities? I believe this is exactly what it is. I also believe that there is an answer to any question a person has, in our bible. The person just really needs have the desire to seek it out.

This leads us to what He was talking about in Hebrew 12:6 For whom the Lord loveth he chasteneth, and scourgeth every son whom he receiveth. 7 If ye endure chastening, God dealeth with you as with sons; for what son is he whom the father chasteneth not? 8 But if ye be without chastisement, whereof all are partakers, then are ye bastards, and not sons. Now Io know that there are a lot of people that think a bastard is a child that is born outside a man-made marriage, but this is far from the truth. No where in the bible does it talk about making a marriage legal by the law. Sex in agreement constitutes a marriage in the bible and yes, this is how they had many wives in the old testament, and we have many wives or husbands today.

I know that there are many that think that their loved ones are in heaven now but the covenant not over yet. Our bible tells us that no man has been to heaven, so why does man think that some are in heaven? John 3:13 And no man hath ascended up to heaven, but he that came down from heaven, even the Son of man which is in heaven. I am sure that there are many in which have passed, are still walking with us today. But now in a different body. Now let us listen to what we are told about a bastard in the old testament. Deuteronomy 23 He that is wounded in the stones, or hath his privy member cut off, shall not enter into the congregation of the Lord. 2 A bastard shall not enter into the congregation of the Lord; even to his tenth generation shall he not enter into the congregation of the Lord. I showed in the chapter Reigning with Christ, where the congregation of the Lord is. It is that simple to become a bastard, just refuse to listen to our Father. This goes a lot deeper than that though. In the last book we showed how there is 15 verses in the new testament that tell us to be sober, sober minded, or to think sober. There are 30 verses alone that mention our conscience. That is because this is half the battle.

Now we need to look at couple of different things. We are told that the people of Nineveh will be brought up in judgement. Matthew 12:41 The men of Nineveh shall rise in judgment with this generation, and shall condemn it: because they repented at the preaching of Jonas; and, behold, a greater than Jonas is here. Are you thinking these people are still alive? Now let us listen to Ezekiel 37 The hand of the

Lord was upon me, and carried me out in the spirit of the Lord, and set me down in the midst of the valley which was full of bones, 2 And caused me to pass by them round about: and, behold, there were very many in the open valley; and, lo, they were very dry. 3 And he said unto me, Son of man, can these bones live? And I answered, O Lord God, thou knowest. 4 Again he said unto me, Prophesy upon these bones, and say unto them, O ye dry bones, hear the word of the Lord. 5 Thus saith the Lord God unto these bones; Behold, I will cause breath to enter into you, and ye shall live: 6 And I will lay sinews upon you, and will bring up flesh upon you, and cover you with skin, and put breath in you, and ye shall live; and ye shall know that I am the Lord. 7 So I prophesied as I was commanded: and as I prophesied, there was a noise, and behold a shaking, and the bones came together, bone to his bone. 8 And when I beheld, lo, the sinews and the flesh came up upon them, and the skin covered them above: but there was no breath in them. 9 Then said he unto me, Prophesy unto the wind, prophesy, son of man, and say to the wind, Thus saith the Lord God; Come from the four winds, O breath, and breathe upon these slain, that they may live. 10 So I prophesied as he commanded me, and the breath came into them, and they lived, and stood up upon their feet, an exceeding great army. 11 Then he said unto me, Son of man, these bones are the whole house of Israel: behold, they say, Our bones are dried, and our hope is lost: we are cut off for our parts. 12 Therefore prophesy and say unto them, Thus saith the Lord God; Behold, O my people, I will open your graves, and cause you to come up out of your graves, and bring you into the land of Israel.

There are probably some that are thinking that this is about the soul that leaves an actual grave. Remember this is a vision and the bible is spiritual. Then listen to Jesus when he tells us that people are as graves. Luke 11:44 **Woe unto you, scribes and Pharisees, hypocrites! for ye are as graves which appear not, and the men that walk over them are not aware of them.** Then listen to what we are being told in Hebrews 9:27 And as it is appointed unto men once to die, but after this the judgment: Now if men are once appointed to die, and men are graves, then when we think about how these bones come back to life, we realize that it is because these bones are reincarnated back into a different body.

Before I do this next section, I do need to state that I am not a doctor. I do not have any medical background at all, and do not, by any means, make recommendations. This chastisement does not come by observation, just as the kingdom of God doesn't. This chastisement comes through our conscience. This is why we are told things like 1 Timothy 4:2 Speaking lies in hypocrisy; having their conscience seared with a hot iron; Now I know that there are many people that suffer from things like depression, anxiety, and things like that. So here is my thinking. I am also speaking from experience. When a person is depressed or something like that, could it be our Father chastising this person? He talks to us through our conscience. I was taking anti-depressants after I tried to take my life in 09. I did not feel any different when I was taking them. I actually quit taking them because they did not make me feel any different other than being a little hornier. I now know why, but at that time, I didn't have any of the knowledge I have now. When a person gets depressed, could this be because our Father is trying to tell you that you are doing something that He does not want you to do? I am not saying this is what is going on, however I am just asking if that is what could be going on for our Father will not tell me anything about what He wants for another person. He will only tell me what He wants or needs from me. But if it our Father is trying to chastise you and then you take these drugs and block Him out, could this now mean that you are now without chastisement? If so, this means that you become a bastard and will be kept in the out courts as we showed in the book of Reigning with Christ. Or better said in Matthew 8:11 And I say unto you, That many shall come from the east and west, and shall sit down with Abraham, and Isaac, and Jacob, in the kingdom of heaven. 12 But the children of the kingdom shall be cast out into outer darkness: there shall be weeping and gnashing of teeth. Notice how Jesus is telling us right here that we are in the kingdom right here.

WHERE IS SATAN LOCKED UP?

This chapter is going to take a lot of people for surprise. Some people might already be leaning to this idea after reading the chapters of believing and the thousand year reign. We are reigning with Christ now and the end of all things is at hand so we need to be learning where Satan will be loosed from. To understand this fully we will be jumping back in forth through our bibles. So, let us start with Revelation 12:9 **And the great dragon was cast out,** that old serpent, called the Devil, and Satan, which deceiveth the whole world: **he was cast out into the earth, and his angels were cast out with him. 10 And I heard a loud voice saying in heaven, Now is come salvation, and strength, and the kingdom of our God, and the power of his Christ: for the accuser of our brethren is cast down, which accused them before our God day and night. 11 And they overcame him by the blood of the Lamb, and by the word of their testimony; and they loved not their lives unto the death.** This is where Satan and his angels were cast out of heaven. Now let us listen to how many stars the dragon took to earth with him. Revelation 12:4 **And his tail drew the third part of the stars of heaven,** and did cast them to the earth: and the dragon stood before the woman which was ready to be delivered, for to devour her child as soon as it was born.

We are going to cover something right here before we get deep into this chapter. Now what did Adam and Eve do in the very beginning of the bible. Let us listen when God approached Adam. Genesis 3:9 And the Lord God called unto Adam, and said unto him, Where art thou? 10 And he said, I heard thy voice in the garden, and I was afraid, because I was naked; and I hid myself. 11 And he said, Who told thee that thou wast naked? Hast thou eaten of the tree, whereof I commanded thee that thou shouldest not eat? 12 **And the man said, The woman whom thou gavest to be with me, she gave me of the tree, and I did eat.** 13 And the Lord God said unto the woman, What is this that thou hast done? **And the woman said, The serpent beguiled me, and I did eat.** They blamed their disobedience on others. They would not take responsibility for their own actions. Let us just look at the difference between accuse and blame. The difference between BLAME and ACCUSE. BLAME – to say or think that a person is responsible for something wrong; hold someone responsible for an accident, bad situation or a problem. ACCUSE – to say that a person did something wrong or illegal; to charge with offense, fault or crime. We can see that they are pretty much the same thing.

Notice how in verse 10, the accuser was cast down to earth? I hear people say this all the time that it is someone else's fault that they did what they did. If you haven't heard it in this book or any of the other two, everything that goes wrong in our lives is our own fault and nobody else's. How many people today accuse someone else when something is wrong in their life? How many turns to the bible to find out why something is going wrong in their life? How many people make others feel as if they are worthless when they put the blame on others? How many of us ask our Father forgiveness for our trespasses but do not forgive others when they trespass against us?

Now I realize that there a lot of people in which believe that this is something that has not happened yet. I need to ask a question here, how many times do you think Satan is going to be cast out of heaven? Let us listen to our Father tell us that the great dragon is here already. By now we all should be realizing that the world is covered with Egypt and the spiritual waters of Egypt. Ezekiel 29 In the tenth year, in the tenth month, in the twelfth day of the month, the word of the Lord came unto me, saying, 2 Son of man, set thy face against Pharaoh king of Egypt, and prophesy against him, and against all Egypt: 3 Speak, and say, **Thus saith the Lord God; Behold, I am against thee, Pharaoh king of Egypt, the great dragon that lieth in the midst of his rivers, which hath said, My river is mine own, and I have made**

it for myself. As we showed in previous chapters, we are in Satan's kingdom now.

Now remember there was a star born when Jesus was born? Matthew 2 Now when Jesus was born in Bethlehem of Judaea in the days of Herod the king, behold, there came wise men from the east to Jerusalem, 2 Saying, Where is he that is born King of the Jews? **for we have seen his star in the east,** and are come to worship him. Now we showed in the last book that when we lift ourselves about the clouds and look down on the earth from above, we can see almost 8 billion functioning body parts of the son of God. Or almost 8 billion little Jesuses running around like little grasshoppers. Isaiah 40:22 It is he that sitteth upon the circle of the earth, **and the inhabitants thereof are as grasshoppers**; that stretcheth out the heavens as a curtain, and spreadeth them out as a tent to dwell in: I believe that there has been a star born and will be a star born, every time some soul is cast out of heaven.

Deuteronomy 1:10 The Lord your God hath multiplied you, and, behold, **ye are this day as the stars of heaven for multitude.** Deuteronomy 10:22 Thy fathers went down into Egypt with threescore and ten persons; and now the Lord thy God hath made thee as the stars of heaven for multitude. Deuteronomy 28:62 And ye shall be left few in number, **whereas ye were as the stars of heaven for multitude;** because thou wouldest not obey the voice of the Lord thy God. This when we got kicked out of heaven. Remember no man remember anything. This is when we were cast to the lowest part of hell. This probably happened 10's of millions of years ago. But we cleaved onto our Father somehow or another, and that is why our Father brought us to where His son's kingdom was established.

So now we need to go back to Genesis 1 In the beginning God created the heaven and the earth. 2 And the earth was without form, and void; and darkness was upon the face of the deep. And the Spirit of God moved upon the face of the waters. 3 **And God said, Let there be light: and there was light. 4 And God saw the light, that it was good: and God divided the light from the darkness. 5 And God called the light Day, and the darkness he called Night.** And the evening and the morning were the first day. 6 And God said, Let there be a firmament in the midst of the waters, and let it divide the waters from the waters. 7 And God made the firmament, and divided the waters which were under the firmament from the waters which were above the firmament: and it was so. 8 And God called the firmament Heaven. And the evening and the morning were the second day. 9 And God said, Let the waters under the heaven be gathered together unto one place, and let the dry land appear: and it was so. 10 And God called the dry land Earth; and the gathering together of the waters called he Seas: and God saw that it was good. 11 And God said, Let the earth bring forth grass, the herb yielding seed, and the fruit tree yielding fruit after his kind, whose seed is in itself, upon the earth: and it was so. 12 And the earth brought forth grass, and herb yielding seed after his kind, and the tree yielding fruit, whose seed was in itself, after his kind: and God saw that it was good. 13 And the evening and the morning were the third day.

Notice in the very beginning that the earth was without form and nothing but water? As you read you this, note that the human body is made up with 60% water. Note that the earth was full of darkness? That is because we were here and had been cast out of heaven, so we were without form, or light. Remember man was man before our Father breathed life into him. Genesis 2:7 **And the Lord God formed man of the dust of the ground,** and breathed into his nostrils the breath of life; **and man became a living soul.** Now remember that the land wasn't here but our Father brought up the land from under the waters to divide the waters. Then formed man from the dust of the earth. Now let us listen to what Abraham said. Genesis 18:27 And Abraham answered and said, Behold now, I have taken upon me to speak unto the Lord, **which am but dust and ashes:** God formed man from the dust in which our Father brought up from under the water.

This was the process of Satan being lockup right here. When he was cast out of heaven, they rejoiced for he could no longer deceive the nations that are in heaven. Revelation 12:9 **And the great dragon was cast out, that old serpent, called the Devil, and Satan, which deceiveth the whole world: he was cast out into the earth, and his**

angels were cast out with him. 10 And I heard a loud voice saying in heaven, Now is come salvation, and strength, and the kingdom of our God, and the power of his Christ: for the accuser of our brethren is cast down, which accused them before our God day and night. 11 And they overcame him by the blood of the Lamb, and by the word of their testimony; and they loved not their lives unto the death. 12 Therefore rejoice, ye heavens, and ye that dwell in them. **Woe to the inhabiters of the earth and of the sea! for the devil is come down unto you, having great wrath, because he knoweth that he hath but a short time.** We are being told right here that Satan is cast down to the earth so woe, to the inhabiters of the earth. Remember in the spiritual world, a short time could be thousands of years. Where he is locked up, will surprise many.

Remember how Jesus told us to pray. Matthew 6:9 After this manner therefore pray ye: Our Father which art in heaven, Hallowed be thy name. 10 Thy kingdom come, **Thy will be done in earth, as it is in heaven.** 11 Give us this day our daily bread. 12 And forgive us our debts, as we forgive our debtors. 13 And lead us not into temptation, but deliver us from evil: For thine is the kingdom, and the power, and the glory, for ever. Amen.

This is where Satan was sent before our Father formed man from the dust of the ground. This is why we told that the earth is given over to the wicked. Job 9:24 **The earth is given into the hand of the wicked: he covereth the faces of the judges thereof; if not, where, and who is he?** In the last book we showed where the son of perdition sits. We are going to have to cover some of that again. We know that we are the temple of God, right? 1 Corinthians 3:16 **Know ye not that ye are the temple of God, and that the Spirit of God dwelleth in you?** Now let us listen to where the son of perdition sits. 2 Thessalonians 2 Now we beseech you, brethren, by the coming of our Lord Jesus Christ, and by our gathering together unto him, 2 That ye be not soon shaken in mind, or be troubled, neither by spirit, nor by word, nor by letter as from us, as that the day of Christ is at hand. 3 **Let no man deceive you by any means: for that day shall not come, except there come a falling away first, and that man of** sin be revealed, the son of perdition; 4 Who opposeth and exalteth himself above all that is called God, or that is worshipped; so that he as God sitteth in the temple of God, shewing himself that he is God.** The son of perdition sits in each person on the planet as we showed in the last book.

This is when we need to be paying attention to what Jesus was talking about when he said a kingdom cannot be divided. Matthew 12:25 And Jesus knew their thoughts, and said unto them, **Every kingdom divided against itself is brought to desolation; and every city or house divided against itself shall not stand: 26 And if Satan cast out Satan, he is divided against himself; how shall then his kingdom stand?** Remember our Father is working a works that no man will believe. When I went out willingly to die and the spirit of Jesus took over David's body, Satan's kingdom no longer had dominion over me. I forced my house to worship God and God only.

Side note here. This is why it is going to hurt so bad for so many. Remember when Jesus told the parable of the rich man? Matthew 19:21 Jesus said unto him, **If thou wilt be perfect, go and sell that thou hast, and give to the poor, and thou shalt have treasure in heaven: and come and follow me.** 22 But when the young man heard that saying, he went away sorrowful: for he had great possessions. There are going to be so many people that are not willing to give things up of this world. But our Father is going to bring this world to an end. All those that are not willing to give up their possessions, will have them stripped from them and it will hurt. There is no way to stop it. This makes me think of when we are told that a woman forgets the travail after the child is born. John 16:20 Verily, verily, I say unto you, That ye shall weep and lament, but the world shall rejoice: and ye shall be sorrowful, but your sorrow shall be turned into joy. 21 A woman when she is in travail hath sorrow, because her hour is come: but as soon as she is delivered of the child, she remembereth no more the anguish, for joy that a man is born into the world.

These kingdoms are the kingdoms in which we live now. Let us listen to Daniel 2:27 Daniel answered in the presence of the king, and said, The secret which the king hath demanded cannot the wise men, the astrologers, the magicians, the soothsayers, shew unto the king; 28 But there is a God in heaven that revealeth secrets, and maketh known to the king Nebuchadnezzar what shall be in the latter days. Thy dream, and the visions of thy head upon thy bed, are these; 29 As for thee, O king, thy thoughts came into thy mind upon thy bed, what should come to pass hereafter: and he that revealeth secrets maketh known to thee what shall come to pass. 30 But as for me, this secret is not revealed to me for any wisdom that I have more than any living, but for their sakes that shall make known the interpretation to the king, and that thou mightest know the thoughts of thy heart. 31 Thou, O king, sawest, and behold a great image. This great image, whose brightness was excellent, stood before thee; and the form thereof was terrible. 32 This image's head was of fine gold, his breast and his arms of silver, his belly and his thighs of brass, 33 His legs of iron, his feet part of iron and part of clay. 34 Thou sawest till that a stone was cut out without hands, which smote the image upon his feet that were of iron and clay, and brake them to pieces. 35 Then was the iron, the clay, the brass, the silver, and the gold, broken to pieces together, and became like the chaff of the summer threshingfloors; and the wind carried them away, that no place was found for them: and the stone that smote the image became a great mountain, and filled the whole earth. 36 This is the dream; and we will tell the interpretation thereof before the king. 37 Thou, O king, art a king of kings: for the God of heaven hath given thee a kingdom, power, and strength, and glory. 38 And wheresoever the children of men dwell, the beasts of the field and the fowls of the heaven hath he given into thine hand, and hath made thee ruler over them all. Thou art this head of gold. 39 And after thee shall arise another kingdom inferior to thee, and another third kingdom of brass, which shall bear rule over all the earth. 40 And the fourth kingdom shall be strong as iron: forasmuch as iron breaketh in pieces and subdueth all things: and as iron that breaketh all these, shall it break in pieces and bruise. 41 And whereas thou sawest the feet and toes, part of potters' clay, and part of iron, the kingdom shall be divided; but there shall be in it of the strength of the iron, forasmuch as thou sawest the iron mixed with miry clay. 42

And as the toes of the feet were part of iron, and part of clay, so the kingdom shall be partly strong, and partly broken. 43 And whereas thou sawest iron mixed with miry clay, they shall mingle themselves with the seed of men: but they shall not cleave one to another, even as iron is not mixed with clay. 44 And in the days of these kings shall the God of heaven set up a kingdom, which shall never be destroyed: and the kingdom shall not be left to other people, but it shall break in pieces and consume all these kingdoms, and it shall stand for ever. 45 Forasmuch as thou sawest that the stone was cut out of the mountain without hands, and that it brake in pieces the iron, the brass, the clay, the silver, and the gold; the great God hath made known to the king what shall come to pass hereafter: and the dream is certain, and the interpretation thereof sure.

Remember the spiritual mountain that our Father is on? Remember man is not made with hands? This image that king Nebuchadnezzar saw, is the how the man is made. In the last book, we showed that Jesus is building the tabernacle without his hands throughout the entire world. These kingdoms go throughout the entire world as well. These different areas of the body in this image represents parts of us. Now we showed in the last book, how we must get to know the Father and learn of the Father before He raises Jesus up in our bodies. He is in our bodies doing what must be done. As we showed just a bit ago, he is the one that reports to the Father on that mountain shown in Ezekiel. So, no you are not getting to the Father but through Jesus. Notice how the Iron breaks all things.

Then notice how the toes are partly iron and partly clay. Now let us listen to a couple of spots in which we can hear that we are formed out of clay. Job 33:6 **Behold, I am according to thy wish in God's stead: I also am formed out of the clay.** Isaiah 64:8 But now, O Lord, thou art our father; **we are the clay, and thou our potter; and we all are the work of thy hand.** Then notice how the kingdom should be partly strong and then partly broken. That is because Jesus is the Iron made with the toes, we are the clay in the toes. Jesus is the strong part and the people are partly broken. Now let us look at the head of this image. It is made of gold and is said to be king Nebuchadnezzar. Let is look at that Jeremiah 49:28 Concerning Kedar, and concerning the kingdoms of Hazor, which Nebuchadrezzar king of Babylon shall smite, thus saith the Lord; Arise ye, go up to Kedar, and spoil the men of the east. Remember how I told you that I didn't read the bible until I was 41 years of age. I didn't understand it for it confused me. So, let us look up the definition of Babylon. H894 bâbel baw-bel' From H1101; **confusion;** Babel (that is, Babylon), including Babylonia and the Babylonian empire:–Babel, Babylon.

We are going to get side tracked here for a minute for we want to show how this connects to Genesis. Let us listen to Daniel 4 Nebuchadnezzar the king, unto all people, nations, and languages, that dwell in all the earth; Peace be multiplied unto you. 2 I thought it good to shew the signs and wonders that the high God hath wrought toward me. 3 How great are his signs! and how mighty are his wonders! his kingdom is an everlasting kingdom, and his dominion is from generation to generation. 4 I Nebuchadnezzar was at rest in mine house, and flourishing in my palace: 5 I saw a dream which made me afraid, and the thoughts upon my bed and the visions of my head troubled me. 6 Therefore made I a decree to bring in all the wise men of Babylon before me, that they might make known unto me the interpretation of the dream. 7 Then came in the magicians, the astrologers, the Chaldeans, and the soothsayers: and I told the dream before them; but they did not make known unto me the interpretation thereof. 8 But at the last Daniel came in before me, whose name was Belteshazzar, according to the name of my God, and in whom is the spirit of the holy gods: and before him I told the dream, saying, 9 O Belteshazzar, master of the magicians, because I know that the spirit of the holy gods is in thee, and no secret troubleth thee, tell me the visions of my dream that I have seen, and the interpretation thereof. 10 Thus were the visions of mine head in my bed; I saw, and behold a tree in the midst of the earth, and the height thereof was great. 11 The tree grew, and was strong, and the height thereof reached unto heaven, and the sight thereof to the end of all the earth: 12 The leaves thereof were fair, and the fruit thereof much, and in it was meat for all: the beasts of the field had shadow under it, and the fowls of the heaven dwelt in the boughs thereof, and all flesh was fed of it. 13 I saw in the visions of my head upon my bed, and, behold, a watcher and an holy one came down from heaven; 14 He cried aloud, and said thus, Hew down the tree, and cut off his branches, shake off his leaves, and scatter his fruit: let the beasts get away from under it, and the fowls from his branches: 15 Nevertheless leave the stump of his roots in the earth, even with a band of iron and brass, in the tender grass of the field; and let it be wet with the dew of heaven, and let his portion be with the beasts in the grass of the earth: 16 Let his heart be changed from man's, and let a beast's heart be given unto him; and let seven times pass over him. 17 This matter is by the decree of the watchers, and the demand by the word of the holy ones: to the intent that the living may that the most High ruleth in the kingdom of men, and giveth it to whomsoever he will, and setteth up over it the basest of men. 18 This dream I king Nebuchadnezzar have seen. Now thou, O Belteshazzar, declare the interpretation thereof, forasmuch as all the wise men of my kingdom are not able to make known unto me the interpretation: but thou art able; for the spirit of the holy gods is in thee. 19 Then Daniel, whose name was Belteshazzar, was astonied for one hour, and his thoughts troubled him. The king spake, and said, Belteshazzar, let not the dream, or the interpretation thereof, trouble thee. Belteshazzar answered and said, My lord, the dream be to them that hate thee, and the interpretation thereof to thine enemies. 20 **The tree that thou sawest, which grew, and was strong, whose height reached unto the heaven, and the sight thereof to all the earth;** 21 Whose leaves were fair, and the fruit thereof much, and in it was meat for all; under which the beasts of the field dwelt, and upon whose branches the fowls of the heaven had their habitation: 22 It is thou, O king, that art grown and become strong: for thy greatness is grown, and reacheth unto heaven, and thy dominion to the end of the earth. 23 And whereas the king saw a watcher and an holy one coming down from heaven, and saying, Hew the tree down, and destroy it; yet leave the stump of the roots thereof in the earth, even with a band of iron and brass, in the tender grass of the field; and let it be wet with the dew of heaven, and let his portion be with the beasts of the field, till seven times pass over him; 24 This is the interpretation, O king, and this is the decree of the most High, which is come upon my lord the king: 25 That they shall drive thee from men, and thy dwelling shall be with the beasts of the field, and they shall make thee to eat grass as oxen, and they shall wet thee with the dew of heaven, and seven times shall pass over thee, till thou know that the most High ruleth in the kingdom of men, and giveth it to whomsoever he will. 26 And whereas they commanded to leave the stump of the tree roots; thy kingdom shall be sure unto thee, after that thou shalt have known that the heavens do rule. 27 Wherefore, O king, let my counsel be acceptable unto thee, and break off thy sins by righteousness, and thine iniquities by shewing mercy to the poor; if it may be a lengthening of thy tranquillity. 28 All this came upon the king Nebuchadnezzar. 29 At the end of twelve months he walked in the palace of the kingdom of Babylon. 30 The king spake, and said, Is not this great Babylon, that I have built for the house of the kingdom by the might of my power, and for the honour of my majesty? 31 While the word was in the king's mouth, there fell a voice from heaven, saying, O king Nebuchadnezzar, to thee it is spoken; The kingdom is departed from thee. 32 **And they shall drive thee from men, and thy dwelling shall be with the beasts of the field: they shall make thee to eat grass as oxen, and seven times shall pass over thee, until thou know that the most High ruleth in the kingdom of men, and giveth it to whomsoever he will.** 33 The same hour was the thing fulfilled upon Nebuchadnezzar: and he was driven from men, and did eat grass as oxen, and his body was wet with the dew of heaven, till his hairs were grown like eagles' feathers, and his nails like birds' claws. 34 And at the end of the days I Nebuchadnezzar lifted up mine eyes unto heaven, and mine understanding returned unto me, and I blessed the most High, and I praised and honoured him that liveth for ever, whose dominion is an everlasting dominion, and his kingdom is from generation to generation: 35 And all the inhabitants of the earth are reputed as nothing: and he doeth according to his will in the army of heaven, and among the inhabitants of the earth: and none can stay his hand, or say unto him, What doest thou? 36

At the same time my reason returned unto me; and for the glory of my kingdom, mine honour and brightness returned unto me; and my counsellors and my lords sought unto me; and I was established in my kingdom, and excellent majesty was added unto me. 37 Now I Nebuchadnezzar praise and extol and honour the King of heaven, all whose works are truth, and his ways judgment: and those that walk in pride he is able to abase.

Genesis 11 And the whole earth was of one language, and of one speech. 2 And it came to pass, as they journeyed from the east, that they found a plain in the land of Shinar; and they dwelt there. 3 And they said one to another, Go to, let us make brick, and burn them thoroughly. And they had brick for stone, and slime had they for morter. 4 And they said, Go to, let us build us a city and a tower, whose top may reach unto heaven; and let us make us a name, lest we be scattered abroad upon the face of the whole earth. 5 And the Lord came down to see the city and the tower, which the children of men builded. 6 And the Lord said, Behold, the people is one, and they have all one language; and this they begin to do: and now nothing will be restrained from them, which they have imagined to do. 7 Go to, let us go down, and there confound their language, that they may not understand one another's speech. 8 So the Lord scattered them abroad from thence upon the face of all the earth: and they left off to build the city. 9 Therefore is the name of it called Babel; because the Lord did there confound the language of all the earth: and from thence did the Lord scatter them abroad upon the face of all the earth.

Can you hear the similarities here? Are you seeing how the entire bible in connected as one long letter of instructions as to how we are to live our lives today? Then the king was told that He would reign until seven times passed over. Let us do a google search and listen to what a times means. Historicist interpreters have usually understood the "time, times and half a time" (i.e. 1+2+0.5=3.5), "1,260 days" and "42 months" mentioned in Daniel and Revelation to be references to represent a period of 1260 years (based on the 360 day Jewish year multiplied by 3.5) Day-year principle. But yet, this king is commanded to do this for seven times. How many years is that exactly?

Now to get back on track. Notice how these kingdoms have rule over the entire earth. Then pay attention to how at the end of the chapter how we are told that God will set up a kingdom that will destroy all the other kingdoms. It will not be left to the other people. This is after we get to know our Father and He completely raises His invisible son inside of us. This will be the end of the world and everybody will be judged by every word they speak. Matthew 12:36 But I say unto you, **That every idle word that men shall speak, they shall give account thereof in the day of judgment. 37 For by thy words thou shalt be justified, and by thy words thou shalt be condemned.**

Now back to the kingdoms in which cannot be divided. This is where we realize that our Father will not force himself on us. It truly must be our own choice as to which god we will serve. Let us listen to what our Father told Satan after he beguiled Eve. Genesis 3 **Now the serpent was more subtil than any beast of the field which the Lord God had made.** And he said unto the woman, Yea, hath God said, Ye shall not eat of every tree of the garden? 2 And the woman said unto the serpent, We may eat of the fruit of the trees of the garden: 3 But of the fruit of the tree which is in the midst of the garden, God hath said, Ye shall not eat of it, neither shall ye touch it, lest ye die. 4 And the serpent said unto the woman, Ye shall not surely die: 5 For God doth know that in the day ye eat thereof, then your eyes shall be opened, and ye shall be as gods, knowing good and evil. 6 And when the woman saw that the tree was good for food, and that it was pleasant to the eyes, and a tree to be desired to make one wise, she took of the fruit thereof, and did eat, and gave also unto her husband with her; and he did eat. 7 And the eyes of them both were opened, and they knew that they were naked; and they sewed fig leaves together, and made themselves aprons. 8 And they heard the voice of the Lord God walking in the garden in the cool of the day: and Adam and his wife hid themselves from the presence of the Lord God amongst the trees of the garden. 9 And the Lord God called unto Adam, and said unto him, Where art thou? 10 And he said, I heard thy voice in the garden, and I was afraid, because I was naked; and I hid myself. 11

And he said, Who told thee that thou wast naked? Hast thou eaten of the tree, whereof I commanded thee that thou shouldest not eat? 12 And the man said, The woman whom thou gavest to be with me, she gave me of the tree, and I did eat. 13 And the Lord God said unto the woman, What is this that thou hast done? And the woman said, The serpent beguiled me, and I did eat. 14 **And the Lord God said unto the serpent, Because thou hast done this, thou art cursed above all cattle, and above every beast of the field; upon thy belly shalt thou go, and dust shalt thou eat all the days of thy life:**

First thing we need to paying attention to is the very first verse of this chapter. We have touched on this in this book and really laid it out in the last book. Man is counted as beast. Note that our Father did not say that the serpent is a beast. Man has just naturally assumed with his imagination that this must be some creature or something. Notice how He said it is more subtle than any beast. That includes man. This is just another reason our Father had me name the first book as He did. Father, forgive us, we haven't been listening. Now pay attention to where our Father said the serpent would be. Remember how we are made in their image and we have dominion over the beast of the field? Notice how he is above the beast of the field? Many have heard upon thy belly shalt thou go and just naturally figured this to be a snake or something. Let us jump back to Daniel 2:32 This image's head was of fine gold, his breast and his arms of silver, **his belly and his thighs of brass,** Now that we are learning that we are the image in which this king saw, we can know that this is our belly. Our Father cursed Satan to our bellies. God was saying on the man's belly thou shalt go.

Now we are going to look at something that might freak you out as it did me when our Father brought this to my attention. Notice how God said dust shalt thou eat all of the days of thy life. Let us do a google search to show how much dust the human body eats. As it turns out, the average person ingests about 100 milligrams of dirt every single day. Overall, that equates to roughly six pounds of dirt in an average lifespan! That's right, dirt is actually a pretty common staple of the human diet. Apr 29, 2015 Strange Facts–**The Average Person eats 6 LBS of dirt in their lifetime.**

Now let us listen to few things we are told about our belly. Psalm 44:25 For our soul is bowed down to the dust: **our belly cleaveth unto the earth.** Remember we came from the dust. Job 15:2 Should a wise man utter vain knowledge, **and fill his belly with the east wind?** Job 15:35 They conceive mischief, and bring forth vanity, **and their belly prepareth deceit.** Job 20:20 **Surely he shall not feel quietness in his belly,** he shall not save of that which he desired. Job 32:19 Behold, **my belly is as wine which hath no vent; it is ready to burst like new bottles.** Philippians 3:19 **Whose end is destruction, whose God is their belly, and whose glory is in their shame, who mind earthly things.)** Romans 16:18 **For they that are such serve not our Lord Jesus Christ, but their own belly; and by good words and fair speeches deceive the hearts of the simple.**

Now this that we are now hearing in Job 32 is going to take us on a little journey. We need to listen to when Jesus talks about putting wine into old bottles. Matthew 9:17 Neither do men put new wine into old bottles: else the bottles break, and the wine runneth out, and the bottles perish: but they put new wine into new bottles, and both are preserved. This is where we need to realize that wine in knowledge in the bible. So, when Jesus turned water in wine, he actually turned basic knowledge into a more in-depth knowledge. Remember this was what happened to me when I willingly gave everything I owned to the poor and needy and went out in the wilderness to die. When I went out, that was me giving up the things and ways of this world. That was the old wine being poured out and then I had this new wine poured into me. If our Father would have tried to pour this knowledge into me while I was yet in the old body of David, I would have lost my mind. I would have not understood of what I am being taught and would have vomited it up. It would not have broken the kingdom in which was in my belly. To help some to understand this, just read the books and listen to how a 49-year old man that failed at school, marriage (by mans terms), and college can understand the bible in the fashion that I do. Then wrap all that up into one shot.

This is what Jesus was talking about when he said Matthew 9:15 And Jesus said unto them, Can the children of the bridechamber mourn, as long as the bridegroom is with them? but the days will come, when the bridegroom shall be taken from them, and then shall they fast. 16 No man putteth a piece of new cloth unto an old garment, for that which is put in to fill it up taketh from the garment, and the rent is made worse. 17 Neither do men put new wine into old bottles: else the bottles break, and the wine runneth out, and the bottles perish: but they put new wine into new bottles, and both are preserved. This was me, when I went into the wilderness to die. I got rid of all the old wine when I willingly gave up everything of this world and even a place to lay my head. To this day, I have no place to call home.

Now to get back on the belly. Proverbs 13:25 The righteous eateth to the satisfying of his soul: **but the belly of the wicked shall want.** Habakkuk 3:16 When I heard, **my belly trembled;** my lips quivered at the voice: rottenness entered into my bones, and I trembled in myself, that I might rest in the day of trouble: when he cometh up unto the people, he will invade them with his troops. Now when we read this it makes me think of James 2:19 Thou believest that there is one God; thou doest well: **the devils also believe, and tremble.** That is where these devils are. We all think of these things as being things we should be able to see, however just as our Father and Jesus are invisible, so are all these spirits.

This is how Satan is able to walk to and fro in the earth even though he is locked up. He is locked up inside of man. Listen to God and Satan talked with one another in Job 1:7 And the Lord said unto Satan, Whence comest thou? **Then Satan answered the Lord, and said, From going to and fro in the earth, and from walking up and down in it.** God dwells inside us and so does Satan.

Remember how Jesus said the kingdom of God does not come with observation, but the kingdom is within you. Luke 17:20 And when he was demanded of the Pharisees, when the kingdom of God should come, he answered them and said, **The kingdom of God cometh not with observation: 21 Neither shall they say, Lo here! or, lo there! for, behold, the kingdom of God is within you.** This is the kingdom that is made up iron and clay. Remember how Satan will bruise the feet of the son of God. Genesis 3:15 And I will put enmity between thee and the woman, and between thy seed and her seed; **it shall bruise thy head, and thou shalt bruise his heel.** Bruising the head is bruising our conscience for that is where are minds are. And look at what we walk on all the time. Are you starting to see this image in your head as the king seen it? Remember how everybody is part of the son of God.

This is why we are told that many people will not inherit the kingdom of God. 1 Corinthians 6:9 Know ye not that the unrighteous shall not inherit the kingdom of God? Be not deceived: neither fornicators, nor idolaters, nor adulterers, nor effeminate, nor abusers of themselves with mankind, 10 Nor thieves, nor covetous, nor drunkards, nor revilers, nor extortioners, shall inherit the kingdom of God. 11 And such were some of you: but ye are washed, but ye are sanctified, but ye are justified in the name of the Lord Jesus, and by the Spirit of our God. 12 All things are lawful unto me, but all things are not expedient: all things are lawful for me, but I will not be brought under the power of any. 13 Meats for the belly, and the belly for meats: but God shall destroy both it and them. Now the body is not for fornication, but for the Lord; and the Lord for the body. Galatians 5:19 Now the works of the flesh are manifest, which are these; Adultery, fornication, uncleanness, lasciviousness, 20 Idolatry, witchcraft, hatred, variance, emulations, wrath, strife, seditions, heresies, 21 Envyings, murders, drunkenness, revellings, and such like: of the which I tell you before, as I have also told you in time past, that they which do such things shall not inherit the kingdom of God.

So, this is where I ask you to look deep into yourself and really think about what you think of other people. Then remember the cross that they are carrying. It is not gold, silver, wooden, or any other kind of material in which is a graven image. It is a spiritual cross built into their bodies. I am not talking about just the people in your immediate family. I am talking about any person you see with your eyes in your life. If you lay your eyes on them, they are now your neighbor. We are in the kingdom of God if it is within a person, even though most can't see it. Quick example, I cannot see you reading this book, does that mean you are not reading it?

Now we need to be realizing something else too. 2 Corinthians 2:15 For we are unto God a sweet savour of Christ, in them that are saved, and in them that perish: 16 **To the one we are the savour of death unto death; and to the other the savour of life unto life.** And who is sufficient for these things. 17 For we are not as many, which corrupt the word of God: but as of sincerity, but as of God, in the sight of God speak we in Christ. Remember how a sacrifice can be a sweet savour unto our Father? Leviticus 3:5 And Aaron's sons shall burn it on the altar upon the burnt sacrifice, which is upon the wood that is on the fire: **it is an offering made by fire, of a sweet savour unto the Lord.** Ezra 6:9 And that which they have need of, both young bullocks, and rams, and lambs, for the burnt offerings of the God of heaven, wheat, salt, wine, and oil, according to the appointment of the priests which are at Jerusalem, let it be given them day by day without fail: 10 **That they may offer sacrifices of sweet savours unto the God of heaven, and pray for the life of the king, and of his sons.** 11 Also I have made a decree, **that whosoever shall alter this word,** let timber be pulled down from his house, and being set up, let him be hanged thereon; and let his house be made a dunghill for this. How many people make sacrifices and make sure others know about it. Such as doing you alms to be seen by man. How many will drive by the poor and needy and ignore them so that they can give some guy standing behind a pulpit so that he can make his garments enlarge. Remember Jesus said to follow him, take up your cross and follow him. In other words, take up a bubble of love and give it unto others just as Jesus did.

I am going to post something that just happened minutes ago. I decided to take a little break and go for a walk. It is now after 1 am, so when I went outside, I could see lightning and could hear thunder in the distance. As I am walking, I hear this guy yell something towards me. I crossed the street to get closer. As I approached, he explained that he has been asking people for just some change, he was trying to get $10 for he and his family needed to get into their room but needed $10 more. He told me that he had been asking for a few hours now. If

I loose my reward for telling this, then so be it. I gave him $20. You could just hear the sigh of relief in his voice. I didn't look at his skin color, I didn't think about whether or not he deserved it. I saw a fellow servant of God in need of some help. It is not for me to judge whether or not if this man is going to do right or wrong with this money. I know that if he does wrong or get the money on false pretenses, then he is the one that must answer for that. I have done well no matter what. Now if I would have just thought he is not worth it, even he was doing wrong, then we both would have had to answer to our Father.

I am sure it was our Father in which caused me to go for the short walk because about 10 -15 minutes after I gave him the money, and he got his family in the room, it started to downpour. But this just reminds me of the scriptures that tell us that everyman is out for his own gain. Philippians 2:21 For all seek their own, not the things which are Jesus Christ's. Isaiah 56:10 His watchmen are blind: they are all ignorant, they are all dumb dogs, they cannot bark; sleeping, lying down, loving to slumber. 11 Yea, they are greedy dogs which can never have enough, and they are shepherds that cannot understand: they all look to their own way, every one for his gain, from his quarter. Now we can understand what the scriptures are saying when we hear they serve their own belly. Philippians 3:18 (For many walk, of whom I have told you often, and now tell you even weeping, that they are the enemies of the cross of Christ:19 **Whose end is destruction, whose God is their belly, and whose glory is in their shame, who mind earthly things.)**

Now listen to what we are being told in Ephesians 4:28 Let him that stole steal no more: but rather let him labour, working with his hands the thing which is good, that he may have to give to him that needeth. When we listen to this, we can hear that the reason we work is so that we can help others. How is buying fancy cars, fancy boats, fancy clothes, and any other thing that is not a basic need to survive, working to help others? This was really shown in the chapter of Jesus the Carpenter in the last book. These are those that have not had Christ come into them and flip the tables of their hearts. 2 Corinthians 3:3 Forasmuch as ye are manifestly declared to be the epistle of Christ ministered by us, written not with ink, but with the Spirit of the living God; not in tables of stone, **but in fleshy tables of the heart.** Psalm 69:22 Let their table become a snare before them: and that which should have been for their welfare, let it become a trap. Romans 11:9 And David saith, Let their table be made a snare, and a trap, and a stumblingblock, and a recompence unto them: These tables are full of things of this world for yourself and not others. Notice how these tables are fleshy and not of God.

This is where we realize that man is Satan. Listen to Jesus when he rebuked Satan. Matthew 16:21 From that time forth began Jesus to shew unto his disciples, how that he must go unto Jerusalem, and suffer many things of the elders and chief priests and scribes, and be killed, and be raised again the third day. 22 Then Peter took him, and began to rebuke him, saying, Be it far from thee, Lord: this shall not be unto thee. 23 **But he turned, and said unto Peter, Get thee behind me, Satan: thou art an offence unto me: for thou savourest not the things that be of God, but those that be of men.** Wait, I thought Peter is a disciple? Yea that is right, instantly turned into Satan when he didn't think Jesus should die the way that he said. John 2:23 Now when he was in Jerusalem at the passover, in the feast day, many believed in his name, when they saw the miracles which he did. 24 **But Jesus did not commit himself unto them, because he knew all men, 25 And needed not that any should testify of man: for he knew what was in man.**

Now we need to go back and listen to what the serpent told Eve. Genesis 3:4 And the serpent said unto the woman, Ye shall not surely die: Hear what he is telling Eve? He is saying you will not die. Let us listen to why our Father hated Esau. Let us listen to the story of Jacob and Esau. Genesis 25:27 And the boys grew: and Esau was a cunning hunter, a man of the field; and Jacob was a plain man, dwelling in tents. 28 And Isaac loved Esau, because he did eat of his venison: but Rebekah loved Jacob. 29 And Jacob sod pottage: and Esau came from the field, and he was faint: 30 And Esau said to Jacob, Feed me, I pray thee, with that same red pottage; for I am faint: therefore was his name called Edom. 31 And Jacob said, Sell me this day thy birthright. 32 **And Esau said, Behold, I am at the point to die: and what profit shall this birthright do to me?** 33 And Jacob said, Swear to me this day; and he sware unto him: and he sold his birthright unto Jacob. 34 Then Jacob gave Esau bread and pottage of lentiles; and he did eat and drink, and rose up, and went his way: thus Esau despised his birthright.

Now this is where we going to have to listen what the outcome was for Esau when Esau sold his birthright for a morsel of meat. Genesis 27 And it came to pass, that when Isaac was old, and his eyes were dim, so that he could not see, he called Esau his eldest son, and said unto him, My son: and he said unto him, Behold, here am I. 2 And he said, Behold now, I am old, I know not the day of my death: 3 Now therefore take, I pray thee, thy weapons, thy quiver and thy bow, and go out to the field, and take me some venison; 4 And make me savoury meat, such as I love, and bring it to me, that I may eat; that my soul may bless thee before I die. 5 And Rebekah heard when Isaac spake to Esau his son. And Esau went to the field to hunt for venison, and to bring it. 6 And Rebekah spake unto Jacob her son, saying, Behold, I heard thy father speak unto Esau thy brother, saying, 7 Bring me venison, and make me savoury meat, that I may eat, and bless thee before the Lord before my death. 8 Now therefore, my son, obey my voice according to that which I command thee. 9 Go now to the flock, and fetch me from thence two good kids of the goats; and I will make them savoury meat for thy father, such as he loveth: 10 And thou shalt bring it to thy father, that he may eat, and that he may bless thee before his death. 11 And Jacob said to Rebekah his mother, Behold, Esau my brother is a hairy man, and I am a smooth man: 12 My father peradventure will feel me, and I shall seem to him as a deceiver; and I shall bring a curse upon me, and not a blessing. 13 And his mother said unto him, Upon me be thy curse, my son: only obey my voice, and go fetch me them. 14 And he went, and fetched, and brought them to his mother: and his mother made savoury meat, such as his father loved. 15 And Rebekah took goodly raiment of her eldest son Esau, which were with her in the house, and put them upon Jacob her younger son: 16 And she put the skins of the kids of the goats upon his hands, and upon the smooth of his neck: 17 And she gave the savoury meat and the bread, which she had prepared, into the hand of her son Jacob. 18 And he came unto his father, and said, My father: and he said, Here am I; who art thou, my son? 19 And Jacob said unto his father, I am Esau thy first born; I have done according as thou badest me: arise, I pray thee, sit and eat of my venison, that thy soul may bless me. 20 And Isaac said unto his son, How is it that thou hast found it so quickly, my son? And he said, Because the Lord thy God brought it to me. 21 And Isaac said unto Jacob, Come near, I pray thee, that I may feel thee, my son, whether thou be my very son Esau or not. 22 And Jacob went near unto Isaac his father; and he felt him, and said, The voice is Jacob's voice, but the hands are the hands of Esau. 23 And he discerned him not, because his hands were hairy, as his brother Esau's hands: so he blessed him. 24 And he said, Art thou my very son Esau? And he said, I am. 25 And he said, Bring it near to me, and I will eat of my son's venison, that my soul may bless thee. And he brought it near to him, and he did eat: and he brought him wine and he drank. 26 And his father Isaac said unto him, Come near now, and kiss me, my son. 27 And he came near, and kissed him: and he smelled the smell of his raiment, and blessed him, and said, See, the smell of my son is as the smell of a field which the Lord hath blessed: 28 Therefore God give thee of the dew of heaven, and the fatness of the earth, and plenty of corn and wine: 29 Let people serve thee, and nations bow down to thee: be lord over thy brethren, and let thy mother's sons bow down to thee: cursed be every one that curseth thee, and blessed be he that blesseth thee. 30 And it came to pass, as soon as Isaac had made an end of blessing Jacob, and Jacob was yet scarce gone out from the presence of Isaac his father, that Esau his brother came in from his hunting. 31 And he also had made savoury meat, and brought it unto his father, and said unto his father, Let my father arise, and eat of his son's venison, that thy soul may bless me. 32 And Isaac his father said unto him, Who art thou? And he said, I am thy son, thy firstborn Esau. 33 And Isaac trembled very exceedingly, and said, Who? where is he that hath taken venison, and brought it me, and I have eaten of all before thou camest, and have blessed him?

yea, and he shall be blessed. 34 And when Esau heard the words of his father, he cried with a great and exceeding bitter cry, and said unto his father, Bless me, even me also, O my father. 35 And he said, **Thy brother came with subtilty, and hath taken away thy blessing. 36 And he said, Is not he rightly named Jacob? for he hath supplanted me these two times: he took away my birthright; and, behold, now he hath taken away my blessing.** And he said, Hast thou not reserved a blessing for me? 37 And Isaac answered and said unto Esau, Behold, I have made him thy lord, and all his brethren have I given to him for servants; and with corn and wine have I sustained him: and what shall I do now unto thee, my son? 38 And Esau said unto his father, Hast thou but one blessing, my father? bless me, even me also, O my father. And Esau lifted up his voice, and wept. 39 And Isaac his father answered and said unto him, Behold, thy dwelling shall be the fatness of the earth, and of the dew of heaven from above; 40 And by thy sword shalt thou live, and shalt serve thy brother; and it shall come to pass when thou shalt have the dominion, that thou shalt break his yoke from off thy neck. 41 **And Esau hated Jacob because of the blessing wherewith his father blessed him: and Esau said in his heart, The days of mourning for my father are at hand; then will I slay my brother Jacob. 42 And these words of Esau her elder son were told to Rebekah: and she sent and called Jacob her younger son, and said unto him, Behold, thy brother Esau, as touching thee, doth comfort himself, purposing to kill thee.**

Now we didn't post everything that happened after the deal went down for that would just take too much room. Notice how after that Jacob received the blessing, Esau was very angry for what his brother had done. I won't post it again however, isn't this the same thing Adam and Eve did in the very beginning? Jacob did not force Esau to give up his birthright. Esau did not have to give up his birthright. But, because Esau was mad at himself for doing so, he hated his brother. That would be like me driving my semi down the interstate at 100 mph in a 65-mph speed zone and getting stopped by the police and thinking it was officer's fault that I was getting a ticket.

Now let us listen to what we are told about Esau in the new testament. Hebrew 12:16 Lest there be any fornicator, or profane person, as Esau, **who for one morsel of meat sold his birthright. 17 For ye know how that afterward, when he would have inherited the blessing, he was rejected: for he found no place of repentance, though he sought it carefully with tears.** Are you hearing why Esau was hated by our Father? Most are probably thinking it is because he sold his birthright for a morsel of meat. That is only part of it, he sold it so that he wouldn't die. We all know that our Father and Jesus are not of this world. This is because this is Satan's world or kingdom. When we want to live in this world longer than our Father needs us to be here, we are loving Satan's kingdom. That is why we are told several times that those that save their lives will lose it. Matthew 16:25 **For whosoever will save his life shall lose it: and whosoever will lose his life for my sake shall find it.** Luke 17:33 **Whosoever shall seek to save his life shall lose it; and whosoever shall lose his life shall preserve it.**

This is why we are told that the last enemy that must destroyed is death. This is not a physical death, but rather a spiritual death. It is letting go of the ways and things of this world. Let us listen to 1 Corinthians 13:24 Then cometh the end, when he shall have delivered up the kingdom to God, even the Father; when he shall have put down all rule and all authority and power. 25 For he must reign, till he hath put all enemies under his feet.26 **The last enemy that shall be destroyed is death.** We are made to naturally want to live. We are brought up in a world in which we learn that we must take care of ourselves before we can help others, but we just heard in Luke 17, that if we will lose our life, we will save preserve it. This entire bible is about learning how to love other as you love yourself. If we were to supposed to try and live a long as we can, then why do we hear this in 1 Timothy 4:8 **For bodily exercise profiteth little: but godliness is profitable unto all things, having promise of the life that now is, and of that which is to come.** It is not about actually dying, but rather about dying to the things and ways of the world.

Now we know of police officers, and military put their lives in danger to help others, right? When someone runs into a burning building or a good Samaritan helps someone from extreme dangers and loses his or her life, this world marks them for a hero. And rightfully so. But now let us reflect back to the last book our Father had me write. We showed that we are in hell now and that we all are walking through spiritual fire. That includes the homeless, poor and needy, widows, handicap, homosexuals, etc. But yet there are so many people that will just ignore these people and let them burn. Can you see how trying to save your own life will hurt others? And then when our Father see you allowing this servant, child of His, and vessel of God burn, your provoking Him to anger. This person is in the fire the same as you are. Be the hero without being the known hero.

Now this does not mean that people should run out and kill yourself or anything like that because if our Father has allowed you to live, you are still needed in the flesh. Philippians 1:21 For to me to live is Christ, and to die is gain. 22 But if I live in the flesh, this is the fruit of my labour: yet what I shall choose I wot not. 23 For I am in a strait betwixt two, having a desire to depart, and to be with Christ; which is far better: 24 **Nevertheless to abide in the flesh is more needful for you.**

This is where we need to remember that Jesus dwells in everybody on the earth and is using you to finish building the body. What I mean by that is our Father has allowed you to live and if you know Him, you know that He is the one that kills as Jesus told us in Luke 12:5 But I will forewarn you whom ye shall fear: **Fear him, which after he hath killed hath power to cast into hell; yea, I say unto you, Fear him.** Satan or man does not have the authority to kill as we heard in the book of Job.

Now that have learned that man is Satan, we need to listen to a few things about seeking glory of men. John 12:42 Nevertheless among the chief rulers also many believed on him; but because of the Pharisees they did not confess him, lest they should be put out of the synagogue: 43 **For they loved the praise of men more than the praise of God.** Matthew 6 **Take heed that ye do not your alms before**

men, to be seen of them: otherwise ye have no reward of your Father which is in heaven. 2 Therefore when thou doest thine alms, do not sound a trumpet before thee, as the hypocrites do in the synagogues and in the streets, that they may have glory of men. Verily I say unto you, **They have their reward.** 3 But when thou doest alms, let not thy left hand know what thy right hand doeth: 4 That thine alms may be in secret: and thy Father which seeth in secret himself shall reward thee openly. 5 **And when thou prayest, thou shalt not be as the hypocrites are: for they love to pray standing in the synagogues and in the corners of the streets, that they may be seen of men. Verily I say unto you, They have their reward.** 6 **But thou, when thou prayest, enter into thy closet, and when thou hast shut thy door, pray to thy Father which is in secret; and thy Father which seeth in secret shall reward thee openly.** 7 **But when ye pray, use not vain repetitions, as the heathen do: for they think that they shall be heard for their much speaking.** I must break here for a second for I know that there are many that do not realize that this door we are to shut is our lips. Psalm 141:3 Set a watch, **O Lord, before my mouth; keep the door of my lips.** Our Father is inside of you and knows all of your thoughts, He does not need you to pray out loud.

8 Be not ye therefore like unto them: for your Father knoweth what things ye have need of, before ye ask him. 9 After this manner therefore pray ye: Our Father which art in heaven, Hallowed be thy name. 10 Thy kingdom come, Thy will be done in earth, as it is in heaven. 11 Give us this day our daily bread. 12 And forgive us our debts, as we forgive our debtors. 13 And lead us not into temptation, but deliver us from evil: For thine is the kingdom, and the power, and the glory, for ever. Amen. 14 For if ye forgive men their trespasses, your heavenly Father will also forgive you: 15 But if ye forgive not men their trespasses, neither will your Father forgive your trespasses. 16 Moreover when ye fast, be not, as the hypocrites, of a sad countenance: for they disfigure their faces, that they may appear unto men to fast. Verily I say unto you, They have their reward. 17 But thou, when thou fastest, anoint thine head, and wash thy face; 18 That thou appear not unto men to fast, but unto thy Father which is in secret: and thy

Father, which seeth in secret, shall reward thee openly. 19 Lay not up for yourselves treasures upon earth, where moth and rust doth corrupt, and where thieves break through and steal: 20 But lay up for yourselves treasures in heaven, where neither moth nor rust doth corrupt, and where thieves do not break through nor steal: 21 For where your treasure is, there will your heart be also.

Now it probably makes a little more since as to why we are told everyman sins. Romans 3:23 **For all have sinned, and come short of the glory of God;** Now we can really understand why we are told to do all these things so that man cannot see or hear what we do. This is how Satan is turned into an angel of light. 2 Corinthians 11:12 But what I do, that I will do, that I may cut off occasion from them which desire occasion; that wherein they glory, they may be found even as we. 13 For such are false apostles, deceitful workers, transforming themselves into the apostles of Christ. 14 And no marvel; **for Satan himself is transformed into an angel of light.** The God of this world makes people feel as if they are doing right by our Father by thinking of themselves before they think of others. He makes people feel as if they should want to live in this world as long as they can. He makes people feel as if their life is measured by what they have and not what they can give. This is where we need to listen to Psalm 109:6 **Set thou a wicked man over him: and let Satan stand at his right hand.** There are so many people that believe in the power of prayer is working for them. I mean like groups of people praying out loud so that man or Satan can hear. Listen to what you just heard. There is no reward from our Father if you do any of these things so that man can hear or see of what you are doing. Remember that Satan will do many wonders. 2 Thessalonians 2:8 And then shall that Wicked be revealed, whom the Lord shall consume with the spirit of his mouth, and shall destroy with the brightness of his coming: 9 **Even him, whose coming is after the working of Satan with all power and signs and lying wonders, 10 And with all deceivableness of unrighteousness in them that perish; because they received not the love of the truth, that they might be saved.** 11 And for this cause God shall send them strong delusion, that they should believe a lie:

12 That they all might be damned who believed not the truth, but had pleasure in unrighteousness.

Now I know there are a lot of people think that there is no harm in having things like pictures, statues, nick knacks, models, crosses, or anything that resembles anything in the heavens, in the earth, or in the water beneath the earth. Let us listen to what our Father says about that. 2 Kings 17:38 And the covenant that I have made with you ye shall not forget; neither shall ye fear other gods. 39 But the Lord your God ye shall fear; and he shall deliver you out of the hand of all your enemies. 40 Howbeit they did not hearken, but they did after their former manner. 41 So these nations feared the Lord, **and served their graven images, both their children, and their children's children: as did their fathers, so do they unto this day.** Now let us listen to the 2nd commandment, Exodus 20:4 **Thou shalt not make unto thee any graven image, or any likeness of any thing that is in heaven above, or that is in the earth beneath, or that is in the water under the earth. 5 Thou shalt not bow down thyself to them, nor serve them: for I the Lord thy God am a jealous God, visiting the iniquity of the fathers upon the children unto the third and fourth generation of them that hate me;** It does not matter, if it is in the image of anything in the heavens, earth or the water, it is a graven image. When people buy these things, what are they for? They are to impress others to let them know what you are about. We are supposed to become as living waters. Jeremiah 2:13 For my people have committed two evils; they have forsaken me the fountain of living waters, and hewed them out cisterns, broken cisterns, that can hold no water. Remember that we showed that water is knowledge? That knowledge is the knowledge of a love for others. This is why we are told to just be content with the very basics. 1 Timothy 6:8 **And having food and raiment let us be therewith content.** Now I am sure there are many that are going to try and defraud me for having my picture on the back cover over the last book, and the front cover of this book. That is so that this world can truly see that Jesus is here! Other than that, I do not have any graven images. I will not even let people send me pictures.

Now look how man is rewarded by man for his deeds. Look how man feels that they have to look good in the eyes of others. Look how this world thinks that if a person is not cleaned up and dressed to impress, they are unworthy. I have heard so many people say that they dress nice to feel better about themselves and not to impress. I will say that is just another way of trying to justify yourself. You do not put on nice clothes or fix your makeup unless you are somewhat trying to look good for the opinion of others. Then people will go and spend a lot of money on themselves instead of helping others. I personally feel that if you think you need makeup or to fancy up to be around people, you are not allowing the inner self to be seen. As we are told in 1 Peter 3:3 Whose adorning let it not be that **outward adorning of plaiting the hair, and of wearing of gold, or of putting on of apparel;** 4 But let it be the hidden man of the heart, in that which is not corruptible, even the ornament of a meek and quiet spirit, which is in the sight of God of great price. Then listen to what we are told in Galatians 1:10 **For do I now persuade men, or God? or do I seek to please men? for if I yet pleased men, I should not be the servant of Christ.** John 12:42 Nevertheless among the chief rulers also many believed on him; but because of the Pharisees they did not confess him, lest they should be put out of the synagogue: 43 **For they loved the praise of men more than the praise of God.** Who are you trying to be praised by when you dress in skimpy clothes, suites, or put on expensive jewelry? I could go on forever in the ways this world ignores the ways of God, but if you have read any or all of the three books our Father has had me write, listen to your conscience and decide who your heart will be for.

I hope I am placing in a spot that fits but our Father has brought something to my attention once again after the initial manuscript was sent to publishers. Look at how this world allows children to do whatever they want. It seems as if parents are afraid of disciplining their children. And this is not what our Father tells us to do. Proverbs 23:13 **Withhold not correction from the child: for if thou beatest him with the rod, he shall not die. 14 Thou shalt beat him with the rod, and shalt deliver his soul from hell.** Which would you rather, your child to be happy for just a short time or would you rather your child be happy for all eternity? Just as our Father does with us, He chastises us and if we harken to His voice, He promises to provide everything we need and so much more. This correction does hurt for a while, but it will be worth it.

This leads us into the last part of this chapter. There are any people that are watching for the anti-Christ and the mark of the beast. Our Father had me show in the first book, that this mark is not going to be a computer chip or anything like that. By now I hope people can tell that the bible is spiritual, and this mark is spiritual. Let us listen to Revelation 13 And I stood upon the sand of the sea, and saw a beast rise up out of the sea, having seven heads and ten horns, and upon his horns ten crowns, and upon his heads the name of blasphemy. 2 And the beast which I saw was like unto a leopard, and his feet were as the feet of a bear, and his mouth as the mouth of a lion: and the dragon gave him his power, and his seat, and great authority. 3 And I saw one of his heads as it were wounded to death; and his deadly wound was healed: and all the world wondered after the beast. 4 And they worshipped the dragon which gave power unto the beast: and they worshipped the beast, saying, Who is like unto the beast? who is able to make war with him? 5 And there was given unto him a mouth speaking great things and blasphemies; and power was given unto him to continue forty and two months. 6 And he opened his mouth in blasphemy against God, to blaspheme his name, and his tabernacle, and them that dwell in heaven. 7 And it was given unto him to make war with the saints, and to overcome them: and power was given him over all kindreds, and tongues, and nations. 8 And all that dwell upon the earth shall worship him, whose names are not written in the book of life of the Lamb slain from the foundation of the world. 9 If any man have an ear, let him hear. 10 He that leadeth into captivity shall go into captivity: he that killeth with the sword must be killed with the sword. Here is the patience and the faith of the saints. 11 And I beheld another beast coming up out of the earth; and he had two horns like a lamb, and he spake as a dragon. 12 And he exerciseth all the power of the first beast before him, and causeth the earth and them which dwell therein to worship the first beast, whose deadly wound was healed. 13 And he doeth great wonders, so that he maketh fire come down from heaven on the earth in the sight of men, 14 And deceiveth them that dwell on the earth by the means of those miracles which he had power to do in the sight of the beast; saying to them that dwell on the earth, that they should make an image to the beast, which had the wound by a sword, and did live. 15 And he had power to give life unto the image of the beast, that the image of the beast should both speak, and cause that as many as would not worship the image of the beast should be killed. 16 And he causeth all, both small and great, rich and poor, free and bond, to receive a mark in their right hand, or in their foreheads: 17 And that no man might buy or sell, save he that had the mark, or the name of the beast, or the number of his name. 18 **Here is wisdom. Let him that hath understanding count the number of the beast: for it is the number of a man; and his number is Six hundred threescore and six.**

Let us listen to the two greatest commandments. Mathew 22:36 Master, which is the great commandment in the law? 37 Jesus said unto him, **Thou shalt love the Lord thy God with all thy heart, and with all thy soul, and with all thy mind. 38 This is the first and great commandment. 39 And the second is like unto it, Thou shalt love thy neighbour as thyself. 40 On these two commandments hang all the law and the prophets.** Now we need to be thinking of when our Father created man. Genesis 1:26 And God said, Let us make man in our image, after our likeness: and let them have dominion over the fish of the sea, and over the fowl of the air, and over the cattle, and over all the earth, and over every creeping thing that creepeth upon the earth. 27 So God created man in his own image, in the image of God created he him; male and female created he them. 28 And God blessed them, and God said unto them, Be fruitful, and multiply, and replenish the earth, and subdue it: and have dominion over the fish of the sea, and over the fowl of the air, and over every living thing that moveth upon the earth. 29 And God said, Behold, I have given you every herb bearing seed, which is upon the face of all the earth, and every tree, in the which is the fruit of a tree yielding seed; to you it shall be for meat. 30 And to every beast of the earth, and to every fowl of the air, and to every thing that creepeth upon the earth, wherein there is life, I have given every green herb for meat: and it was so. 31 **And God saw every thing that he had made, and, behold, it was very good. And the evening and the morning were the sixth day.**

    Man was created on the sixth day of creation, so when a man chooses not to love God with all of his heart, one six. When a man chooses not to love God with all of his soul, second six. When a man chooses not to love God with all of his mind, third six. Now I know that there are many that believe there will come a day in which we will not be able to buy and sell. This transaction has already been completed. Remember our Father has purchased us with the blood of His son. Isaiah 44:22 I have blotted out, as a thick cloud, thy transgressions, and, as a cloud, thy sins: return unto me; **for I have redeemed thee.** That is why we are now in the thousand year reign with Christ. You got here by cleaving onto our Father somehow or another. This is when our Father has put man to the test to see who's heart would be for Him, and who's would not. Deuteronomy 8 All the commandments which I command thee this day shall ye observe to do, that ye may live, and multiply, and go in and possess the land which the Lord sware unto your fathers. 2 And thou shalt remember all the way which the Lord thy God led thee these forty years in the wilderness, to humble thee, and to prove thee, **to know what was in thine heart, whether thou wouldest keep his commandments, or no.** When you decide not to love God just by not trying to take the time to get to know Him, you are taking the spiritual mark.

    Now we also need to be looking at how many believe that there will be a new world order before the end. This new world order has been set up for a long time. Let us listen to Luke 2 And it came to pass in those days, **that there went out a decree from Caesar Augustus that all the world should be taxed.** 2 (And this taxing was first made when Cyrenius was governor of Syria.) 3 And all went to be taxed, every one into his own city. Obviously, this was new at the time. It went throughout the world. **There is the new world order.** There is not going to be a time in which you will not be able to physically buy your food. You were purchased already buy our Father and He is the master mind behind it all. It is your choice as to which king, lord, or spirit has dominion over you, but you still belong to our Father. Are you starting to see why our Father has raised me to be the ensign of the end of the world? It is part of all this being hidden from the wise and prudent.

Now if you are seeing how this beast is devouring this world, you should be able to start understanding 1 John 2:18 Little children, it is the last time: and as ye have heard that antichrist shall come, even now are there many antichrists; whereby we know that it is the last time. Now from the last book and we touched on it in this one, many people can and do represent one person, or one person can represent many people in our bible. Judges 20:1 Then all the children of Israel went out, **and the congregation was gathered together as one man,** from Dan even to Beersheba, with the land of Gilead, unto the Lord in Mizpeh. 2 And the chief of all the people, even of all the tribes of Israel, presented themselves in the assembly of the people of God, four hundred thousand footmen that drew sword. 3 (Now the children of Benjamin heard that the children of Israel were gone up to Mizpeh.) Then said the children of Israel, Tell us, how was this wickedness? 4 And the Levite, the husband of the woman that was slain, answered and said, I came into Gibeah that belongeth to Benjamin, I and my concubine, to lodge. 5 And the men of Gibeah rose against me, and beset the house round about upon me by night, and thought to have slain me: and my concubine have they forced, that she is dead. 6 And I took my concubine, and cut her in pieces, and sent her throughout all the country of the inheritance of Israel: for they have committed lewdness and folly in Israel. 7 Behold, ye are all children of Israel; give here your advice and counsel. 8 **And all the people arose as one man,** saying, We will not any of us go to his tent, neither will we any of us turn into his house. 9 But now this shall be the thing which we will do to Gibeah; we will go up by lot against it; 10 And we will take ten men of an hundred throughout all the tribes of Israel, and an hundred of a thousand, and a thousand out of ten thousand, to fetch victual for the people, that they may do, when they come to Gibeah of Benjamin, according to all the folly that they have wrought in Israel. 11 **So all the men of Israel were gathered against the city, knit together as one man.** Nehemiah 8:1 **And all the people gathered themselves together as one man into the street that was before the water gate;** and they spake unto Ezra the scribe to bring the book of the law of Moses, which the Lord had commanded to Israel.

This antichrist that everybody is looking for is and has been here since the beginning. Remember we are hearing conversations being held in heaven when we listen to the bible. This antichrist does not believe the bible. He believes God changed so that man can do as he wants, and his sins are automatically forgiven. He believes that the bible is about people of the past. This antichrist believes his life matters more than others. This antichrist believes that he does not have to take the time to get to know our Father. This antichrist thinks he is doing right in his own eyes. Proverbs 21:2 **Every way of a man is right in his own eyes:** but the Lord pondereth the hearts. This antichrist loves this world and the things of it. 1 John 2:15 **Love not the world, neither the things that are in the world. If any man love the world, the love of the Father is not in him. 16 For all that is in the world, the lust of the flesh, and the lust of the eyes, and the pride of life, is not of the Father, but is of the world.**

Notice how the pride of life is not of the Father? Look at how this world wants to live longer. Then listen to this in Proverbs 16:5 **Every one that is proud in heart is an abomination to the Lord: though hand join in hand, he shall not be unpunished.** Isaiah 28 **Woe to the crown of pride,** to the drunkards of Ephraim, whose glorious beauty is a fading flower, which are on the head of the fat valleys of them that are overcome with wine! 2 Behold, the Lord hath a mighty and strong one, which as a tempest of hail and a destroying storm, as a flood of mighty waters overflowing, shall cast down to the earth with the hand. 3 **The crown of pride, the drunkards of Ephraim, shall be trodden under feet:**

Now I have shown you of many witnesses showing that I am the son of man that has been prophesied about. And I know that there are many that think this is something that happened in the past or is way off in the future for many don't think it can happen in their lifetime. Here is the catch, it was then, and it is now. Just as I showed in the chapter of believing, the first time I read the bible, I believed it was about our lives today. So now listen to 1 John 4 Beloved, believe not every spirit, but try the spirits whether they are of God: because many false prophets are gone out into the world. 2 Hereby know ye the Spirit of God: **Every spirit that confesseth that Jesus Christ is come in the flesh is of God: 3 And every spirit that confesseth not that Jesus Christ is come in the flesh is not of God: and this is that spirit of antichrist, whereof ye have heard that it should come; and even now already is it in the world.** 4 Ye are of God, little children, and have overcome them: because greater is he that is in you, than he that is in the world. 5 They are of the world: therefore speak they of the world, and the world heareth them. 6 We are of God: he that knoweth God heareth us; he that is not of God heareth not us. Hereby know we the spirit of truth, and the spirit of error. 7 Beloved, let us love one another: for love is of God; and every one that loveth is born of God, and knoweth God. 8 He that loveth not knoweth not God; for God is love. 9 In this was manifested the love of God toward us, because that God sent his only begotten Son into the world, that we might live through him. 10 Herein is love, not that we loved God, but that he loved us, and sent his Son to be the propitiation for our sins. 11 Beloved, if God so loved us, we ought also to love one another. 12 No man hath seen God at any time. If we love one another, God dwelleth in us, and his love is perfected in us. 13 Hereby know we that we dwell in him, and he in us, because he hath given us of his Spirit. 14 And we have seen and do testify that the Father sent the Son to be the Saviour of the world. 15 Whosoever shall confess that Jesus is the Son of God, God dwelleth in him, and he in God. 16 And we have known and believed the love that God hath to us. God is love; and he that dwelleth in love dwelleth in God, and God in him. 17 Herein is our love made perfect, that we may have boldness in the day of judgment: because as he is, so are we in this world. 18 There is no fear in love; but perfect love casteth out fear: because fear hath torment. He that feareth is not made perfect in love. 19 We love him, because he first loved us. 20 If a man say, I love God, and hateth his brother, he is a liar: for he that loveth not his brother whom he hath seen, how can he love God whom he hath not seen? 21 And this commandment have we from him, That he who loveth God love his brother also.

The anti-Chris is not going to be one man like the president of a country or something like that. Many people represent one person as shown earlier in the book. Or one person can represent one person. This anti-Christ is already here and not going to be set up or coming in the future.

Now let us listen to 2 John 1:7 For many deceivers are entered into the world, who confess not that Jesus Christ is come in the flesh. This is a deceiver and an antichrist. Notice how this tells us that Jesus Christ is come in the flesh. It does not say that Jesus came in the flesh, however he is in the flesh. This is why believing is about believing that the bible is one long letter from our Father, giving us instructions on how we are to live our lives today and not just for the people of the past. And this is not some plot to say that you better believe or else or something like that. If you have made it this far in the book, than obviously you believe.

In the last book, our Father had me show what makes a man desolate. Psalm 34:22 The Lord redeemeth the soul of his servants: **and none of them that trust in him shall be desolate.** These books that our Father has had me write will bring people back to learn of Him and His ways. They will start putting their trust back into our Father and stop listening to Satan. So, I am saying that I believe I am the abomination of desolation spoken of in the book of Daniel. Matthew 24:15 **When ye therefore shall see the abomination of desolation, spoken of by Daniel the prophet, stand in the holy place, (whoso readeth, let him understand:)** Remember our Father did say that He will make a people from those that are not His people. Hosea 2:23 **And I will sow her unto me in the earth; and I will have mercy upon her that had not obtained mercy; and I will say to them which were not my people, Thou art my people; and they shall say, Thou art my God.** I am not in the country we call Israel, but I am married to our Father as explained in the last book.

Now I know that there are many that are going to try and figure out the day. Daniel 12 And at that time shall Michael stand up, the great prince which standeth for the children of thy people: and there shall be a time of trouble, such as never was since there was a nation even to that same time: and at that time thy people shall be delivered, every one that shall be found written in the book. 2 And many of them that sleep in the dust of the earth shall awake, some to everlasting life, and some to shame and everlasting contempt. 3 And they that be wise shall shine as the brightness of the firmament; and they that turn many to righteousness as the stars for ever and ever. 4 But thou, O Daniel, shut up the words, and seal the book, even to the time of the end: many shall run to and fro, and knowledge shall be increased. 5 Then I Daniel looked, and, behold, there stood other two, the one on this side of the bank of the river, and the other on that side of the bank of the river. 6 And one said to the man clothed in linen, which was upon the waters of the river, How long shall it be to the end of these wonders? 7 And I heard the man clothed in linen, which was upon the waters of the river, when he held up his right hand and his left hand unto heaven, and sware by him that liveth for ever that it shall be for a time, times, and an half; and when he shall have accomplished to scatter the power of the holy people, all these things shall be finished. 8 And I heard, but I understood not: then said I, O my Lord, what shall be the end of these things? 9 And he said, Go thy way, Daniel: for the words are closed up and sealed till the time of the end. 10 Many shall be purified, and made white, and tried; but the wicked shall do wickedly: and none of the wicked shall understand; but the wise shall understand. 11 And from the time that the daily sacrifice shall be taken away, and the abomination that maketh desolate set up, there shall be a thousand two hundred and ninety days. 12 Blessed is he that waiteth, and cometh to the thousand three hundred and five and thirty days. 13 But go thou thy way till the end be: for thou shalt rest, and stand in thy lot at the end of the days.

For those that want to try and figure this out. When was this set up? March of 2016? October of 2018, or maybe even after this book is published. Even if you do figure it something out, remember the day will be cut short. Matthew 24:22 **And except those days should be shortened, there should no flesh be saved: but for the elect's sake those days shall be shortened.** Isaiah 14 For the Lord will have mercy on Jacob, and will yet choose Israel, and set them in their own land: and the strangers shall be joined with them, and they shall cleave to the house of Jacob. 2 And the people shall take them, and bring them to their place: and the house of Israel shall possess them in the land of the Lord for servants and handmaids: and they shall take them captives, whose captives they were; and they shall rule over their oppressors. 3 And it shall come to pass in the day that the Lord shall give thee rest from thy sorrow, and from thy fear, and from the hard bondage wherein thou wast made to serve, 4 That thou shalt take up this proverb against the king of Babylon, and say, How hath the oppressor ceased! the golden city ceased! 5 The Lord hath broken the staff of the wicked, and the sceptre of the rulers. 6 He who smote the people in wrath with a continual stroke, he that ruled the nations in anger, is persecuted, and none hindereth. 7 The whole earth is at rest, and is quiet: they break forth into singing. 8 Yea, the fir trees rejoice at thee, and the cedars of Lebanon, saying, Since thou art laid down, no feller is come up against us. 9 Hell from beneath is moved for thee to meet thee at thy coming: it stirreth up the dead for thee, even all the chief ones of the earth; it hath raised up from their thrones all the kings of the nations. 10 All they shall speak and say unto thee, Art thou also become weak as we? art thou become like unto us? 11 Thy pomp is brought down to the grave, and the noise of thy viols: the worm is spread under thee, and the worms cover thee. 12 How art thou fallen from heaven, O Lucifer, son of the morning! how art thou cut down to the ground, which didst weaken the nations! 13 For thou hast said in thine heart, I will ascend into heaven, I will exalt my throne above the stars of God: I will sit also upon the mount of the congregation, in the sides of the north: 14 I will ascend above the heights of the clouds; I will be like the most High. 15 Yet thou shalt be brought down to hell, to the sides of the pit. 16 They that see thee shall narrowly look upon thee, and consider thee, saying, Is this the man that made the earth to tremble, that did shake kingdoms; 17 That made the world as a wilderness, and destroyed the cities thereof; that opened not the house of his prisoners? 18 All the kings of the nations, even all of them, lie in glory, every one in his own house. 19 But thou art cast out of thy grave like an abominable branch, and as the raiment of those that are slain, thrust through with a sword, that go down to the stones of the pit; as a carcase trodden under feet. 20 Thou shalt not be joined with them in burial, because thou hast destroyed thy land, and slain thy people: the seed of evildoers shall never be renowned. 21 Prepare slaughter for his children for the iniquity of their fathers; that they do not rise, nor possess the land, nor fill the face of the world with cities. 22 For I will rise up against them, saith the Lord of hosts, and cut off from Babylon the name, and remnant, and son, and nephew, saith the Lord. 23 I will also make it a possession for the bittern, and pools of water: and I will sweep it with the besom of destruction, saith the Lord of hosts. **24 The Lord of hosts hath sworn, saying, Surely as I have thought, so shall it come to pass; and as I have purposed, so shall it stand: 25 That I will break the Assyrian in my land, and upon my mountains tread him under foot: then shall his yoke depart from off them, and his burden depart from off their shoulders. 26 This is the purpose that is purposed upon the whole earth: and this is the hand that is stretched out upon all the nations. 27 For the Lord of hosts hath purposed, and who shall disannul it? and his hand is stretched out, and who shall turn it back? 28 In the year that king Ahaz died was this burden. 29 Rejoice not thou, whole Palestina, because the rod of him that smote thee is broken: for out of the serpent's root shall come forth a cockatrice, and his fruit shall be a fiery flying serpent. 30 And the firstborn of the poor shall feed, and the needy shall lie down in safety: and I will kill thy root with famine, and he shall slay thy remnant. 31 Howl, O gate; cry, O city; thou, whole Palestina, art dissolved: for there shall come from the north a smoke, and none shall be alone in his appointed times. 32 What shall one then answer the messengers of the nation? That the Lord hath founded Zion, and the poor of his people shall trust in it.**

In closing of this chapter, I want to talk about a movie that I have seen that is based on a true story. Earlier in the book, I told you all that I think out our Father every moment of the day. I am giving an example of this now. Have you ever seen the movie of The Exorcism of Emily Rose? She was possessed. Toward the end of the movie, when they did the exorcism on her, they asked what the name of the demon was. She replied with, one, two, three, four, five, six. I am the one the dwells within. This movie is based on a true story and her grave can be visited still. Without getting into all the details of the movie, that was our Father showing the world that Satan is locked up inside of us and yes, he wants out. I know that there are some that believe that it is just a movie. To that I say, you do not believe that our Father is the creator of everything. Our Father has the ultimate dominion over every person on this planet. And yes, He has the power to make movies also.

THE ROCK

This chapter is going to cover a few different topics. It is mainly going to be focusing what is that rock in which we are to build our house. It is not a physical house nor is it a physical rock. The house in which we build is our own body and the rock is our Father. The reason we need to do this chapter is because there a lot of people in which believe that Jesus changed God, our Father. There are a lot of people that believe that the old testament is only for the people of the past. There are a lot of people in which still believe that celebrating holidays and such are okay with our Father.

One of the first things we want to bring up is Matthew 7:21 **Not every one that saith unto me, Lord, Lord, shall enter into the kingdom of heaven; but he that doeth the will of my Father which is in heaven.** 22 Many will say to me in that day, Lord, Lord, have we not prophesied in thy name? and in thy name have cast out devils? and in thy name done many wonderful works? 23 And then will I profess unto them, I never knew you: depart from me, ye that work iniquity. 24 **Therefore whosoever heareth these sayings of mine, and doeth them, I will liken him unto a wise man, which built his house upon a rock:** 25 And the rain descended, and the floods came, and the winds blew, and beat upon that house; and it fell not: for it was founded upon a rock. 26 And every one that heareth these sayings of mine, and doeth them not, shall be likened unto a foolish man, which built his house upon the sand: 27 And the rain descended, and the floods came, and the winds blew, and beat upon that house; and it fell: and great was the fall of it.

Jesus is telling us right hear that whosoever heareth these sayings of mine and do them, that is the person in which will build his house on a rock. Where in the bible does Jesus say that he came to change our Father? I will guarantee you that Jesus did not come to change one jot or tittle of the law. Matthew 5:17 **Think not that I am come to destroy the law, or the prophets: I am not come to destroy, but to fulfil. 18 For verily I say unto you, Till heaven and** earth pass, one jot or one tittle shall in no wise pass from the law, till all be fulfilled.

Where did Jesus say that we no longer needed the old testament? He didn't, however we are going to look at several spots in which Jesus is telling us to that we need the old testament just as well as we do the new testament, without actually coming right out and saying it. But people refuse to listen, hence the name of the first book, Father, forgive us, we haven't been listening. Matthew 4 Then was Jesus led up of the Spirit into the wilderness to be tempted of the devil. 2 And when he had fasted forty days and forty nights, he was afterward an hungred. 3 And when the tempter came to him, he said, If thou be the Son of God, command that these stones be made bread. 4 **But he answered and said, It is written, Man shall not live by bread alone, but by every word that proceedeth out of the mouth of God.** 5 Then the devil taketh him up into the holy city, and setteth him on a pinnacle of the temple, 6 And saith unto him, If thou be the Son of God, cast thyself down: for it is written, He shall give his angels charge concerning thee: and in their hands they shall bear thee up, lest at any time thou dash thy foot against a stone. 7 **Jesus said unto him, It is written again, Thou shalt not tempt the Lord thy God.** 8 Again, the devil taketh him up into an exceeding high mountain, and sheweth him all the kingdoms of the world, and the glory of them; 9 And saith unto him, All these things will I give thee, if thou wilt fall down and worship me. 10 **Then saith Jesus unto him, Get thee hence, Satan: for it is written, Thou shalt worship the Lord thy God, and him only shalt thou serve.**

11 Then the devil leaveth him, and, behold, angels came and ministered unto him. Okay, do you think Jesus knew all of these things by just reading the first three books of the new testament? Matthew

21:42 Jesus saith unto them, **Did ye never read in the scriptures,** The stone which the builders rejected, the same is become the head of the corner: this is the Lord's doing, and it is marvellous in our eyes? Matthew 22:29 Jesus answered and said unto them, **Ye do err, not knowing the scriptures,** nor the power of God. Matthew 26:54 But how then shall the scriptures be fulfilled, that thus it must be? 55 In that same hour said Jesus to the multitudes, Are ye come out as against a thief with swords and staves for to take me? I sat daily with you teaching in the temple, and ye laid no hold on me. 56 But all this was done, **that the scriptures of the prophets might be fulfilled.** Then all the disciples forsook him, and fled. Luke 24:27 **And beginning at Moses and all the prophets, he expounded unto them in all the scriptures the things concerning himself.** Luke 24:32 And they said one to another, Did not our heart burn within us, while he talked with us by the way, **and while he opened to us the scriptures?**

What scriptures is he referring to if we do not need the old testament anymore? So now let us listen to a few spots other than the words of Jesus that we can hear that we need the scriptures or the old testament. Acts 17:2 And Paul, as his manner was, **went in unto them, and three sabbath days reasoned with them out of the scriptures,** 3 Opening and alleging, that Christ must needs have suffered, and risen again from the dead; and that this Jesus, whom I preach unto you, is Christ. 4 And some of them believed, and consorted with Paul and Silas; and of the devout Greeks a great multitude, and of the chief women not a few. 5 But the Jews which believed not, moved with envy, took unto them certain lewd fellows of the baser sort, and gathered a company, and set all the city on an uproar, and assaulted the house of Jason, and sought to bring them out to the people. 6 And when they found them not, they drew Jason and certain brethren unto the rulers of the city, crying, These that have turned the world upside down are come hither also; 7 Whom Jason hath received: and these all do contrary to the decrees of Caesar, saying that there is another king, one Jesus. 8 And they troubled the people and the rulers of the city, when they heard these things. 9 And when they had taken security of Jason, and of the other, they let them go. 10 And the brethren immediately sent away Paul and Silas by night unto Berea: who coming thither went into the synagogue of the Jews. 11 These were more noble than those in Thessalonica, **in that they received the word with all readiness of mind, and searched the scriptures daily, whether those things were so.** 12 Therefore many of them believed; also of honourable women which were Greeks, and of men, not a few.

Romans 1 Paul, a servant of Jesus Christ, called to be an apostle, separated unto the gospel of God, 2 **(Which he had promised afore by his prophets in the holy scriptures,)** 3 Concerning his Son Jesus Christ our Lord, which was made of the seed of David according to the flesh; Romans 16:26 **But now is made manifest, and by the scriptures of the prophets,** according to the commandment of the everlasting God, made known to all nations for the obedience of faith: 2 Peter 3:16 As also in all his epistles, speaking in them of these things; in which are some things hard to be understood, which they that are unlearned and unstable wrest, **as they do also the other scriptures, unto their own destruction.** This is why we are told that God's people will be destroyed for their lack of knowledge. Hosea 4:6 **My people are destroyed for lack of knowledge: because thou hast rejected knowledge, I will also reject thee, that thou shalt be no priest to me: seeing thou hast forgotten the law of thy God, I will also forget thy children.**

Beings how I am a truck driver and drive all over the country, I see many signs or billboards saying that real Christians obey the teaching of Christ. First and foremost, that statement alone condemns. It is telling people that if they don't believe the same way as they do, then there not a Christian. As we showed in the last book, nobody knows what God wants for each person other than to love as we have heard from the beginning. But at the same time, I know they do not even believe in the teachings of Jesus for Jesus did not come into this world to condemn it, neither do I. I come in my Father's name to show how easy it is to learn what our Father has wanted from us if we just listen to Him and not man.

I just walked out of a truck stop that has a stack of free new testament bibles. Where does any scripture say that we do not need the old testament? I will guarantee that there is not one scripture that even hints to this. In fact, we just read several scriptures that in reality are telling us to seek the old testament. Let us listen to what Jesus said in John 5:44 How can ye believe, which receive honour one of another, and seek not the honour that cometh from God only? 45 **Do not think that I will accuse you to the Father: there is one that accuseth you, even Moses, in whom ye trust. 46 For had ye believed Moses, ye would have believed me; for he wrote of me. 47 But if ye believe not his writings, how shall ye believe my words?** Then let us listen to what he said in John 6:44 No man can come to me, except the Father which hath sent me draw him: and I will raise him up at the last day. 45 **It is written in the prophets, And they shall be all taught of God. Every man therefore that hath heard, and hath learned of the Father, cometh unto me.**

These two sections of the new testament alone give us direct instructions from Jesus himself to seek Moses and the prophets. But more importantly let us listen to when we are told that a lot of people have a vail on their hearts when it comes to reading Moses. This is in the new testament. 2 Corinthians 3:12 Seeing then that we have such hope, we use great plainness of speech: 13 And not as Moses, which put a veil over his face, that the children of Israel could not stedfastly look to the end of that which is abolished: 14 **But their minds were blinded: for until this day remaineth the same vail untaken away in the reading of the old testament; which vail is done away in Christ. 15 But even unto this day, when Moses is read, the vail is upon their heart. 16 Nevertheless when it shall turn to the Lord, the vail shall be taken away.**

Let us listen to when this vail was on Moses. Exodus 34:29 And it came to pass, when Moses came down from mount Sinai with the two tables of testimony in Moses' hand, when he came down from the mount, that Moses wist not that the skin of his face shone while he talked with him. 30 And when Aaron and all the children of Israel saw Moses, behold, the skin of his face shone; and they were afraid to come nigh him. 31 And Moses called unto them; and Aaron and all the rulers of the congregation returned unto him: and Moses talked with them. 32 And afterward all the children of Israel came nigh: and he gave them in commandment all that the Lord had spoken with him in mount Sinai. 33 **And till Moses had done speaking with them, he put a vail on his face.** 34 But when Moses went in before the Lord to speak with him, he took the vail off, until he came out. And he came out, and spake unto the children of Israel that which he was commanded. 35 And the children of Israel saw the face of Moses, that the skin of Moses' face shone: **and Moses put the vail upon his face again,** until he went in to speak with Him.

The people couldn't handle the brightness of Moses's face after He had spoken with our Father. Now think about this for a minute, how do you react when you think about reading or listening to the old testament? This world has allowed their imagination to run wild when they read the old testament and automatically think our Father is cruel, mean vindictive, or something like that. They put the same vail on their hearts. Then most refuse to look into the books of Moses. There is the first commandment being broken. Exodus 20 And God spake all these words, saying, 2 I am the Lord thy God, which have brought thee out of the land of Egypt, out of the house of bondage. 3 **Thou shalt have no other gods before me.** Now listen to what Jesus said in Matthew 4:4 But he answered and said, It is written, **Man shall not live by bread alone, but by every word that proceedeth out of the mouth of God.** How can man live by every word that proceedeth out of the mouth of God if they will not even go and see the words in which God spoke? 1 John 1:5 This then is the message which we have heard of him, and declare unto you, that God is light, and in him is no darkness at all. This also mean He is all love and man does not want to love in the same manner as He does. Now though these three books our Father has had me write, we have been finding out that the bible is not at all what it seems when you first read it. In the last book we showed what the forbidden fruit is, as man calls it. We showed that our Father never commanded us to sacrifice animals, but man let his imagination run wild. We have showed in this book that our Father never commanded man to starve themselves. We have showed you the sacrifice of Abraham and his son and how I did the same thing, but yet was there never any threat to the life of my son. But all along, we have been told God is love. 1 John 4:8 **He that loveth not knoweth not God; for God is love.** We all know that God is spirit, Galatians 5:22 **But the fruit of the Spirit is love, joy, peace, longsuffering, gentleness, goodness,** faith,23 Meekness, temperance: against such there is no law.

So now let us listen to a few times that our Father tells us what He will do with those that have went a whoring after their own imagination. Jeremiah 7:21 Thus saith the Lord of hosts, the God of Israel; Put your burnt offerings unto your sacrifices, and eat flesh. 22 For I spake not unto your fathers, nor commanded them in the day that I brought them out of the land of Egypt, concerning burnt offerings or sacrifices: 23 But this thing commanded I them, saying, Obey my voice, and I will be your God, and ye shall be my people: and walk ye in all the ways that I have commanded you, that it may be well unto you. 24 **But they hearkened not, nor inclined their ear, but walked in the counsels and in the imagination of their evil heart, and went backward, and not forward.** 25 Since the day that your fathers came forth out of the land of Egypt unto this day I have even sent unto you all my servants the prophets, daily rising up early and sending them: 26 **Yet they hearkened not unto me, nor inclined their ear, but hardened their neck: they did worse than their fathers.** 27 Therefore thou shalt speak all these words unto them; but they will not hearken to thee: thou shalt also call unto them; but they will not answer thee. 28 But thou shalt say unto them, This is a nation that obeyeth not the voice of the Lord their God, nor receiveth correction: truth is perished, and is cut off from their mouth. 29 **Cut off thine hair, O Jerusalem, and cast it away, and take up a lamentation on high places; for the Lord hath rejected and forsaken the generation of his wrath.**

Just want to make a quick side note here. Remember we are hearing conversations being held in heaven when we read or listen to the bible. Remember that they have dominion over our bodies. I am not saying this is what is going on for sure for our Father will not tell me what He has wants or needs from any other person on the planet, as explained in the last book. But look at all the men that are shaving their heads. I truly do believe the bible is about us and not the people of the past. And remember Jesus saying that not one jot nor tittle of the law shall in no wise pass until all be fulfilled?

Jeremiah 11 The word that came to Jeremiah from the Lord saying, 2 Hear ye the words of this covenant, and speak unto the men of Judah, and to the inhabitants of Jerusalem; 3 And say thou unto them, Thus saith the Lord God of Israel; Cursed be the man that obeyeth not the words of this covenant, 4 Which I commanded your fathers in the day that I brought them forth out of the land of Egypt, from the iron furnace, saying, Obey my voice, and do them, according to all which I command you: so shall ye be my people, and I will be your God: 5 That I may perform the oath which I have sworn unto your fathers, to give them a land flowing with milk and honey, as it is this day. Then answered I, and said, So be it, O Lord. 6 Then the Lord said unto me, Proclaim all these words in the cities of Judah, and in the streets of Jerusalem, saying, Hear ye the words of this covenant, and do them. 7 For I earnestly protested unto your fathers in the day that I brought them up out of the land of Egypt, even unto this day, rising early and protesting, saying, Obey my voice. 8 **Yet they obeyed not, nor inclined their ear, but walked every one in the imagination of their evil heart: therefore I will bring upon them all the words of this covenant, which I commanded them to do: but they did them not.** 9 And the Lord said unto me, A conspiracy is found among the men of Judah, and among the inhabitants of Jerusalem. 10 They are turned back to the iniquities of their forefathers, **which refused to hear my words; and they went after other gods to serve them:** the house of Israel and the house of Judah have broken my covenant which I made with their fathers. 11 **Therefore thus saith the Lord, Behold, I will bring evil upon them, which they shall not be able to escape; and though they shall cry unto me, I will not hearken unto them.** 12 Then shall the cities of Judah and inhabitants of Jerusalem go, and cry unto the gods unto whom they offer incense: but they shall not save them at all in the time of their trouble. 13 For according to the number of thy cities were thy gods, O Judah; and according to the number of the streets of Jerusalem have ye set up altars to that shameful thing, even altars to burn incense unto Baal. 14 Therefore pray not thou for this people, neither lift up a cry or prayer for them: **for I will not hear them in the time that they cry unto me for their trouble.** This right here makes me think of what we are told in Romans 10:11 For the scripture saith, Whosoever believeth on him shall not be ashamed. 12 For there is no difference between the Jew and the Greek: for the same Lord over all is rich unto all that call upon him. 13 For whosoever shall call upon the name of the Lord shall be saved. 14 **How then shall they call on him in whom they have not believed? and how shall they believe in him of whom they have not heard? and how shall they hear without a preacher?** How can one call on our Father if you do not believe that He truly is love? Or you believe He is cruel and wrong for doing what He is doing?

Jeremiah 13:8 Then the word of the Lord came unto me, saying, 9 Thus saith the Lord, After this manner will I mar the pride of Judah, and the great pride of Jerusalem. 10 This evil people, which refuse to hear my words, **which walk in the imagination of their heart, and walk after other gods, to serve them, and to worship them, shall even be as this girdle, which is good for nothing.** I am going to have to place the entire chapter of Jeremiah 23 for there is so much that is being said by our Father and I feel it fits right here.

Jeremiah 23 Woe be unto the pastors that destroy and scatter the sheep of my pasture! saith the Lord. 2 Therefore thus saith the Lord God of Israel against the pastors that feed my people; Ye have scattered my flock, and driven them away, and have not visited them: behold, I will visit upon you the evil of your doings, saith the Lord. 3 And I will gather the remnant of my flock out of all countries whither I have driven them, and will bring them again to their folds; and they shall be fruitful and increase. 4 And I will set up shepherds over them which shall feed them: and they shall fear no more, nor be dismayed, neither shall they be lacking, saith the Lord. 5 Behold, the days come, saith the Lord, that I will raise unto David a righteous Branch, and a

King shall reign and prosper, and shall execute judgment and justice in the earth. 6 In his days Judah shall be saved, and Israel shall dwell safely: and this is his name whereby he shall be called, The Lord Our Righteousness. 7 Therefore, behold, the days come, saith the Lord, that they shall no more say, The Lord liveth, which brought up the children of Israel out of the land of Egypt; 8 But, The Lord liveth, which brought up and which led the seed of the house of Israel out of the north country, and from all countries whither I had driven them; and they shall dwell in their own land. 9 Mine heart within me is broken because of the prophets; all my bones shake; I am like a drunken man, and like a man whom wine hath overcome, because of the Lord, and because of the words of his holiness. 10 **For the land is full of adulterers; for because of swearing the land mourneth; the pleasant places of the wilderness are dried up, and their course is evil, and their force is not right.** 11 For both prophet and priest are profane; yea, in my house have I found their wickedness, saith the Lord. 12 Wherefore their way shall be unto them as slippery ways in the darkness: they shall be driven on, and fall therein: for I will bring evil upon them, even the year of their visitation, saith the Lord. 13 And I have seen folly in the prophets of Samaria; they prophesied in Baal, and caused my people Israel to err. 14 I have seen also in the prophets of Jerusalem an horrible thing: they commit adultery, and walk in lies: they strengthen also the hands of evildoers, that none doth return from his wickedness; they are all of them unto me as Sodom, and the inhabitants thereof as Gomorrah. 15 Therefore thus saith the Lord of hosts concerning the prophets; Behold, I will feed them with wormwood, and make them drink the water of gall: for from the prophets of Jerusalem is profaneness gone forth into all the land. 16 Thus saith the Lord of hosts, Hearken not unto the words of the prophets that prophesy unto you: they make you vain: they speak a vision of their own heart, and not out of the mouth of the Lord. 17 **They say still unto them that despise me, The Lord hath said, Ye shall have peace; and they say unto every one that walketh after the imagination of his own heart, No evil shall come upon you.** 18 For who hath stood in the counsel of the Lord, and hath perceived and heard his word? who hath marked his word, and heard it? 19 Behold, a whirlwind of the Lord is gone forth in fury, even a grievous whirlwind: it shall fall grievously upon the head of the wicked. 20 The anger of the Lord shall not return, until he have executed, and till he have performed the thoughts of his heart: in the latter days ye shall consider it perfectly. 21 I have not sent these prophets, yet they ran: I have not spoken to them, yet they prophesied. 22 But if they had stood in my counsel, and had caused my people to hear my words, then they should have turned them from their evil way, and from the evil of their doings. 23 Am I a God at hand, saith the Lord, and not a God afar off? 24 Can any hide himself in secret places that I shall not see him? saith the Lord. Do not I fill heaven and earth? saith the Lord. 25 I have heard what the prophets said, that prophesy lies in my name, saying, I have dreamed, I have dreamed. 26 How long shall this be in the heart of the prophets that prophesy lies? yea, they are prophets of the deceit of their own heart; 27 **Which think to cause my people to forget my name by their dreams which they tell every man to his neighbour, as their fathers have forgotten my name for Baal.** 28 The prophet that hath a dream, let him tell a dream; and he that hath my word, let him speak my word faithfully. What is the chaff to the wheat? saith the Lord. 29 **Is not my word like as a fire? saith the Lord; and like a hammer that breaketh the rock in pieces?** 30 Therefore, behold, **I am against the prophets, saith the Lord, that steal my words every one from his neighbour.** 31 Behold, I am against the prophets, saith the Lord, that use their tongues, and say, He saith. 32 Behold, I am against them that prophesy false dreams, saith the Lord, and do tell them, and cause my people to err by their lies, and by their lightness; yet I sent them not, nor commanded them: therefore they shall not profit this people at all, saith the Lord. 33 **And when this people, or the prophet, or a priest, shall ask thee, saying, What is the burden of the Lord? thou shalt then say unto them, What burden? I will even forsake you, saith the Lord.** 34 And as for the prophet, and the priest, and the people, that shall say, The burden of the Lord, I will even punish that man and his house. 35 Thus shall ye say every one to his neighbour, and every one to his brother, What hath the Lord answered? and, What hath the Lord spoken? 36 And the burden of the Lord shall ye mention no more: for every man's word shall be his burden; for ye have perverted the words of the living God, of the Lord of hosts our God. 37 Thus shalt thou say to the prophet, What hath the Lord answered thee? and, What hath the Lord spoken? 38 But since ye say, The burden of the Lord; therefore thus saith the Lord; Because ye say this word, The burden of the Lord, and I have sent unto you, saying, Ye shall not say, The burden of the Lord; 39 **Therefore, behold, I, even I, will utterly forget you, and I will forsake you, and the city that I gave you and your fathers, and cast you out of my presence:** 40 **And I will bring an everlasting reproach upon you, and a perpetual shame, which shall not be forgotten.**

Now let us listen to a couple of times in which we can even hear that it is pastors and such in which lead people to their own destruction. Jeremiah 10 Hear ye the word which the Lord speaketh unto you, O house of Israel: 2 Thus saith the Lord, Learn not the way of the heathen, and be not dismayed at the signs of heaven; for the heathen are dismayed at them. 3 For the customs of the people are vain: for one cutteth a tree out of the forest, the work of the hands of the workman, with the axe. 4 They deck it with silver and with gold; they fasten it with nails and with hammers, that it move not. 5 They are upright as the palm tree, but speak not: they must needs be borne, because they cannot go. Be not afraid of them; for they cannot do evil, neither also is it in them to do good. 6 Forasmuch as there is none like unto thee, O Lord; thou art great, and thy name is great in might. 7 Who would not fear thee, O King of nations? for to thee doth it appertain: forasmuch as among all the wise men of the nations, and in all their kingdoms, there is none like unto thee. 8 But they are altogether brutish and foolish: the stock is a doctrine of vanities. 9 Silver spread into plates is brought from Tarshish, and gold from Uphaz, the work of the workman, and of the hands of the founder: blue and purple is their clothing: they are all the work of cunning men. 10 But the Lord is the true God, he is the living God, and an everlasting king: at his wrath the earth shall tremble, and the nations shall not be able to abide his indignation. 11 Thus shall ye say unto them, The gods that have not made the heavens and the earth, even they shall perish from the earth, and from under these heavens. 12 He hath made the earth by his power, he hath established the world by his wisdom, and hath stretched out the heavens by his discretion. 13 When he uttereth his voice, there is a multitude of waters in the heavens, and he causeth the vapours to ascend from the ends of the earth; he maketh lightnings with rain, and bringeth forth the wind out of his treasures. 14 Every man is brutish in his knowledge: every founder is confounded by the graven image: for his molten image is falsehood, and there is no breath in them. 15 They are vanity, and the work of errors: in the time of their visitation they shall perish. 16 The portion of Jacob is not like them: for he is the former of all things; and Israel is the rod of his inheritance: The Lord of hosts is his name. 17 Gather up thy wares out of the land, O inhabitant of the fortress. 18 For thus saith the Lord, Behold, I will sling out the inhabitants of the land at this once, and will distress them, that they may find it so. 19 Woe is me for my hurt! my wound is grievous; but I said, Truly this is a grief, and I must bear it. 20 **My tabernacle is spoiled, and all my cords are broken: my children are gone forth of me, and they are not: there is none to stretch forth my tent any more, and to set up my curtains.** 21 **For the pastors are become brutish, and have not sought the Lord: therefore they shall not prosper, and all their flocks shall be scattered.**

Remember how we showed that the curtain is the sky that was being made in the books of Moses and the prophets? We showed how that the instructions for us to build our house in the prophets. Now let us listen to a couple of times we can hear them talk about the tents in which men we to dwell in. Exodus 35:10 And every wise hearted among you shall come, and make all that the Lord hath commanded; 11 **The tabernacle, his tent, and his covering, his taches, and his boards, his bars, his pillars, and his sockets, Exodus 26:36 And thou shalt make an hanging for the door of the tent, of blue, and purple, and scarlet, and fine twined linen, wrought with needlework.**

These tents are spiritual tents in which we put around us when as we build our house. Our bodies being the house of God. Obviously, we will not show all of the instructions for that is not what these books are about. They are about getting people to turn back to our Father. Now remember that we must worship God in spirit and in truth. As you seen on my picture on the cover of this book, I wear fringes. Now check this out, the atmosphere protects the earth from things falling from space onto it. Just as these tents that we put around us, protect us from the ways of this world. Remember thy kingdom come in earth as it is in heaven. Now I will speak about my tent and the door of my tent. But first let us listen to Ephesian 6:11 **Put on the whole armour of God, that ye may be able to stand against the wiles of the devil. 12 For we wrestle not against flesh and blood, but against principalities, against powers, against the rulers of the darkness of this world, against spiritual wickedness in high places. 13 Wherefore take unto you the whole armour of God, that ye may be able to withstand in the evil day, and having done all, to stand.** 14 Stand therefore, having your loins girt about with truth, **and having on the breastplate of righteousness;** 15 And your feet shod with the preparation of the gospel of peace; 16 Above all, taking the shield of faith, wherewith ye shall be able to quench all the fiery darts of the wicked. 17 **And take the helmet of salvation, and the sword of the Spirit, which is the word of God: 18 Praying always with all prayer and supplication in the Spirit, and watching thereunto with all perseverance and supplication for all saints;**

The armour of God that I have put on is the entire bible and not just bits and pieces. I have learned of our Father through Moses and the prophets so that I could build my house (my body), and I have made this tent to be around me at all times so that all the things of the world do no harm to me. But what about the door to my tent. Numbers 15:38 Speak unto the children of Israel, **and bid them that they make them fringes in the borders of their garments throughout their generations, and that they put upon the fringe of the borders a ribband of blue: 39 And it shall be unto you for a fringe, that ye may look upon it, and remember all the commandments of the**

Lord, and do them ; and that ye seek not after your own heart and your own eyes, after which ye use to go a whoring: 40 That ye may remember, and do all my commandments, and be holy unto your God. 41 I am the Lord your God, which brought you out of the land of Egypt, to be your God: I am the Lord your God. Let us listen to this again, Exodus 26:36 And thou shalt make an hanging for the door of the tent, **of blue, and purple, and scarlet, and fine twined linen, wrought with needlework.** I do not have scarlet in my fringes but the blue is a blue violet in which is a form of purple.

Notice how we are told to make these fringes for ourselves. You used or heard the expression made with my own sweat and blood? The scarlet is me making the fringes myself and not having others make them for me. I use my own sweat and blood to make them. Because we can here that it tells us to make them ourselves. Then can you hear now why we are told to write the commandments on our door post? Without showing all the laws and such, let us just listen to where we are told this. Deuteronomy 6:9 And thou shalt write them upon the posts of thy house, and on thy gates. You are the house of God, so write these within yourself by meditating on all of God's word all of the time.

I confess, I am just learning this as I am writing it. I have always worn my fringes to remind me that I will do as I am commanded. Well I think it was the later part of 2012 when I first started to make and ware them for myself and not so that I could be seen for wearing them. And yes, it does take a little needlework, well a safety pin. But now we are seeing that these fringes are the door to my tent. Now I can relate to this firsthand. I told you all in the chapter of believing, that I am sometimes rebellious and do mess up. It is a learning process and I do know that, but there have been times that this learning process has been difficult. Our Father has been bringing me into His world, without leaving this one. Sometimes it gets to be hard to understand of what I am supposed to be doing. So, there has been a couple of times in which I took the fringes off. Big mistake, my mood was foul. I didn't realize what I was doing, I was opening that door and telling our Father that I didn't want His instructions. Needless to say, I think the longest they stayed off of me is almost three days. I do remember about six months ago I did take a shower and decided not to put them back on before I went in. I always listen to some of the bible as soon as I am done showering, so by the time I was walking out the door of the shower, the fringes were back on. I knew within myself, that I did not like feeling like I did before when I had kept them off for the almost three days, and I just couldn't keep them off. Now I know why. I will keep my door shut. Are you all starting to hear how the old testament is showing us how to build our house and how to protect our house? I will also mention one more thing about my fringes. For about two weeks before I received the commandment to make my name known, I started to think about making new fringes for the ones that I was wearing were getting to be stained and a little frayed. I just figured, oh I will soon, then when I finally made them and put them on, it wasn't but a day or two when I received the commandment to make my name known and to get the book done. There is absolutely no way anyone will tell me that they do not work.

    Now without showing that all the instructions for building the tabernacle, let us just know that we are to build our own personal tabernacle. Let us look at a couple of times where they are instructed to build the tabernacle. Exodus 25:9 According to all that I shew thee, after the pattern of the tabernacle, and the pattern of all the instruments thereof, **even so shall ye make it.** Exodus 26:1 **Moreover thou shalt make the tabernacle with ten curtains of fine twined linen, and blue, and purple, and scarlet: with cherubims of cunning work shalt thou make them.** Now let us look up the definition of tabernacle on E-sword, the online bible concordance. H4908 mishkân mish-kawn' From H7931; a residence (including a shepherd's hut, the lair of animals, figuratively the grave; **also the Temple**); specifically the Tabernacle (properly its wooden walls):–dwelleth, dwelling (place), **habitation,** tabernacle, tent. We are the temple of God and God habitats or dwells within each person. Can you see how we are being instructed on how to build our house of God within ourselves and not for everyone else. Listen to how we are being told that these tabernacles are for individual people. Luke 9:33 And it came to pass, as they departed from him, Peter said unto Jesus, Master, it is good for us to be here: **and let us make three tabernacles; one for thee, and one for Moses, and one for Elias: not knowing what he said.** Notice how it shows us how Peter did not know what he said. We cannot make tabernacles for others. Each individual must make their own. That is that engrafted word in which can save our souls. James 1:21 Wherefore lay apart all filthiness and superfluity of naughtiness, **and receive with meekness the engrafted word,** which is able to save your souls.

Just to make a side note here, this is because man has allowed his imagination to run wild as to why they cannot hear what our Father has been saying along. Many imaginations have run wild and made our Father out to be a completely different God than He really is. And I am living proof that it truly does take a complete desire to learn of Him and His ways if you want Him to teach you the proper way instead of the ways of man.

In the last book, we showed that most of the laws, rules, judgements, statues, ordinances, and commandments were for most of them in heaven in which have dominion over our bodies. Now we are leaning that we really need to be thinking about how Jesus told us to pray. Matthew 6:9 After this manner therefore pray ye: Our Father which art in heaven, Hallowed be thy name. 10 **Thy kingdom come, Thy will be done in earth, as it is in heaven.** 11 Give us this day our daily bread. 12 And forgive us our debts, as we forgive our debtors. 13 And lead us not into temptation, but deliver us from evil: For thine is the kingdom, and the power, and the glory, for ever. Amen. We are to be doing the same thing, but in a spiritual realm. We are actually hearing how to build our lives so that we can be doing what our Father needs us to be doing. We are being told of how to do it without being told directly how to build our lives.

Remember how we showed, in the last book, that there are 15 verses that tell us to be sober, sober minded, or to think soberly in the new testament. Then we showed that there are 30 verses that mention our conscience. This is where we put on the helmet of salvation. God the Father is our salvation. When we let the bible, bible verses, and or just meditate on the word of God all the time. And that means all of the bible and not just bits and pieces or a couple hours a day. We are putting on the helmet of salvation.

How can anyone build their house on this rock (the old testament), if they think this rock is ugly, defiled, unjust, and most of all, not perfect in all that He is doing, done, and will do? Let us listen to the two greatest commandments again. Matthew 22:36 Master, which is the great commandment in the law? 37 Jesus said unto him, **Thou shalt love the Lord thy God with all thy heart, and with all thy soul, and with all thy mind. 38 This is the first and great commandment. 39 And the second is like unto it, Thou shalt love thy neighbour as thyself. 40 On these two commandments hang all the law and the prophets.**

How can anyone love God with all of their heart, soul, and mind if they do not want to get to know everything about Him? As we showed in the last book, one of the main things the old testament does, is shows us how to love our neighbor as ourselves. That is why we are told to hang all of the law and prophets on these two commandments.

But now listen to what our Father will do because so many people have chosen not to get to know Him and just live off their imagination of Him. Jeremiah 9 Oh that my head were waters, and mine eyes a fountain of tears, that I might weep day and night for the slain of the daughter of my people! 2 Oh that I had in the wilderness a lodging place of wayfaring men; that I might leave my people, and go from them! for they be all adulterers, an assembly of treacherous men. 3 And they bend their tongues like their bow for lies: but they are not valiant for the truth upon the earth; for they proceed from evil to evil, and they know not me, saith the Lord. 4 Take ye heed every one of his neighbour, and trust ye not in any brother: for every brother will utterly supplant, and every neighbour will walk with slanders. 5 And they will deceive every one his neighbour, and will not speak the truth: they have taught their tongue to speak lies, and weary themselves to commit iniquity. 6 **Thine habitation is in the midst of deceit; through deceit they refuse to know me, saith the Lord.** 7 Therefore thus saith the Lord of hosts, Behold, I will melt them, and try them; for how shall I do for the daughter of my people? 8 Their tongue is as an arrow shot out; it speaketh deceit: one speaketh peaceably to his neighbour with his mouth, but in heart he layeth his wait. 9 Shall I not visit them for these things? saith the Lord: shall not my soul be avenged on such a nation as this? 10 For the mountains will I take up a weeping and wailing, and for the habitations of the wilderness a lamentation, because they are burned up, so that none can pass through them; neither can men hear the voice of the cattle; both the fowl of the heavens and the beast are fled; they are gone. 11 And I will make Jerusalem heaps, and a den of dragons; and I will make the cities of Judah desolate, without an inhabitant. 12 Who is the wise man, that may understand this? and who is he to whom the mouth of the Lord hath spoken, that he may declare it, for what the land perisheth and is burned up like a wilderness, that none passeth through? 13 **And the Lord saith, Because they have forsaken my law which I set before them, and have not obeyed my voice, neither walked therein; 14 But have walked after the imagination of their own heart, and after Baalim, which their fathers taught them:** 15 Therefore thus saith the Lord of hosts, the God of Israel; Behold, I will feed them, even this people, with wormwood, and give them water of gall to drink. 16 I will scatter them also among the heathen, whom neither they nor their fathers have known: and I will send a sword after them, till I have consumed them. 17 Thus saith the Lord of hosts, Consider ye, and call for the mourning women, that they may come; and send for cunning women, that they may come: 18 And let them make haste, and take up a wailing for us, that our eyes may run down with tears, and our eyelids gush out with waters. 19 For a voice of wailing is heard out of Zion, How are we spoiled! we are greatly confounded, because we have forsaken the land, because our dwellings have cast us out. 20 Yet hear the word of the Lord, O ye women, and let your ear receive the word of his mouth, and teach your daughters wailing, and every one her neighbour lamentation. 21 For death is come up into our windows, and is entered into our palaces, to cut off the children from without, and the young men from the streets. 22 Speak, Thus saith the Lord, Even the carcases of men shall fall as dung upon the open field, and as the handful after the harvestman, and none shall gather them. 23 Thus saith the Lord, Let not the wise man glory in his wisdom, neither let the mighty man glory in his might, let not the rich man glory in his riches: 24 **But let him that glorieth glory in this, that he understandeth and knoweth me, that I am the Lord which exercise lovingkindness, judgment, and righteousness, in the earth: for in these things I delight, saith the Lord.** 25 Behold, the days come, saith the Lord, that I will punish all them which are circumcised with the uncircumcised; 26 Egypt, and Judah, and Edom, and the children of Ammon, and Moab, and all that are in the utmost corners, that dwell in the wilderness: for all these nations are uncircumcised, and all the house of Israel are uncircumcised in the heart.

Now I am sure that there are many that are wondering how God can do this if He is all about love. Remember we all have transgressed his law. That is why are souls were cast out of heaven, probably billions of years ago, and were given another chance to learn how to love in the same manner that He loves. Our Father has had me show in all three books that He is about love, but people refuse to learn about Him. Remember in the last book of how every person is a part of the son of God? When we do something to one of His children, He is the one that justifies your actions by making sure the same thing happens to you. That is a fair love for all and not just a few. Now He is getting ready to bring this world to an end and welcome some back into heaven. His house in which is perfect. It is perfect because it is built on love. Why would He allow anyone to come into His house that does not want anything to do with His perfect love? I mean, that is why we got cast out, we thought our own ways were better. Why would He allow someone in that does not have a desire to be obedient to everything He commands? If you do not believe He is perfect than you will try to run things differently then He already has it functioning perfectly. In reality, it isn't Him it, it is our own selves. Because we refuse to listen to Him and trust His perfection.

Now maybe we can all see why Jesus said many will not make it to eternal life. Let us listen to Matthew 7:13 Enter ye in at the strait gate: for wide is the gate, and broad is the way, that leadeth to destruction, and many there be which go in there at: 14 **Because strait is the gate, and narrow is the way, which leadeth unto life, and few there be that find it.** 15 Beware of false prophets, which come to you in sheep's clothing, but inwardly they are ravening wolves. 16 Ye shall know them by their fruits. Do men gather grapes of thorns, or figs of thistles. 17 Even so every good tree bringeth forth good fruit; but a corrupt tree bringeth forth evil fruit. 18 A good tree cannot bring forth evil fruit, neither can a corrupt tree bring forth good fruit. 19 Every tree that bringeth not forth good fruit is hewn down, and cast into the fire. 20 Wherefore by their fruits ye shall know them. 21 **Not every one that saith unto me, Lord, Lord, shall enter into the kingdom of heaven; but he that doeth the will of my Father which is in heaven. 22 Many will say to me in that day, Lord, Lord, have we not prophesied in thy name? and in thy name have cast out devils? and in thy name done many wonderful works? 23 And then will I profess unto them, I never knew you: depart from me, ye that work iniquity.**

This leads us to Isaiah 27 n that day the Lord with his sore and great and strong sword shall punish leviathan the piercing serpent, even leviathan that crooked serpent; and he shall slay the dragon that is in the sea. 2 In that day sing ye unto her, A vineyard of red wine. 3 I the Lord do keep it; I will water it every moment: lest any hurt it, I will keep it night and day. 4 Fury is not in me: who would set the briers and thorns against me in battle? I would go through them, I would burn them together. 5 Or let him take hold of my strength, that he may make peace with me; and he shall make peace with me. 6 He shall cause them that come of Jacob to take root: Israel shall blossom and bud, and fill the face of the world with fruit. 7 Hath he smitten him, as he smote those that smote him? or is he slain according to the slaughter of them that are slain by him? 8 In measure, when it shooteth forth, thou wilt debate with it: he stayeth his rough wind in the day of the east wind. 9 By this therefore shall the iniquity of Jacob be purged; and this is all the fruit to take away his sin; when he maketh all the stones of the altar as chalkstones that are beaten in sunder, the groves and images shall not stand up. 10 Yet the defenced city shall be desolate, and the habitation forsaken, and left like a wilderness: there shall the calf feed, and there shall he lie down, and consume the branches thereof. 11 When the boughs thereof are withered, they shall be broken off: the women come, and set them on fire: **for it is a people of no understanding: therefore he that made them will not have mercy on them, and he that formed them will shew them no favour.** 12 And it shall come to pass in that day, that the Lord shall beat off from the channel of the river unto the stream of Egypt, and ye shall be gathered one by one, O ye children of Israel. 13 And it shall come to pass in that day, that the great trumpet shall be blown, and they shall come which were ready to perish in the land of Assyria, and the outcasts in the land of Egypt, and shall worship the Lord in the holy mount at Jerusalem.

This leads us to where we need to say that it is nobodies' fault that you have not been able to understand this but your own. Don't be like Adam and Eve in the very beginning and try to say that someone taught me. You have heard of the bible, so what you did with it is your own fault. Even if you want to say that your pastor, preacher, priest, or any other teacher has taught you differently, it is still your own fault that you didn't build your house as instructed in our bibles. Ephesians 4:18 **Having the understanding darkened, being alienated from the life of God through the ignorance that is in them, because of the blindness of their heart:** 19 Who being past feeling have given themselves over unto lasciviousness, to work all uncleanness with greediness. Isaiah 44 et now hear, O Jacob my servant; and Israel, whom I have chosen: 2 Thus saith the Lord that made thee, and formed thee from the womb, which will help thee; Fear not, O Jacob, my servant; and thou, Jesurun, whom I have chosen. 3 For I will pour water upon him that is thirsty, and floods upon the dry ground: I will pour my spirit upon thy seed, and my blessing upon thine offspring: 4 And they shall spring up as among the grass, as willows by the water courses. 5 One shall say, I am the Lord's; and another shall call himself by the name of Jacob; and another shall subscribe with his hand unto the Lord, and surname himself by the name of Israel.

6 Thus saith the Lord the King of Israel, and his redeemer the Lord of hosts; I am the first, and I am the last; and beside me there is no God. 7 And who, as I, shall call, and shall declare it, and set it in order for me, since I appointed the ancient people? and the things that are coming, and shall come, let them shew unto them. 8 Fear ye not, neither be afraid: have not I told thee from that time, and have declared it? ye are even my witnesses. Is there a God beside me? yea, there is no God; I know not any. 9 They that make a graven image are all of them vanity; and their delectable things shall not profit; and they are their own witnesses; they see not, nor know; that they may be ashamed. 10 Who hath formed a god, or molten a graven image that is profitable for nothing? 11 Behold, all his fellows shall be ashamed: and the workmen, they are of men: let them all be gathered together, let them stand up; yet they shall fear, and they shall be ashamed together. 12 The smith with the tongs both worketh in the coals, and fashioneth it with hammers, and worketh it with the strength of his arms: yea, he is hungry, and his strength faileth: he drinketh no water, and is faint. 13 The carpenter stretcheth out his rule; he marketh it out with a line; he fitteth it with planes, and he marketh it out with the compass, and maketh it after the figure of a man, according to the beauty of a man; that it may remain in the house. 14 He heweth him down cedars, and taketh the cypress and the oak, which he strengtheneth for himself among the trees of the forest: he planteth an ash, and the rain doth nourish it. 15 Then shall it be for a man to burn: for he will take thereof, and warm himself; yea, he kindleth it, and baketh bread; yea, he maketh a god, and worshippeth it; he maketh it a graven image, and falleth down thereto. 16 He burneth part thereof in the fire; with part thereof he eateth flesh; he roasteth roast, and is satisfied: yea, he warmeth himself, and saith, Aha, I am warm, I have seen the fire: 17 And the residue thereof he maketh a god, even his graven image: he falleth down unto it, and worshippeth it, and prayeth unto it, and saith, Deliver me; for thou art my god. 18 **They have not known nor understood: for he hath shut their eyes, that they cannot see; and their hearts, that they cannot understand. 19 And none** considereth in his heart, neither is there knowledge nor

understanding to say, I have burned part of it in the fire; yea, also I have baked bread upon the coals thereof; I have roasted flesh, and eaten it: and shall I make the residue thereof an abomination? shall I fall down to the stock of a tree? 20 He feedeth on ashes: a deceived heart hath turned him aside, that he cannot deliver his soul, nor say, Is there not a lie in my right hand?

Our Father does not respect or favor any person as you just read a bit ago. It does not matter who you are or who you know, if you do not understand Him and what He is doing, He is not allowing you into His perfect house. I know that there are probably some that are thinking that this is not fair for our Father could have shown us in an easier way. Remember we were told that He hid this knowledge. He hid it for there is no thief getting into His house. Our hearts must be right with Him and not man. To this I must say, I don't think it has been hidden. It has been in our bible all along. Man, just don't take the time to listen to Him. Luke 12:2 For there is nothing covered, that shall not be revealed; neither hid, that shall not be known. All of my knowledge comes from the King James bible and the King James bible only.

So, let us listen to where our Father explains this very well. Ezekiel 18 The word of the Lord came unto me again, saying, 2 What mean ye, that ye use this proverb concerning the land of Israel, saying, The fathers have eaten sour grapes, and the children's teeth are set on edge? 3 As I live, saith the Lord God, ye shall not have occasion any more to use this proverb in Israel. 4 Behold, all souls are mine; as the soul of the father, so also the soul of the son is mine: the soul that sinneth, it shall die. 5 But if a man be just, and do that which is lawful and right, 6 And hath not eaten upon the mountains, neither hath lifted up his eyes to the idols of the house of Israel, neither hath defiled his neighbour's wife, neither hath come near to a menstruous woman, 7 And hath not oppressed any, but hath restored to the debtor his pledge, hath spoiled none by violence, hath given his bread to the hungry, and hath covered the naked with a garment; 8 He that hath not given forth upon usury, neither hath taken any increase, that hath withdrawn his hand from iniquity, hath executed true judgment between man and man, 9 Hath walked in my statutes, and hath kept my judgments, to deal truly; he is just, he shall surely live, saith the Lord God. 10 If he beget a son that is a robber, a shedder of blood, and that doeth the like to any one of these things, 11 And that doeth not any of those duties, but even hath eaten upon the mountains, and defiled his neighbour's wife, 12 Hath oppressed the poor and needy, hath spoiled by violence, hath not restored the pledge, and hath lifted up his eyes to the idols, hath committed abomination, 13 Hath given forth upon usury, and hath taken increase: shall he then live? he shall not live: he hath done all these abominations; he shall surely die; his blood shall be upon him. 14 Now, lo, if he beget a son, that seeth all his father's sins which he hath done, and considereth, and doeth not such like, 15 That hath not eaten upon the mountains, neither hath lifted up his eyes to the idols of the house of Israel, hath not defiled his neighbour's wife, 16 Neither hath oppressed any, hath not withholden the pledge, neither hath spoiled by violence, but hath given his bread to the hungry, and hath covered the naked with a garment, 17 That hath taken off his hand from the poor, that hath not received usury nor increase, hath executed my judgments, hath walked in my statutes; he shall not die for the iniquity of his father, he shall surely live. 18 As for his father, because he cruelly oppressed, spoiled his brother by violence, and did that which is not good among his people, lo, even he shall die in his iniquity. 19 Yet say ye, Why? doth not the son bear the iniquity of the father? When the son hath done that which is lawful and right, and hath kept all my statutes, and hath done them, he shall surely live. 20 The soul that sinneth, it shall die. The son shall not bear the iniquity of the father, neither shall the father bear the iniquity of the son: the righteousness of the righteous shall be upon him, and the wickedness of the wicked shall be upon him. 21 But if the wicked will turn from all his sins that he hath committed, and keep all my statutes, and do that which is lawful and right, he shall surely live, he shall not die. 22 All his transgressions that he hath committed, they shall not be mentioned unto him: in his righteousness that he hath done he shall live. 23 Have I any pleasure at all that the wicked should die? saith the Lord God: and not that he should return from his ways, and live?

24 But when the righteous turneth away from his righteousness, and committeth iniquity, and doeth according to all the abominations that the wicked man doeth, shall he live? All his righteousness that he hath done shall not be mentioned: in his trespass that he hath trespassed, and in his sin that he hath sinned, in them shall he die. 25 Yet ye say, The way of the Lord is not equal. Hear now, O house of Israel; Is not my way equal? are not your ways unequal? 26 When a righteous man turneth away from his righteousness, and committeth iniquity, and dieth in them; for his iniquity that he hath done shall he die. 27 Again, when the wicked man turneth away from his wickedness that he hath committed, and doeth that which is lawful and right, he shall save his soul alive. 28 Because he considereth, and turneth away from all his transgressions that he hath committed, he shall surely live, he shall not die. 29 Yet saith the house of Israel, The way of the Lord is not equal. O house of Israel, are not my ways equal? are not your ways unequal? 30 Therefore I will judge you, O house of Israel, every one according to his ways, saith the Lord God. Repent, and turn yourselves from all your transgressions; so iniquity shall not be your ruin. 31 Cast away from you all your transgressions, whereby ye have transgressed; and make you a new heart and a new spirit: for why will ye die, O house of Israel? 32 For I have no pleasure in the death of him that dieth, saith the Lord God: wherefore turn yourselves, and live ye.

Now at the same time that we can hear that each person must pay for their own sins and no one else's, we can hear that anyone that is alive can still repent and change his or her ways and turn back to our Father and seek His perfection. Jeremiah 3 They say, If a man put away his wife, and she go from him, and become another man's, shall he return unto her again? shall not that land be greatly polluted? but thou hast played the harlot with many lovers; yet return again to me, saith the Lord. 2 Lift up thine eyes unto the high places, and see where thou hast not been lien with. In the ways hast thou sat for them, as the Arabian in the wilderness; and thou hast polluted the land with thy whoredoms and with thy wickedness. 3 Therefore the showers have been withholden, and there hath been no latter rain; and thou hadst a whore's forehead, thou refusedst to be ashamed. 4 Wilt thou not from this time cry unto me, My father, thou art the guide of my youth? 5 Will he reserve his anger for ever? will he keep it to the end? Behold, thou hast spoken and done evil things as thou couldest. 6 The Lord said also unto me in the days of Josiah the king, Hast thou seen that which backsliding Israel hath done? she is gone up upon every high mountain and under every green tree, and there hath played the harlot. 7 And I said after she had done all these things, Turn thou unto me. But she returned not. And her treacherous sister Judah saw it. 8 **And I saw, when for all the causes whereby backsliding Israel committed adultery I had put her away, and given her a bill of divorce;** yet her treacherous sister Judah feared not, but went and played the harlot also. 9 And it came to pass through the lightness of her whoredom, that she defiled the land, and committed adultery with stones and with stocks. 10 And yet for all this her treacherous sister Judah hath not turned unto me with her whole heart, but feignedly, saith the Lord. 11 And the Lord said unto me, The backsliding Israel hath justified herself more than treacherous Judah. 12 Go and proclaim these words toward the north, **and say, Return, thou backsliding Israel, saith the Lord; and I will not cause mine anger to fall upon you: for I am merciful, saith the Lord, and I will not keep anger for ever. 13 Only acknowledge thine iniquity, that thou hast transgressed against the Lord thy God, and hast scattered thy ways to the strangers under every green tree, and ye have not obeyed my voice, saith the Lord. 14 Turn, O backsliding children, saith the Lord; for I am married unto you: and I will take you one of a city, and two of a family, and I will bring you to Zion:**

We showed int the first book, that the bill of divorcement that our Father gave us is not final. Without having to go over all of it again, we can see in verse 8 that He gave us a bill of divorcement and then in verse 14, that the divorce is not final. But at the same time listen to what needs to be done to keep the marriage alive. And neither of you will wear rings. Our Father never said this was going to be easy, nor did He say that He will make it simple. But He did tell us that He comes to us in a cloud. Exodus 19:9 And the Lord said unto Moses, **Lo, I come unto thee in a thick cloud, that the people may hear**

when I speak with thee, and believe thee for ever. And Moses told the words of the people unto the Lord. How hard is it to see when the fog is thick? Now think of the bible as being the cloud in which our Father comes to us. This is why we are to diligently seek Him. Hebrews 11:6 But without faith it is impossible to please him: for he that cometh to God must believe that he is, **and that he is a rewarder of them that diligently seek him.** My King James bible has just over 2000 pages in it. That is a pretty thick cloud, if you will. And a pretty dark cloud if you allow your imagination to run wild. Continue to seek Him through the entire cloud and you will see that this cloud will change your life. So now that we have done this chapter, we ask you, where are you going to build your house?

How will the truth ever set you free if you refuse to listen to the word of God? John 8 :31 Then said Jesus to those Jews which believed on him, If ye continue in my word, then are ye my disciples indeed; **32 And ye shall know the truth, and the truth shall make you free**. Remember we showed in the first book that the truth is the law. Note that this next verse was written before the new testament. Psalm 119:142 Thy righteousness is an everlasting righteousness, **and thy law is the truth**. Then as shown in the second book, the royal law is James 2:8 **If ye fulfil the royal law according to the scripture, Thou shalt love thy neighbour as thyself, ye do well**: Now with just listening to everything that we have been hearing, listen to what we are told about the doctrine of God our Father. Deuteronomy 32 Give ear, O ye heavens, and I will speak; and hear, O earth, the words of my mouth. 2 My doctrine shall drop as the rain, my speech shall distil as the dew, as the small rain upon the tender herb, and as the showers upon the grass: 3 Because I will publish the name of the Lord: ascribe ye greatness unto our God. Try to listen to all of God's doctrine and watch how everything around you starts to bloom.

CONCLUSION

First thing that we want to bring up is I stated that this will be the final book in which I will write of this trilogy of books. I cannot say that, for my knowledge will continue to grow as long as I am in the flesh. And I have to say here something that I tell people all the time. It is not up to me; it is up to our Father for He is my boss. And when I say He is my boss; I mean He is my boss in everything that I do. He is the reason I awake; He is the reason I am alive; He is my dispatcher at my job; I drive the truck He tells me to drive; He is my doctor or medical advisor. He is my rock; He is my fortress and most of all He is my salvation.

I mentioned in the chapter of believing that it took me about a week to find a job after the day of dispute with my brother and his wife in South Dakota. Beings how we just mentioned that our Father is my dispatcher and I drive the truck that He wants me in, we need to explain this a bit further. When I was at my brother's, I did not know this that I was being led to the company I drive for. I know this for a fact for there was a time about a year after I started here that I was going to quit. I was tired of not going out west for this company usually stays east of Denver, Co. And at that time our truck only went 63-64 mph, depending on the ware on the tires. It was a Thursday in which I sent a message to my dispatcher telling him that I am officially giving my two weeks' notice. I did not give him the reasons I was quitting but I was quitting.

Then come Saturday, I got dispatched on a load going to Oregon. It is a state that is on the west coast for those not familiar with geography of the country. It was Monday when I called my dispatcher and cancelled my notice. I got back from Oregon and was dispatched on a load that was going to Las Angeles, Ca. I was at total awe. I couldn't believe what was happening. Then on my way back from California I had to take a 34-hour restart on my hours so that I could make delivery on time. Well I would be an hour late but if I would have just run my recap, then I would have been an entire day late. I will not try and explain the laws that I must follow for if you do not drive truck, it won't make since to you. This too, was touched on in the first book. Anyway, when I got to customers in Chicago, I called my dispatcher and told him I got there as fast as I could with a 63-mph truck. I already had my plans for my next load in which was picking up in Waterloo, Ia. He stated that they are turning trucks up now. I asked how soon can we have them turned up? He told me as soon as I can get by a terminal. The load that was picking up in Waterloo, Ia. took me right by the East Dubuque, Il terminal. I got my truck turned up that day.

This all happened within two weeks of me giving my notice of quitting. Just another example of how our Father is the one in control over everything. It isn't up to me on who I work for or when I get days off and such. He is my true boss in everything. Yes, there are days in which I hate it but overall I will not give any of it up for all the money, gold, silver, diamonds, emeralds, and rubies in the world combined.

I want to show one chapter of many in our bible that really makes me feel this way. Psalm 139 O lord, thou hast searched me, and known me. 2 Thou knowest my downsitting and mine uprising, thou understandest my thought afar off. 3 Thou compassest my path and my lying down, and art acquainted with all my ways. 4 For there is not a word in my tongue, but, lo, O Lord, thou knowest it altogether. 5 Thou hast beset me behind and before, and laid thine hand upon me. 6 Such knowledge is too wonderful for me; it is high, I cannot attain unto it. 7 Whither shall I go from thy spirit? or whither shall I flee from thy presence? 8 If I ascend up into heaven, thou art there: if I make my bed in hell, behold, thou art there. 9 If I take the wings of the morning, and dwell in the uttermost parts of the sea; 10 Even there shall thy hand lead me, and thy right hand shall hold me. 11 If

I say, Surely the darkness shall cover me; even the night shall be light about me. 12 Yea, the darkness hideth not from thee; but the night shineth as the day: the darkness and the light are both alike to thee. 13 For thou hast possessed my reins: thou hast covered me in my mother's womb. 14 I will praise thee; for I am fearfully and wonderfully made: marvellous are thy works; and that my soul knoweth right well. 15 My substance was not hid from thee, when I was made in secret, and curiously wrought in the lowest parts of the earth. 16 Thine eyes did see my substance, yet being unperfect; and in thy book all my members were written, which in continuance were fashioned, when as yet there was none of them. 17 How precious also are thy thoughts unto me, O God! how great is the sum of them! 18 If I should count them, they are more in number than the sand: when I awake, I am still with thee. 19 Surely thou wilt slay the wicked, O God: depart from me therefore, ye bloody men. 20 For they speak against thee wickedly, and thine enemies take thy name in vain. 21 Do not I hate them, O Lord, that hate thee? and am not I grieved with those that rise up against thee? 22 I hate them with perfect hatred: I count them mine enemies. 23 Search me, O God, and know my heart: try me, and know my thoughts: 24 And see if there be any wicked way in me, and lead me in the way everlasting.

Now let us listen to who our enemies are by our Father's definition. Psalm74:4 **Thine enemies roar in the midst of thy congregations; they set up their ensigns for signs.** They do not take the time to try and understand who our Father is and what He is all about. They would rather look for things in which indicate the end is near in which keeps people away from the truth. They are not learning how to love others and they are not teaching others how we should love.

As we have went through this book, we have learned some very important things about our bibles and how it is about our lives today. For anyone that still has any doubt as to whether or not we are in the end times; let us listen to Ecclesiastes 3 To every thing there is a season, and a time to every purpose under the heaven: 2 A time to be born, and a time to die; a time to plant, and a time to pluck up that which is planted; 3 A time to kill, and a time to heal; a time to break down, and a time to build up; 4 A time to weep, and a time to laugh; a time to mourn, and a time to dance; 5 A time to cast away stones, and a time to gather stones together; a time to embrace, and a time to refrain from embracing; 6 A time to get, and a time to lose; a time to keep, and a time to cast away; 7 A time to rend, and a time to sew; a time to keep silence, and a time to speak; 8 A time to love, and a time to hate; a time of war, and a time of peace. 9 What profit hath he that worketh in that wherein he laboureth? 10 I have seen the travail, which God hath given to the sons of men to be exercised in it. 11 **He hath made every thing beautiful in his time: also he** hath set the world in their heart, so that no man can find out the work that God maketh from the beginning to the end.

Through these three books that our Father has had me write, we can all agree that the bible is making a lot more since. Our Father has made sure that no man would be able to understand how He is doing this until the time of the end as we just read. Now that we can know that the old testament is about how we are to build our own personal house of God, we can know that we are getting very close to the end.

Remember there is nothing new under the sun as shown in Ecclesiastes 1 earlier. Can you now see how Moses parted the Red Sea? We are in that sea now and this sea is full of man's blood. Now we truly know what it means when we are told it will be just like the days of Noah. Luke 17:26 **And as it was in the days of Noe, so shall it be also in the days of the Son of man. 27 They did eat, they drank, they married wives, they were given in marriage, until the day that Noah entered into the ark, and the flood came, and destroyed them all. 28 Likewise also as it was in the days of Lot; they did eat, they drank, they bought, they sold, they planted, they builded; 29 But the same day that Lot went out of Sodom it rained fire and brimstone from heaven, and destroyed them all. 30 Even thus shall it be in the day when the Son of man is revealed.** Makes you think about the bible completely different doesn't it? This world is covered in water just as it was in the days of Noah. Notice how the same time that we all are being shown that this world is covered in a spiritual water at the same time the son of man, or I am being revealed.

Knowing that there are a couple more things that we need to consider. There are a lot of people out here that keep wondering why things just keep happening to them the way they do. This is because most do not realize that our Father has always gave us an opportunity to learn why these things happen. Yes, we just heard that He put it in man's heart not to know until the time of the end, but why did He do this. It is because this world goes chasing after their imagination of God, instead of just listening to Him.

Now we need to listen to Psalm 83 Keep not thou silence, O God: hold not thy peace, and be not still, O God. 2 For, lo, thine enemies make a tumult: and they that hate thee have lifted up the head. 3 They have taken crafty counsel against thy people, and consulted against thy hidden ones. 4 They have said, Come, and let us cut them off from being a nation; that the name of Israel may be no more in remembrance. 5 For they have consulted together with one consent: they are confederate against thee: 6 The tabernacles of Edom, and the Ishmaelites; of Moab, and the Hagarenes; 7 Gebal, and Ammon, and Amalek; the Philistines with the inhabitants of Tyre; 8 Assur also is joined with them: they have holpen the children of Lot. Selah. 9 Do unto them as unto the Midianites; as to Sisera, as to Jabin, at the brook of Kison: 10 Which perished at Endor: they became as dung for the earth. 11 Make their nobles like Oreb, and like Zeeb: yea, all their princes as Zebah, and as Zalmunna: 12 Who said, Let us take to ourselves the houses of God in possession. 13 O my God, make them like a wheel; as the stubble before the wind. 14 As the fire burneth a wood, and as the flame setteth the mountains on fire; 15 So persecute them with thy tempest, and make them afraid with thy storm. 16 Fill their faces with shame; that they may seek thy name, O Lord. 17 Let them be confounded and troubled for ever; yea, let them be put to shame, and perish: 18 **That men may know that thou, whose name alone is Jehovah, art the most high over all the earth.**

In the last book, we showed that the name Jehovah means to self-exist. Yes, God our Father is sitting right inside of you. I am going to tell you a little bit of a story so you all can hear how our Father told me that He wants this in the book. We mentioned earlier in the book, that I know a woman that has marital problems going on in here life and that her 18-year-old daughter was moving out. We showed how that was putting salt on an open wound. Remember I am married to our Father and there is absolutely no chance of me allowing any woman into my house of God. Me being the house of God as we all have learned, for that would take my mind off of our Father and that is something I will not allow. But anyway, I was talking with her on the phone a few days ago and she said she knows what it feels like to love somebody and still feel alone. As soon as we got off the phone, the name Jehovah came to mind and I have known for some while now that He is self-existing, I knew right away that this is exactly how are Father feels. He is inside each and every one of us. He is sitting there wanting to share His love with us, but this world doesn't want Him. As we have shown, He will not force Himself on anyone, it is your choice.

I will guarantee you this though, once you get a taste of how deep and strong His love is for you, you will never look back. Okay I cannot say this for all for the scriptures do warn of this. Hebrews 6 Therefore leaving the principles of the doctrine of Christ, let us go on unto perfection; not laying again the foundation of repentance from dead works, and of faith toward God, 2 Of the doctrine of baptisms, and of laying on of hands, and of resurrection of the dead, and of eternal judgment. 3 And this will we do, if God permit. **4 For it is impossible for those who were once enlightened, and have tasted of the heavenly gift, and were made partakers of the Holy Ghost, 5 And have tasted the good word of God, and the powers of the world to come, 6 If they shall fall away, to renew them again unto repentance; seeing they crucify to themselves the Son of God afresh, and put him to an open shame. 7 For the earth which drinketh in the rain that cometh oft upon it, and bringeth forth herbs meet for them by whom it is dressed, receiveth blessing from God:** 8 But that which beareth thorns and briers is rejected, and is nigh unto cursing; whose end is to be burned. 9 But, beloved, we are persuaded better things of you, and things that accompany salvation, though we thus speak.

His love is so profound that I can't even imagine a woman being able to make me feel as He does. I truly feel that I am a spoiled little brat. I own nothing and I live paycheck to paycheck, okay, I do have one weeks' worth of clothes, four or five short sleeve shirts and four or five long sleeve shirts plus undershirts, a cell phone, a microwave, laptop for writing, CB for safety reasons, a tablet, and a large duffle bag for traveling out of the country if needed. yet I feel I have more than I need. Remember how Jesus said unless you become as a little child, you will not enter the kingdom of God. Just as our Father had me put in the first book, I feel my Father can do no wrong and there is (I will say it) no way that your dad is better than my dad. I am laughing when I say that but that is exactly how I feel. I am His little boy and He makes sure I have everything my heart desires. I have been married and have children. None of them has ever come close to making me feel as loved as I do by our Father.

This is where I want to mention that I have been told by some people that I am supposed to be with a woman for that is what the bible states. To that I will say if that is what you believe than you do not know the scriptures. Jesus stated himself that some are born that way and some that will become alone for the kingdom. Let us listen to what he says in Matthew 19:9 And I say unto you, Whosoever shall put away his wife, except it be for fornication, and shall marry another, committeth adultery: and whoso marrieth her which is put away doth commit adultery. **10 His disciples say unto him, If the case of the man be so with his wife, it is not good to marry. 11 But he said unto them, All men cannot receive this saying, save they to whom it is given. 12 For there are some eunuchs, which were so born from their mother's womb: and there are some eunuchs, which were made eunuchs of men: and there be eunuchs, which have made themselves eunuchs for the kingdom of heaven's sake. He that is able to receive it, let him receive it.**

Then let us listen to a little of 1 Corinthians 7. Now concerning the things whereof ye wrote unto me: It is good for a man not to touch a woman. 2 Nevertheless, to avoid fornication, let every man have his own wife, and let every woman have her own husband. 3

Let the husband render unto the wife due benevolence: and likewise also the wife unto the husband. 4 The wife hath not power of her own body, but the husband: and likewise also the husband hath not power of his own body, but the wife. 5 Defraud ye not one the other, except it be with consent for a time, that ye may give yourselves to fasting and prayer; and come together again, that Satan tempt you not for your incontinency. 6 But I speak this by permission, and not of commandment. **7 For I would that all men were even as I myself. But every man hath his proper gift of God, one after this manner, and another after that. 8 I say therefore to the unmarried and widows, it is good for them if they abide even as I.** 9 But if they cannot contain, let them marry: for it is better to marry than to burn. And I will assure you all, I can and will contain. Now I realize that we need to look at what eunuchs means on the E-sword, the online bible concordance. G2134 εὐνουχίζω eunouchizō yoo-noo-khid'-zo From G2135; to castrate **(figuratively live unmarried)**: - make . . . eunuch. As shown in the last book, if you are married, then you tend to care for the ways of the world to please your spouse, but if you are singe it is a lot easier to care for the ways of God.

Now we can understand why Jesus said there is no marriage in the resurrection. Matthew 22:24 Saying, Master, Moses said, If a man die, having no children, his brother shall marry his wife, and raise up seed unto his brother. 25 Now there were with us seven brethren: and the first, when he had married a wife, deceased, and, having no issue, left his wife unto his brother: 26 Likewise the second also, and the third, unto the seventh. 27 And last of all the woman died also. 28 Therefore in the resurrection whose wife shall she be of the seven? for they all had her. 29 Jesus answered and said unto them, **Ye do err, not knowing the scriptures, nor the power of God. 30 For in the resurrection they neither marry, nor are given in marriage, but are as the angels of God in heaven. 31 But as touching the resurrection of the dead, have ye not read that which was spoken unto you by God, saying, 32 I am the God of Abraham, and the God of Isaac, and the God of Jacob? God is not the God of the dead, but of the living.**

And to make another note here, the clothes that I wear are from Walmart. I will not spend extra money on clothes that only cover my body. I will not dress in a fashion that might intimidate some o make others feel as if I deserve better. I do not deserve any better than anyone else. I will say though; I do by my cowboy boots at a boot store for Walmart does not carry boots. And because I wear them most of the time, I need a boot that will last longer. And I will say that if we ever meet, you will know what I am about for I will not allow a conversation to go on for more than five minutes without bringing our Father into the conversation for He is my true love. You will know what I am about by the love you will hear come from my heart and not the clothes that I wear.

Now this is something that I am not sure if I should be putting in here or not, but I am going to throw this in here for this is something that I heard in the bible the very first time I read it. I will warn you though, this could freak you out a little. One thing in the book of Revelation that I am sure hasn't happened yet, and this is the supper of the great God. Revelation 19:17 **And I saw an angel standing in the sun; and he cried with a loud voice, saying to all the fowls that fly in the midst of heaven, Come and gather yourselves together unto the supper of the great God; 18 That ye may eat the flesh of kings, and the flesh of captains, and the flesh of mighty men, and the flesh of horses, and of them that sit on them, and the flesh of all men, both free and bond, both small and great.** The very first time I read the bible back in 2011, I thought and still think that this is our dead bodies. This is when our Father calls all the fowls of the heavens to come and eat. Yes, I believe in aliens, as we call them, but they too, are children of our Father for our Father created them also. Our souls will be gone at this time and they will only be eating our dead bodies. Remember our flesh is dung. Jeremiah 9:22 Speak, Thus saith the Lord, **Even the carcases of men shall fall as dung upon the open field, and as the handful after the harvestman, and none shall gather them.** 23 Thus saith the Lord, Let not the wise man glory in his wisdom, neither let the mighty man glory in his might, let not the rich man glory in his riches: 24 But let him that glorieth glory in this, that he understandeth and knoweth me, that I am the Lord which exercise lovingkindness, judgment, and righteousness, in the earth: for in these things I delight, saith the Lord. 25 Behold, the days come, saith the Lord, that I will punish all them which are circumcised with the uncircumcised; 26 Egypt, and Judah, and Edom, and the children of Ammon, and Moab, and all that are in the utmost corners, that dwell in the wilderness: for all these nations are uncircumcised, and all the house of Israel are uncircumcised in the heart. Jeremiah 25:33 **And the slain of the Lord shall be at that day from one end of the earth even unto the other end of the earth: they shall not be lamented, neither gathered, nor buried; they shall be dung upon the ground.**

This is where we really need to be thinking about what we said in the last book. We showed that the son of God is made up with about eight billion functioning body parts. Everybody on this planet. We will be in travail when we give birth to the son of God. This is when everybody will be changed in the blink of an eye.1 Corinthians 15:51 Behold, I shew you a mystery; We shall not all sleep, but we shall all be changed, 52 **In a moment, in the twinkling of an eye, at the last trump: for the trumpet shall sound, and the dead shall be raised incorruptible, and we shall be changed.** But before this happens we must go through labor pains.

This is when we really need to realize that our Father's hand is stretched out still. Isaiah 9 Nevertheless the dimness shall not be such as was in her vexation, when at the first he lightly afflicted the land of Zebulun and the land of Naphtali, and afterward did more grievously afflict her by the way of the sea, beyond Jordan, in Galilee of the nations. 2 The people that walked in darkness have seen a great light: they that dwell in the land of the shadow of death, upon them hath the light shined. 3 Thou hast multiplied the nation, and not increased the joy: they joy before thee according to the joy in harvest, and as men rejoice when they divide the spoil. 4 For thou hast broken the yoke of his burden, and the staff of his shoulder, the rod of his oppressor, as in the day of Midian. 5 For every battle of the warrior is with confused noise, and garments rolled in blood; but this shall be with burning and fuel of fire. 6 For unto us a child is born, unto us a son is given: and the government shall be upon his shoulder: and his name shall be called Wonderful, Counsellor, The mighty God, The everlasting Father, The Prince of Peace. 7 Of the increase of his government and peace there shall be no end, upon the throne of David, and upon his kingdom, to order it, and to establish it with judgment and with justice from henceforth even for ever. The zeal of the Lord of hosts will perform this. 8 The Lord sent a word into Jacob, and it hath lighted upon Israel. 9 And all the people shall know, even Ephraim and the inhabitant of Samaria, that say in the pride and stoutness of heart, 10 The bricks are fallen down, but we will build with hewn stones: the sycomores are cut down, but we will change them into cedars. 11 Therefore the Lord shall set up the adversaries of Rezin against him, and join his enemies together; 12 **The Syrians before, and the Philistines behind; and they shall devour Israel with open mouth. For all this his anger is not turned away, but his hand is stretched out still.** 13 For the people turneth not unto him that smiteth them, neither do they seek the Lord of hosts. 14 Therefore the Lord will cut off from Israel head and tail, branch and rush, in one day. 15 The ancient and honourable, he is the head; and the prophet that teacheth lies, he is the tail. 16 For the leaders of this people cause them to err; and they that are led of them are destroyed. 17 **Therefore the Lord shall have no joy in their young men, neither shall have mercy on their fatherless and widows: for every one is an hypocrite and an evildoer, and every mouth speaketh folly. For all this his anger is not turned away, but his hand is stretched out still.** 18 For wickedness burneth as the fire: it shall devour the briers and thorns, and shall kindle in the thickets of the forest, and they shall mount up like the lifting up of smoke. 19 Through the wrath of the Lord of hosts is the land darkened, and the people shall be as the fuel of the fire: no man shall spare his brother. 20 And he shall snatch on the right hand, and be hungry; and he shall eat on the left hand, and they shall not be satisfied: they shall eat every man the flesh of his own arm: 21 **Manasseh, Ephraim; and Ephraim, Manasseh: and they**

together shall be against Judah. For all this his anger is not turned away, but his hand is stretched out still.

He has not ended this world so that can only mean that there is room for repentance. I have told you all that I read the bible twice and have listened to it more than 20 times. I will continue to listen to the bible until the day I die. The reason I share this is because I really feel that the bible truly came to life once I started to listen to the word of God. From Genesis 1 through all the books of Revelation. I mean I believed the bible the first time I read it as described in the chapter believing but once I started listening, it became like a drug and I was and am addicted. So yes, if you have the will to learn, our Father has the power to show you.

Now I told you all in the chapter of believing of how I heard what the spirit said. I was commanded to get the book done and make my name known. I am going to give a little detail on that for there is something that I did not tell you. There was more that the spirit said but I didn't want to mention what else the spirit said till now. Now with all my understanding of the scriptures, I know what it meant when I heard a servant directly say to me. Hear what the spirit says. We all know that God is spirit, right. John 4:23 But the hour cometh, and now is, when the true worshippers shall worship the Father in spirit and in truth: for the Father seeketh such to worship him. 24 **God is a Spirit:** and they that worship him must worship him in spirit and in truth. I was told to get the book done on the 17th of June. Just under three weeks ago. Yes, I had started the book, but only had about 30,000 words or so before then. I am writing the conclusion now with over 100,000 words, and I feel as if maybe I didn't get everything in that is needed to be said. That is why I say there might be another. But at the same time that I heard the spirit say get the book done, I was also told something else. I was told that if I didn't get the book done, I would have to do it all over and start from the beginning. As we showed in the last book and in the chapter of reincarnation in this book, that means another 70-80,000 years without being with my Father.

But with Him telling me this, it makes me think of a couple of areas of the bible in which we need to look at. Because Jehovah is self- existing and now that the world is learning where Satan is, we are getting ready to meet our Father. Amos 4 Hear this word, ye kine of Bashan, that are in the mountain of Samaria, which oppress the poor, which crush the needy, which say to their masters, Bring, and let us drink. 2 The Lord God hath sworn by his holiness, that, lo, the days shall come upon you, that he will take you away with hooks, and your posterity with fishhooks. 3 And ye shall go out at the breaches, every cow at that which is before her; and ye shall cast them into the palace, saith the Lord. 4 Come to Bethel, and transgress; at Gilgal multiply transgression; and bring your sacrifices every morning, and your tithes after three years: 5 And offer a sacrifice of thanksgiving with leaven, and proclaim and publish the free offerings: for this liketh you, O ye children of Israel, saith the Lord God. 6 And I also have given you cleanness of teeth in all your cities, and want of bread in all your places: yet have ye not returned unto me, saith the Lord. 7 And also I have withholden the rain from you, when there were yet three months to the harvest: and I caused it to rain upon one city, and caused it not to rain upon another city: one piece was rained upon, and the piece whereupon it rained not withered. 8 So two or three cities wandered unto one city, to drink water; but they were not satisfied: yet have ye not returned unto me, saith the Lord. 9 I have smitten you with blasting and mildew: when your gardens and your vineyards and your fig trees and your olive trees increased, the palmerworm devoured them: yet have ye not returned unto me, saith the Lord. 10 I have sent among you the pestilence after the manner of Egypt: your young men have I slain with the sword, and have taken away your horses; and I have made the stink of your camps to come up unto your nostrils: yet have ye not returned unto me, saith the Lord. 11 I have overthrown some of you, as God overthrew Sodom and Gomorrah, and ye were as a firebrand plucked out of the burning: yet have ye not returned unto me, saith the Lord. 12 **Therefore thus will I do unto thee, O Israel: and because I will do this unto thee, prepare to meet thy God, O Israel.** 13 For, lo, he that formeth the mountains, and createth the wind, and declareth unto man what is his thought, that maketh the morning darkness, and treadeth upon the high places of the earth, The Lord, The God of hosts, is his name.

Now we are going to look at one more spot. This is an area that caught my attention the very first time that I listened to the bible. I am going to place the entire chapter so that maybe you can hear how this is all connected even more than you have already. Ezekiel 12 The word of the Lord also came unto me, saying, 2 **Son of man, thou dwellest in the midst of a rebellious house, which have eyes to see, and see not; they have ears to hear, and hear not: for they are a rebellious house.** 3 Therefore, thou son of man, prepare thee stuff for removing, and remove by day in their sight; and thou shalt remove from thy place to another place in their sight: it may be they will consider, though they be a rebellious house. 4 Then shalt thou bring forth thy stuff by day in their sight, as stuff for removing: and thou shalt go forth at even in their sight, as they that go forth into captivity. 5 Dig thou through the wall in their sight, and carry out thereby. 6 In their sight shalt thou bear it upon thy shoulders, and carry it forth in the twilight: thou shalt cover thy face, that thou see not the ground: for I have set thee for a sign unto the house of Israel. 7 And I did so as I was commanded: I brought forth my stuff by day, as stuff for captivity, and in the even I digged through the wall with mine hand; I brought it forth in the twilight, and I bare it upon my shoulder in their sight. 8 And in the morning came the word of the Lord unto me, saying, 9 Son of man, hath not the house of Israel, the rebellious house, said unto thee, What doest thou? 10 Say thou unto them, Thus saith the Lord God; This burden concerneth the prince in Jerusalem, and all the house of Israel that are among them. 11 Say, I am your sign: like as I have done, so shall it be done unto them: they shall remove and go into captivity. 12 And the prince that is among them shall bear upon his shoulder in the twilight, and shall go forth: they shall dig through the wall to carry out thereby: he shall cover his face, that he see not the ground with his eyes. 13 My net also will I spread upon him, and he shall be taken in my snare: and I will bring him to Babylon to the land of the Chaldeans; yet shall he not see it, though he shall die there. 14 And I will scatter toward every wind all that are about him to help him, and all his bands; and I will draw out the sword after them. 15 And they shall know that I am the Lord, when I shall scatter them among the nations, and disperse them in the countries. 16 But I will leave a few men of them from the sword, from the famine, and from the pestilence; that they may declare all their abominations among the heathen whither they come; and they shall know that I am the Lord. 17 Moreover the word of the Lord came to me, saying, 18 Son of man, eat thy bread with quaking, and drink thy water with trembling and with carefulness; 19 And say unto the people of the land, Thus saith the Lord God of the inhabitants of Jerusalem, and of the land of Israel; They shall eat their bread with carefulness, and drink their water with astonishment, that her land may be desolate from all that is therein, because of the violence of all them that dwell therein. 20 And the cities that are inhabited shall be laid waste, and the land shall be desolate; and ye shall know that I am the Lord. 21 And the word of the Lord came unto me, saying, 22 **Son of man, what is that proverb that ye have in the land of Israel, saying, The days are prolonged, and every vision faileth? 23 Tell them therefore, Thus saith the Lord God; I will make this proverb to cease, and they shall no more use it as a proverb in Israel; but say unto them, The days are at hand, and the effect of every vision. 24 For there shall be no more any vain vision nor flattering** divination within the house of Israel. 25 For I am the Lord: I will speak, and the word that I shall speak shall come to pass; it shall be no more prolonged: for in your days, O rebellious house, will I say the word, and will perform it, saith the Lord God. 26 Again the word of the Lord came to me, saying. 27 Son of man, behold, they of the house of Israel say, The vision that he seeth is for many days to come, and he prophesieth of the times that are far off. 28 Therefore say unto them, Thus saith the Lord God; There shall none of my words be prolonged any more, but the word which I have spoken shall be done, saith the Lord God.

Listen to verse two for a second. I was living in the Lake of the Ozarks, MO. area when I first heard this. That is only 400 miles from the dead center of the United Sates. I remember this for my brother offered to take me there for he could not stand how much I listened to the bible and talked about nothing but God, our Father. When he offered to do this, I was at my mom's for the three weeks right after the baptism. And from there I was less than 400 miles away from the center of the United States.

Believe the bible is about us today and notice how the bible will come to life in our very own life. And then try to remember the only thing our Father commanded us to do is to love one another. In the beginning He said be fruitful, multiply, and replenish the earth. This cannot be done without love. AMEN!

One last thing that I feel our Father is telling me to add in here. Remember how Jesus states in Matthew 6, to go into the closet when we pray and shut the door? Matthew 6:5 And when thou prayest, thou shalt not be as the hypocrites are: for they love to pray standing in the synagogues and in the corners of the streets, that they may be seen of men. Verily I say unto you, They have their reward. **6 But thou, when thou prayest, enter into thy closet, and when thou hast shut thy door, pray to thy Father which is in secret; and thy Father which seeth in secret shall reward thee openly. 7 But when ye pray, use not vain repetitions, as the heathen do: for they think that they shall be heard for their much speaking. 8 Be not ye therefore like unto them: for your Father knoweth what things ye have need of, before ye ask him.** 9 After this manner therefore pray ye: Our Father which art in heaven, Hallowed be thy name. 10 Thy kingdom come, Thy will be done in earth, as it is in heaven. 11 Give us this day our daily bread. 12 And forgive us our debts, as we forgive our debtors. 13 And lead us not into temptation, but deliver us from evil: For thine is the kingdom, and the power, and the glory, for ever. Amen.

Now we need to listen to where that door is. Psalm 141:3 Set a watch, O Lord, before my mouth; keep the door of my lips. After learning that Satan is locked up inside of man, and that Satan can hear everything that man says, can you start to understand why our Father only rewards those that pray in secret? Satan does not hear our thoughts as our Father does.

www.ingramcontent.com/pod-product-compliance
Lightning Source LLC
LaVergne TN
LVHW021655060526
838200LV00050B/2370